On Sondheim

On Sondheim
An Opinionated Guide

Ethan Mordden

OXFORD
UNIVERSITY PRESS

OXFORD
UNIVERSITY PRESS

Oxford University Press is a department of the University of Oxford.
It furthers the University's objective of excellence in research, scholarship,
and education by publishing worldwide. Oxford is a registered trade mark of
Oxford University Press in the UK and certain other countries.

Published in the United States of America by Oxford University Press
198 Madison Avenue, New York, NY 10016, United States of America

Library of Congress Cataloging-in-Publication Data
Mordden, Ethan, 1947–.
On Sondheim : an opinionated guide / Ethan Mordden.
pages   cm
Includes bibliographical references and index.
ISBN 978-0-19-939481-4 (alk. paper)
1. Sondheim, Stephen—Criticism and interpretation.
2. Musicals—United States—History and criticism.   I. Title.
ML410.S6872M67   2015
782.1'4092—dc23
2015027518

Stephen Sondheim at New York Philharmonic performance of *Sweeney Todd*:
© 2014 Chris Lee, used with gracious permission of Chris Lee Photographer.

Other illustrations courtesy of The Billy Rose Theatre Collection,
the New York Public Library For the Performing Arts, Astor, Lenox,
and Tilden Foundations; Culver Pictures; and private collections.

A portion of the passage on the *Into the Woods* film appeared
in somewhat different form in the author's blog,
Blogger: Cultural Advantages.

1 3 5 7 9 8 6 4 2

Printed in the United States of America
on acid-free paper

CONTENTS

PREFACE

This is not a reference work. A superb database is available online at www
.sondheimguide.com, so comprehensive that it includes all the pertinent
details of Sondheim's stage shows from the first production to the last revival. The site is extremely easy to navigate and, incidentally, has no affilia-
tion with the present volume.

My intention is to bring the reader closer to Sondheim's oeuvre, to explore
his unique approach to the creation of musicals while trying to position him
in relation to developments in Western art, especially in twentieth-century
music and theatre. Sondheim is, after all, the man who intellectualized
the American musical, much as Eugene O'Neill intellectualized American
drama and William Faulkner intellectualized American fiction, and Sondheim should—where it is relevant—be viewed as much in the broader perspective of the arts as in the more limited survey of the musical per se.

I have endeavored to address all readers simultaneously, from the aficionado through the average theatregoer to the newcomer whose familiarity
with the subject is still in process. While doing so, I have left out or skipped
lightly through the Sondheim clichés—his collection of antique games, for
instance—in trying to keep the book fresh. A great deal has been written
about him, and he has added more information in his many interviews;
I have tried as much as possible to strike out on my own. Except for statements specifically attributed to others within the text itself, all observations and interpretations are mine. The bibliographical essay at the end of
the book is not meant as a list of works consulted, because in many cases
I didn't examine these books till I had finished this one. Rather, the bibliog-
raphy is intended to lead the reader to other works, some of which offer
compelling discussions among Sondheim and his collaborators, or fascinating analyses of Sondheim's work. For my own part, I think the best
source in Sondheim study is the black and white of his compositions—the
scripts and the scores, with a healthy overlay of quotations from the most
eloquent Sondheim expert of all, the man himself.

ACKNOWLEDGMENTS

To my close friend and agent, Joe Spieler; to fellow musical-theatre buffs Jon Cronwell and Ken Mandelbaum; to Ian Marshall Fisher in London; to Chris Lee and Edward Yim of the New York Philharmonic; and, at Oxford, to designer Jack Donner; to savvy Ken Bloom; to Joellyn Ausanka, mistress of all she surveys; and to my wonderful editor, Norm Hirschy.

SONDHEIM'S CHRONOLOGY

1930   Stephen Sondheim (SS) is born on March 22 in New York City. Parents: Herbert and Janet "Foxy" Sondheim.

1942   SS's parents separate, pending divorce. SS moves with Foxy to rural Doylestown, Pennsylvania, attends the Quaker-run George School, and becomes a regular drop-in at the neighboring farm of Oscar Hammerstein, destined to be SS's major mentor figure in the writing of musicals.

1946   SS matriculates at Williams College, takes part in theatricals, and writes musicals for performance by his fellow students.

1947   SS works as a "gofer" on the production of *Allegro*, Rodgers and Hammerstein's experimental musical that inspires SS in the formatting of his own experimental shows.

1950   After graduation from Williams, SS pursues two years of musical study with the cutting-edge composer Milton Babbitt.

1955   SS writes his first full Broadway score for *Saturday Night*, cancelled when its producer dies of leukemia.

1956   SS's first original music is heard on Broadway in *Girls of Summer*, by N. Richard Nash in the William Inge manner, very fashionable at the time. The program credit is "Song by Stephen Sondheim," though it is in fact a trumpet solo (in the Harold Arlen manner), to which SS writes lyrics for promotional purposes.

1957   SS's first Broadway show, *West Side Story*. Lyrics only.

1959   SS's second Broadway show, *Gypsy*. Lyrics only.

1960   SS buys a house on Manhattan's East Forty-Ninth Street, his home from then on.

1962   SS's first full Broadway score to be produced, *A Funny Thing Happened On the Way To the Forum*. *West Side Story* was an artistic breakthrough and *Gypsy* the unique triumph of Ethel Merman, one of Broadway's greatest stars. But *Forum* is a sheer musical-comedy smash.

1964   SS's second full Broadway score, *Anyone Can Whistle*. A failure but, through its cast recording, a cult favorite.

1965   SS collaborates with Richard Rodgers on *Do I Hear a Waltz?*, the older composer at odds with his younger lyricist (as well as with the rest of the creative outfit). It is the Old Musical versus the New Musical. A sour experience.

1970   *Company*, SS's third full Broadway score, inaugurates the era of Sondheim-[Hal] Prince, with *Follies* (1971), *A Little Night Music* (1973), *Pacific Overtures* (1976), *Sweeney Todd* (1979), and *Merrily We Roll Along* (1981) to follow. Though only *Company* and *Night Music* make money in their first run, and accepting that *Merrily* takes a beating in its original production, the series as a whole arouses intense interest. The triumph of the New Musical.

1971   SS inaugurates an eight-year reign as president of the Dramatists' Guild. Meanwhile, *Sondheim: A Musical Tribute* (a star-filled charity benefit) and a *Newsweek* cover hailing SS as "Broadway's Music Man" affirm his growing reputation as Broadway's unofficial composer-in-chief.

1977   Another turning point: the 1976 English revue *Side By Side By Sondheim*, seen on Broadway with (at first) its original cast of Julia McKenzie, David Kernan, and Millicent Martin, is greeted enthusiastically by even SS's former critics. Extracted from the sometimes dense psychology of their settings within the shows themselves, SS's songs step forward as enjoyable as sheer music-making.

1979   Suffering a heart attack at age forty-nine, SS abruptly institutes a healthful diet and now takes in a great love, old Hollywood films, while pedaling on a stationary bicycle.

1984   SS inaugurates his post-Prince era: *Sunday in the Park With George* (1984), *Into the Woods* (1987), *Assassins* (1990), *Passion* (1994), *The Frogs* (2004; revision of shorter work, 1974), *Wise Guys/Bounce/ Road Show* (1999/2003/2008). Generally smaller-scaled than the Prince set, these later shows are just as adventurous, particularly the freely structured *Sunday* and the flowingly composed *Passion*. Sondheim has created the Newer Musical.

1985   An all-star New York Philharmonic concert of *Follies* reaffirms its importance. Originally thought popular/controversial, it now seems only popular—and the performance generates the show's first complete recording. Meanwhile, Barbra Streisand's *The Broadway Album*, programming eight Sondheim numbers (six with his music and two with lyrics only) charts at the highest level.

1990   With all of America's musicians to choose from, Warren Beatty asks SS to write the songs for *Dick Tracy*. "Sooner or Later," introduced in the film by Madonna, wins the Oscar for Best Original Song. At the 1991 awards telecast, she performs the number in a backless white gown, skinny white sable shoulder-throw, and long white gloves in classy-floozy style. Ovation ensues.

1993   SS is one of the year's Kennedy Center honorees.

1995   A fire at SS's house makes it uninhabitable for two years, with a loss of much personal memorabilia.

2010   Henry Miller's Theatre, opened in 1918, has played host to the original American productions of such titles as *Journey's End*, *Our Town*, *Born Yesterday*, and *Witness For the Prosecution*. A Broadway fixture till 1969, it then becomes a gay porn cinema, then a discothèque, and has lately returned to its original calling. Now it is named after SS, who becomes one of only three composers (the others are George Gershwin and Richard Rodgers) with a house in his honor. That same year, *Finishing the Hat*, the first of SS's two lyric collections, reaches the top slot on Amazon's book-sales rankings. SS and the New Musical are Number One.

On Sondheim

An Introduction to Sondheim's Life and Art

The essential fact in understanding Stephen Sondheim is that he is a classically trained composer who chose the theatre over the concert hall and Broadway over the opera house: as if Claude Debussy had written musicals. Further, because of expert verbal skills, Sondheim decided to write his own lyrics: as if Debussy had been as much a wit and poet as a musician.

Born the only child of an upper-middle-class family in New York City in 1930, Sondheim enjoyed the advantage of private schooling, a wide cultural perspective, and a secular worldview, free of the occult confusions that religion invents. The Sondheim marriage broke up when Stephen was twelve, and his mother moved with him to Bucks County, Pennsylvania, north of Philadelphia. The area had been colonized by New Yorkers in search of second homes and thus boasted a sub-population of folk connected to the arts; just a year before, in 1941, in the song "Farming," Cole Porter poked fun at the likes of Katharine Cornell, Fanny Brice, and Clifford Odets shelling peas and driving tractors. Porter even slipped in an "encoded" line addressed to sophisticates, concerning the failure of George Raft's cow to produce a calf: "Georgie's bull is beautiful but he's gay." This was the age of the magnificent closet, when the homosexual artist had to observe a cautious etiquette, moving among straights as if one him- or herself and doing what came naturally in secret.

Some of the Bucks County weekenders so enjoyed the rustic life that they virtually lived in the country; Manhattan was their second home. One such was Oscar Hammerstein, the lyricist-librettist of smash twenties musicals like *Rose-Marie*, *The Desert Song*, *The New Moon*, and, above all, *Show Boat*, to Jerome Kern's music and the first of the incontestably great American musicals. By this time, 1942, Hammerstein had recently teamed up with Richard Rodgers to write *Oklahoma!*, the first of their pioneering series instituting story content over diversion as the musical's first element. An enthusiast of the tennis court and the vast sunny calm of a rural morning, Hammerstein maintained an informal hostel in which the guests included his family, a few wards, and young Steve. Mrs. Sondheim had introduced her son to the Hammersteins because James Hammerstein, Oscar's younger son (the older, Bill, was away in uniform), seemed a likely companion for Steve. Only a year younger, James would presumably share Steve's arty interests. After all, James represented the fourth generation of a theatrical dynasty. His father was actually named Oscar Hammerstein II: the grandson of Oscar I, a cigar magnate who obsessively plowed his fortune into producing opera and vaudeville on the grand scale. Oscar II's father and uncle had gone into show business as well.

As it happened, Steve and James were ill-suited, for the younger boy could not keep up with the precocious Sondheim, twelve years old but an accomplished chess player, an aficionado of esoteric corners of classical music, and in many other ways a bright and confident young man. It was Oscar with whom Sondheim forged a bond, for here was a being on Steve's own level. Often folksy in his lyrics (one reason why Hammerstein preferred operetta to musical comedy was the former's emphasis on romance over flash), Hammerstein was in real life a worldly man, given to withering sarcasm and somewhat heedless of his power to hurt. Like Sondheim, he loved games and was extremely competitive. James he found unequal in contest, unwilling to battle in the first place.

But Sondheim was keen. He taught Oscar to play chess, and in three matches the older man had become the practiced boy's equal. Sondheim told this story to his biographer, Meryle Secrest: he executed a trap to create checkmate in just a few turns, but, as Hammerstein was about to fall into it, the older man looked at Sondheim for a bit and then made a different move, foiling the trap. "You saw what I was setting up," Sondheim told him. "No," said Hammerstein. "I heard your heart beating."

Thus the bond between Steve and Oscar grew intense, as each learned from the other. Most important, Oscar gave Steve the stable relationship of an appreciative "parent." Steve did not get along with his mother, and while he loved his father and stepmother (and got on well with his two younger half-brothers), Steve was an artist growing up in a conventionally business-minded family atmosphere. Steve's father sold women's clothing—but Oscar was a maker of theatre. As the cliché phrase has it, they spoke the same language. Years later, Jamey (as he came to be called) told me, "Oscar Hammerstein was a wonderful father to everyone except his children."

Besides music and the stage, Sondheim nurtured a love of Hollywood movies, especially the dark and thrilling kind. (Oddly, he had no use for musicals.) Anyone who writes about Sondheim makes a port of call out of a title Steve was especially fond of, *Hangover Square* (1945), because it is replete with references to Sondheim's later life. For one thing, its protagonist, a classical composer of Edwardian England named George Harvey Bone (played by Laird Cregar), makes his name (like Sondheim) writing the music for popular songs—"All For You [I've changed my way of living]" and "So Close To Paradise."

Bone is caught between two women; the nice one (Faye Marlowe) encourages him to write a piano concerto, but the bad one (Linda Darnell) turns him into her love slave to juice more pop tunes out of him. He even writes her a musical (and here's another apropos reference) called *Gay Love*. Like Sondheim's later anti-hero protagonist Sweeney Todd, Bone becomes a serial killer, murdering in a kind of waking coma, always set off by wildly shrill sounds, like the factory whistle that goes off when Todd cuts someone's throat. Then, too, Bone's concerto, when we finally hear it (as composed by Bernard Herrmann), sounds—as movie concertos were bound to, in the 1940s—like Rachmaninof, one of Sondheim's favorite composers.

Sondheim also loves Ravel, who makes an interesting pairing with Rachmaninof. The latter was the last of the Romantics, while Ravel was one of the outstanding Neo-classicists. That is, the former represents rhapsodic melody and emotionalism while the latter stands for more intellectualized composition, tightly structured and controlled, scorning emotion-driven communication. To put it another way, the Romantic gushes with music; the Neo-classicist reins it in. A third way: Mahler versus Stravinsky. A fourth way: Sondheim himself, rich in sheer songmaking yet intent on craft and the challenge of matching music to its subject. In short: a Neo-classical Romantic.

At sixteen, Sondheim enrolled at Williams College, which, with Amherst and Wesleyan, created the "Little Three," small men's schools on a par with the big Ivy League universities. Williams supported a lively student theatre scene, and Sondheim acted, most notably in Emlyn Williams' *Night Must Fall*. Sondheim played Dan, an appealing vagrant who ingratiates himself with the village tyrant, an old woman in a wheelchair who is nothing but nags, complaints, self-absorption, and irritation at the slightest suggestion that things won't go her way. Dan captivates as well the beldam's frumpy, repressed niece, and he does seem a charming rogue. In fact, he's another of Sondheim's favorite types, a psychotic serial killer. Yet it's a glamor role—MGM had filmed it in 1937, with Robert Montgomery opposite Rosalind Russell as the niece—written full of sneaky subterfuge cut by outbursts of passionate honesty. Once Dan enters, he owns the show. "I been around," he says. "You'd be surprised."

Steve must have seen the film at some point (he was only seven on its original release), and we know that he was determined to play the part. It's tempting to note that Dan is, above all, gifted in his own unique way—and musical as well, constantly singing snatches of popular song. He also murders an irritating mother figure. Still, Dan is above all a fabulously showy role that no young artist could resist.

Elswhere at Williams, Sondheim found a music class taught by Robert Barrow so invigorating that it pushed him toward seeking a career as a composer, as opposed to a movie director (which must have been on his mind as a possibility). Still, the overwhelming influence in Sondheim's life continued to be Oscar Hammerstein, who, in Steve's junior year, proposed a course of informal study in the writing of musicals. Practice makes perfect: first, write a musical based on a play you admire. Then a musical based on a play with problems, so you can log experience in resolving them: a dry run for what happens when you go out of town with a musical that isn't playing well. Then adapt a show from some non-theatrical form—that is, learn how to dramatize from a lyrical point of view. Last, write an original.

Amusingly, Hammerstein was running through the experiments himself, on the professional level; they became the first four Rodgers and Hammerstein titles:

> *Oklahoma!* (1943), which launched the cycle, was the play with problems, based on Lynn Riggs' *Green Grow the Lilacs*, a Broadway failure in 1931.

> *Carousel* (1945) was the play you admire, because the adaptation hewed closely to its source, Ferenc Molnár's *Liliom*, adding in an uplifting final scene.

> *South Pacific* (1949) was the third adaptation, taken from a non-theatrical form, James Michener's story series *Tales of the South Pacific*.

> And *Allegro* (1947) was the original.

Even then, Sondheim was ambitious: the play he admired was George S. Kaufman and Marc Connelly's *Beggar on Horseback* and the one with problems was Maxwell Anderson's *High Tor*—"art" plays rather than the farces and romantic comedies that had provided typical source material for musicals for some thirty years. *High Tor* is a verse play (and a fantasy) and *Beggar on Horseback* is an expressionist comedy, an oxymoron in that expressionism belonged to the visionaries of the serious progressive forms, from Eugene

O'Neill to German horror cinema. The eponymous beggar is a composer who, like Laird Cregar in *Hangover Square*, is trapped between the music he yearns to write and the music that "everyone" wants to hear, classical versus popular. And of course this is a very basic dilemma in American culture, where art and commercialism intermingle in a kind of panic. First staged in 1924, *Beggar on Horseback* remained a vital memory for many, though expressionism's dreamy distortions appeared to lock it into its time. For years, people would approach Kaufman with "You know what play of yours should be revived?" and Kaufman would immediately snap back, "It's dated."*

After being graduated from Williams, Sondheim received three thousand dollars a year for two years from the Hutchinson Prize in which to pursue his musical studies, and he undertook a private course in composition with Milton Babbitt, one of the most experimental of musicians. Oddly, Babbitt and Sondheim would analyze a song by Jerome Kern as often as a movement of a Beethoven symphony. But then Babbitt, like many other "ivory tower" composers, sought financial security in creating something popular, even, say, a musical for Mary Martin. One of the genre's two biggest stars (Ethel Merman was the other), Martin was so versatile that almost everyone offered her the top part in his show, first dibs, from *My Fair Lady* to *Funny Girl*. Again, it's that American dilemma: if you have the skills, shouldn't you invent something dazzling—a *Porgy and Bess*, for instance? It's classical, but it's popular, too.

So: you're twenty-two, smarter than everybody, and ready to start. You've been living rent-free in your father's New York apartment, but he isn't offering an allowance and the Hutchinson money is spent. What next?

For Sondheim, it was scriptwriting for television's *Topper* series, mostly collaborating with George Oppenheimer. A spinoff of Thorne Smith's two *Topper* novels and the films they engendered, the video adaptation told of starchy banker Cosmo Topper (Leo G. Carroll), his fluttery wife (Lee Patrick), and three ghosts (Robert Sterling; his then wife, Anne Jeffreys; and their vast St. Bernard, Neil). The half-hour episodes were based less on plot than on the interaction between the soigné Sterlings and the befuddled Carroll, with his English accent and clipped mustache. Thus, the show's writers had only to mix character ingredients as if tossing a salad. It was labor for money rather than for love, and today *Topper* looks quaintly

---

* *Beggar on Horseback* made it to Broadway as a semi-musical in 1970, at Lincoln Center. The original text was retained, but Stanley Silverman and John Lahr musicalized the central dream sequence as a Ziegfeldian pageant that anticipated parts of Sondheim's *Follies*.

ho-hum next to its coevals, especially the daffy *George Burns and Gracie Allen Show* and *I Love Lucy*. The commercials, however, are bizarre. As so often in the 1950s, the series stars were expected to serve as spokesmen for the sponsor, Camel Cigarettes, staying more or less in character while delivering encomiums:

JEFFREYS: (as Sterling lights her up) Uum, this is going to taste *so* good.
STERLING: (with his own cigarette) And *this* is going to taste even better.

Carroll is on hand for these spiels, too. Everyone smokes but the dog.

It's an odd way to launch a career in music theatre, but we should note that Sondheim later collaborated on play and movie scripts. It's not too early to point out that Sondheim sees his songs as "playwrighting." That is, he is a dramatist more than a songwriter, with an acute sense of when narrative needs to spring into song: his music lies somewhere between dialogue and opera, mixing the former's kinetic motion with the latter's expressive power.

Back in New York after *Topper*, Sondheim set about establishing living quarters on his own and finding work. His first opportunity hit when he was twenty-four: *Saturday Night*, a smallish show about courtship rituals in Brooklyn in the late 1920s, with a book by Julius J. Epstein. One may wonder why Sondheim never considered writing an opera. But then, for all his love of classical music, he wasn't interested in a theatrical form that depended more on lavish vocalism than on crisply dramatic communication, cast for the most part with not singing actors but singing singers. Then, too, in those days before titling was normalized, opera audiences had no idea what the characters were saying from one line to the next. What kind of theatre is that?

Unbeknown to Sondheim, *Saturday Night*'s producer, Lemuel Ayers, suffered from leukemia; he died suddenly while the show was still casting and raising its capitalization, and the production evaporated. There was another project, called *The Last Resorts*, spun off Cleveland Amory's book of essays about the gala vacation haunts of the one per cent, from Newport to Saratoga. Amory was known for two things, pioneering animal-rights activism and writing about Society, and his books were bestsellers. So *The Last Resorts* was designed to take advantage of a pre-sold title, now attached to a wholly original story devised by Walter and Jean Kerr. Sondheim wrote three songs, which the Kerrs didn't like, and the show's producer, Harold S. (more commonly Hal) Prince, didn't like the Kerrs' script. So nothing came of that show, either, though Palm Beach, another of those haunts of the leisure class, would figure in Sondheim's latest work, *Road Show*.

Then Steve got a show destined to make the short list of great musicals, *West Side Story* (1957). This time, he was asked to write only lyrics—worse, only some of the lyrics, collaborating with Leonard Bernstein, to Bernstein's music. This was dismaying, of course: melody centers the art, and juggling rhymes is just so much homework. However, Oscar Hammerstein advised Steve not to pass up the chance to work with top people, for besides Bernstein there was Jerome Robbins, already celebrated not only as a choreographer but also as a director. Hammerstein was well aware of what Robbins could do; hired to stage the numbers on *The King and I*, Robbins became the show's virtual director when John Van Druten, of the spoken stage, proved helpless trying to command a big musical. Further, Hammerstein's professional savvy must have told him that Robbins' reputation was just about to break out spectacularly, and *West Side Story*, made of gangs, jazz, and Shakespeare, might easily be the coronation title. Last, Hammerstein, a lyricist himself, knew that great shows need great words as well as great music. The lyricist matters.

And Hammerstein was right on every point, especially that Steve would find *West Side Story* a veritable college in the making of musicals. But then it happened again: he was invited to write the score to *Gypsy* (1959), yet its star, Ethel Merman, was unwilling to take a chance on an unestablished composer. Maybe the lyricist *doesn't* matter, for Merman must have thought of herself as singing entirely on the music. Starting with her debut in 1930, she had appeared in eleven shows, all boasting major composers. Not just Cole Porter, George Gershwin, and Irving Berlin but Vincent Youmans, Ray Henderson, and Arthur Schwartz. Even Merman's second rank was first rank. Then, on the twelfth show, *Happy Hunting*, in 1956, Merman accepted the unknown composer Harold Karr, and while the show ran a year with the "first months sold out" feeling of a hit, it lost money and the score did not really take off. *Gypsy*, Merman's thirteenth musical, had to revert to the Merman formula: music by Famous and lyrics by whoever's handy.

The chosen composer, Jule Styne, turned out to be a fine partner for Sondheim, a ceaselessly inventive musician and very open to new ideas. "You don't like that tune?" he would ask, from the keyboard. "Let me try another. How about this one?" And Styne would simply start playing as if the piano itself had channeled him.

Nevertheless, Steve would have turned the show down but for, again, Hammerstein's advice. Writing for a star like Merman, he thought, would give Steve another valuable experience. Oddly, Hammerstein himself had seldom written for a star. Yes, in the 1920s, Hammerstein's *Wildflower* (with co-composers Vincent Youmans and Herbert Stothart) was built around the star of *Irene*, Edith Day; and *Sunny* (with Jerome Kern) was made on

Marilyn Miller, the biggest musical star of the age. Still, more often, performers *became* stars in Hammerstein's shows—Mary Ellis and Dennis King in *Rose-Marie*, Helen Morgan in *Show Boat*, Helen Kane in *Good Boy*, Alfred Drake and Celeste Holm in *Oklahoma!*, John Raitt in *Carousel*.

Perhaps it was Hammerstein's belief that Steve needed more exposure to Big Broadway, where the despots of talent turn productions into their own personal banana republic and ego eats ego for snacks. Steve was brighter than anyone, but he was sensitive and needed toughening up.

However, Sondheim was getting acquainted with The Business on his own. One of its most important (and hush-hush) jobs is Play Doctor: a colleague's show is struggling out of town and you are invited to have a look and then outline the required fixes. It's a gig that takes in anything from giving the creative staff a few notes to replacing the director with name billing on the poster in big letters inside a box. Jerome Robbins was notable in the field—and Hammerstein could be counted on for a trip to a matinée and a suggestion or two. Now, at the age of twenty-six, Sondheim attained the position when Bernstein's *Candide* was in trouble in Boston.

At Bernstein's insistence, Steve went up to have a look at what was soon to be the most distinguished flop in Broadway history, with, he thought, a brilliant book (by Lillian Hellman), a brilliant score (taking in a bevy of lyricists, including even Hellman and Bernstein and, for some unknown reason, Dorothy Parker), and a brilliant production (by Tyrone Guthrie). Unfortunately, each of these elements was brilliant in a different way, the book mean and funny, the score now spoofy and now plangent, and the production on the grand scale with infusions of camp. It was Western Civilization in the form of a pageant co-authored by Karl Marx, Oscar Wilde, and Bugs Bunny, and Bernstein induced Sondheim to share his thoughts with Bernstein's collaborators. As Sondheim put it in the second of his lyric collections, *Look, I Made a Hat*, the *Candide* crew "looked balefully at me, with understandable disdain—who was this kid, this latest protégé of Lenny's?" Indeed, they probably took Steve for Bernstein's latest romance; he had a habit of introducing his flames into his world professionally. The episode shows us how sharp Sondheim's theatrical instincts were even without any practical Broadway experience, for *Candide* opened nine months before *West Side Story*, when the latter was still in composition. Ironically, Sondheim himself was to join the ranks of *Candide*'s myriad lyricists for the 1973 Brooklyn (and 1974 Broadway) revision, directed by Hal Prince in a more consistent tone of meta-theatrical clowning.

In the 1960s, making himself at home in the New York theatre world, Sondheim was at last able to present Broadway with scores entirely his own, writing music and lyrics for *A Funny Thing Happened On the Way To the*

Forum (1962) and *Anyone Can Whistle* (1964). They were different from *West Side Story* and *Gypsy*, for the former was experimental and the latter very dark, while *Forum* was sunny and hilarious and *Whistle* offbeat and mischievous. Both were musical comedies in the purest sense, Sondheim's first since the unproduced *Saturday Night*. Thus they stand out in his oeuvre, for his later shows returned him to the dark and experimental. At that, Sondheim's television musical, *Evening Primrose* (1967) was dark, though its plot whimsically concerned people living undetected in a department store, some of them for decades.

Sondheim's next full score would inaugurate his series with Hal Prince, starting with *Company* (1970). But there were detours along the way, writing lyrics only, to Richard Rodgers' music, for *Do I Hear a Waltz?* (1965), then to Leonard Bernstein's music on an adaptation of Bertolt Brecht's *The Exception and the Rule*, starting in 1968 (and ultimately never produced). Sondheim dislikes Brecht's hectoring political statements and automatic characterizations of manipulative authority figures and their pathetic victims; when Sondheim came to write about authority figures and their victims, in *Sweeney Todd*, there was nothing automatic about their character development (though their actions called forth a few of those hectoring political statements).

The Brecht project seemed enticing nonetheless, even if Bernstein had already begun working with another lyricist, Jerry Leiber, a stalwart of rock and roll who with Mike Stoller wrote "Jailhouse Rock" and "[You ain't nothin' but a] Hound Dog," among other definitive titles. Indeed, it's hard to imagine the history of rock without Leiber and Stoller—but what was Leiber doing in Bernstein's company, not to mention that of John Guare (writing the book) and Jerome Robbins (directing)? The lure of working with Robbins again, and possibly coming up with something as distinguished as *West Side Story*, was what led Sondheim to sign on, and he ultimately wrote lyrics for eight numbers. But he found Bernstein as condescending and competitive as he had been on *West Side Story*, relentlessly challenging Sondheim's lines. (Steve: "A boy like that." Lenny: No, how about... "A boy like him"?) Worse, Bernstein was still unaware of how mawkish his instincts were in the matter of the "softer" lyric. His lack of perspective in how words sound led him to insist on calling the musical *A Pray By Blecht*, perhaps the most juvenile and affected title ever proposed for Broadway. It makes one think fondly of the ancient days of *Whoop-De-Doo* and *Piff! Paff!! Pouf!!!*. Sondheim found battling through Bernstein's egomania "tedious and time-consuming and no fun at all," and he dropped out of the project. Sooner or later, one outgrows one's Bernstein—and when Steve wrote a few lyrics for the aforementioned *Candide* revision, he insisted that he work alone with Bernstein's music, not with Bernstein himself.

Company, produced when Sondheim was forty, at last brought him recognition as an author of important musicals. He always gives full credit to his librettists, with whom he exchanges ideas and who write dialogue that he can transform into musical passages. And it must be said that the Sondheim shows' emphasis on literate and imaginative book writing have concentrated attention on the contributions of the librettist as never before. (This is yet another part of Oscar Hammerstein's legacy.) Still, no one thinks of—to cite the librettists—*Company* as a George Furth musical, *Follies* (1971) as a James Goldman musical, *A Little Night Music* (1973) as a Hugh Wheeler musical, *Pacific Overtures* (1976) as a John Weidman musical, or *Sweeney Todd* (1979) as another Hugh Wheeler musical. These are Sondheim musicals.

They are as well the five shows that Sondheim wrote for production and direction by Hal Prince in the 1970s, a body of work that, when new, divided the theatregoing community as never before, though now all five are undisputed classics. As each of the quintet was experimental—and each experimental in a completely different way—some opinion makers felt imposed upon, forced to admire.

This led to what appeared to be a pile-on of anger at the sixth Sondheim-Prince title, *Merrily We Roll Along* (1981). True, the English revue *Side By Side By Sondheim*, seen here between *Pacific Overtures* and *Sweeney Todd*, marked a change in the way Sondheim was perceived by some of his detractors. With three singers, a narrator, and Sondheim's songs presented as stand-alone art, his supposedly difficult music and idea-stuffed lyrics suddenly seemed not difficult but agreeable and not idea-stuffed but stimulating. One reason that some listeners weren't able to assimilate Sondheim's mature style—that is, from *Company* on—is the way the numbers are embedded in each show's action. Once, theatre music was "Tea For Two": you relax and enjoy the song as pure sensuality. By the Rodgers and Hammerstein era—from the 1940s on—theatre music was *Carousel*'s "Soliloquy": you can't relax, because the song provides compelling character information. And Sondheim took the process a step further, adding irony to the mix. In *Company*'s "Side By Side By Side," the character tells us one thing (I'm so happy in my social loop) while the context of the number creates a contradiction (Is he, really?). However, released from their dramatic responsibilities, "Side By Side By Side" and the rest of the program turned out to be easy to enjoy, even relaxing.

But of course the music wasn't meant to be heard outside its theatrical setting. It's narrative tissue, psychologically dense because the shows are. Some musicals are revived because we love the scores: *Show Boat, Finian's*

Rainbow, *La Cage aux Folles*. Sondheim's shows are revived because they're so rich in content that we never quite collect them. We need to see them again just to figure them out. *Company*: marriage robs you of your freedom...and your isolation. *Follies*: why must beautiful youth end in bitter age? *A Little Night Music*: half the world are fools and the other half fall in love and *become* fools. *Pacific Overtures*: a lesson in the transformations of history. *Sweeney Todd*: opera ennobles all its people, even a ragbag nobody who becomes a serial killer. It sounds too tidy to parse them thus, so clear to the view. And, indeed, the development of those themes and procedures is rich, with all the why?s and excepts that we experience in life.

Now for a bit of analysis. The most influential series of shows in the musical's developments are:

The Ned Harrigan-Tony Hart Irish farces of the 1880s, emphasizing immigrant New York as a setting and a style.

The Princess Theatre shows of the late 1910s, natural rather than exotic and boasting the innovatively clever songs of Jerome Kern and P. G. Wodehouse.

The Alex Aarons-Vinton Freedley musical comedies of the 1920s, built around a star performer and a star score (usually by the Gershwins).

Twenties operetta, in which the score was completely at the story's service.

The Richard Rodgers-Oscar Hammerstein musical play of the 1940s and 1950s, reinventing operetta with adult storylines.

The Sondheim-Prince shows of the 1970s.

Note that the consistently evolving element in the list is the power of the narrative. Aarons-Freedley musical comedy is silly, but Rodgers and Hammerstein seek out "big" characters in spiky confrontations over serious issues. And when Sondheim adds to this format the slithery conjugations of his "playwrighting" scores, the musical blends entertainment into enlightenment.

Let's tack a bit to the academic side. The late seventeenth to early eighteenth century Italian historian Giambattista Vico, in his *Scienza Nuova*, saw human events as cyclic, moving from a Theocratic Age through an Aristocratic Age to a Democratic Age, thence to an upheaval ushering in the next Theocratic Age, and so on. More recently, the literary critic Harold Bloom revised Vico's paradigm for his study of Dante, Shakespeare, Tolstoy, Kafka, and others in *The Western Canon*. Bloom proposed an Aristocratic Age, a Democratic Age, and then a Chaotic Age. Ours. And we can, very loosely, apply this to the history of the American musical. The first age favors icons—*Evangeline, Adonis*, fairies, royalty. It is the time of *Robin Hood, The Shogun, The Three Musketeers.* Meanwhile, the Democratic Age has been stealing in, with feisty working-girl heroines and ambitious, up-from-nothing young lads—*The Girl Friend, Babes in Arms, The Pajama Game.*

And the Chaotic Age came in with Sondheim-Prince, for their offbeat subject matter creates offbeat forms, superseding the musical's handbook as it had been developing for some hundred years and thus unsettling less adventurous spectators. Thus, *Company* is constructed of little one-acts, each with its own tiny storyline. In one, a married couple gets on each other's nerves with goading little teases till the tension explodes in a mock karate battle. In another, the show's unmarried hero enjoys a one-night stand until he realizes it might last more than one night. *Company* is a puzzle and these are some of its pieces; when all the pieces are assembled, they give us a narrative by other means. Yes, there is a sort of beginning (the hero is happy as a bachelor), middle (or is he?), and end (he's finally ready for marriage), but they are not clearly demarcated. They are in *My Fair Lady*: the beginning (Higgins will "reclass" Eliza), the middle (she fails at Ascot but Succeeds at the Embassy Ball; they fight; she flees), the end (she returns). Or even in the plotless *A Chorus Line*: the beginning ("I hope I get it"), the middle (confessions), the end ("Will the following people please step forward?"). *Company*, however, is very free in form—or, rather, it is strict in form, but in a form that didn't exist before *Company*. As we'll presently see, Sondheim-Prince is, above all, wholly original.

Innovation in a form that some people still believed was ontologically intended to provide nothing but amusement was bound to prove divisive. Sondheim often tells a story that takes us back to *West Side Story*, at the start of his professional experience. Standing at the back of the orchestra on the second night of the New York run, he saw a man get up and leave a few minutes into the opening, a ballet of rival gangs, before even a note had been sung. Seeing Sondheim and assuming he was connected with the production, the man told him, "Don't ask."

And Steve knew immediately what had happened. This was the Tired Businessman of Broadway lore; he thought he'd drop in on a musical before heading home to the suburbs. He didn't know anything about *West Side Story* itself, but the poster photograph of Tony and Maria running down a Manhattan street looked happy, and this was, after all, the 1950s, when newspaper columnists touted what they called "musigirl" shows—*Top Banana, Wish You Were Here, Can-Can, Ankles Aweigh, Li'l Abner.* And instead this guy gets weird jazzy riffs, unsettling syncopations, teenage hoods snapping their fingers and snarling when they aren't leaping about like angry lizards. Then came the racial aspect, as a rival gang of Latinos challenged the white boys...and the tired businessman departed for Roslyn Heights.

And, says Sondheim, "That's when I knew my career was in trouble."

Of course, *West Side Story* was a hit. Overcapitalized at $300,000,* it made a profit (according to its co-producer, Hal Prince, in his book *Contradictions*) of $1,090,000. *Company* and *A Little Night Music*, says Prince, were profitable in their first runs, too, if considerably less so. But critics and public were—again, at first—ambivalent about Sondheim's shows. Even as they realized how stimulating and original these musicals were, their inner Tired Businessman longed for that old-fashioned show business in which, whatever else happens—despair, murder, the collapse of a democracy in a feudal epoch—the public has a guiltless good time. Thus, while the fresh rehearing of "Too Many Mornings" or "The Little Things You Do Together" in *Side By Side By Sondheim* reintroduced theatregoers to the music's charm, Sondheim still had to persuade the public to think more expansively about his shows as wholes.

But then, why shouldn't they? The cultural upheaval of the American 1960s affected virtually everything—how people regarded social clichés of class, gender, and sexuality; how they dressed; what they expected from the arts. *Psycho, Dr. Strangelove, Bonnie and Clyde, The Graduate*, and many other films marked a breakaway from Hollywood's entertainment models, and rock had unseated theatre songs as the national music. Sondheim-Prince offered Broadway's equivalent of all this, albeit on its own terms, as a kind of liberation of the musical.

Sondheim felt liberated personally: more relaxed. He could be tense with fools, easily irritated; he was less so now. On the other hand, he had always been reluctant to get into the fights that punctuate the rehearsal and tryout periods of every show, especially the musical. Some love a fight—Jerome Robbins, for instance. If there wasn't a scrap in service, he'd provoke one. Some hate a fight but will battle to defend their place in a production. But where does a legitimate argument over art end and a plain old hard-on contest begin? When *Sweeney Todd* premiered in London, at Drury Lane, British television ran a documentary on the piece, including "reality" footage of the rehearsals. At one point, John Aron, playing the barber Pirelli—Todd's first victim—learned that his only musical number was to be cut in half, and, with the camera whirring away, Aron and Prince got into some good old backstage geschrei. Typically, Sondheim was nowhere to be seen during

---

* Only very elaborate musicals of the 1950s cost that much. *My Fair Lady*, the most lavish production of the 1950s before *West Side Story*, cost $360,000, and *Saratoga*, the most lavish production of the 1950s after *West Side Story*, cost $480,000. But *West Side Story* didn't remotely rival their colossal sets-and-costumes bill.

this sequence. If a problem can't be solved in something like a civil tone, he simply moves off the battlefield till order is restored.

Growing comfortable with success in the 1970s, Sondheim adapted to the times. Candid photos of Steve with Bernstein and Robbins during *West Side Story*'s gestation show the debutant smartly turned out in jacket and tie; by the 1970s, he favored casual wear. Further, Sondheim became a magnet for anyone interested in the musical, the leader of the pack. In a novel published in 1977, James Fritzhand's *Starring*, five characters are seen launching careers in show business, and each is an *à clef* figure. Suzann Jaffe is clearly Barbra Streisand; Fritzhand gives us precisely turned counterparts for her first Broadway show, *I Can Get It For You Wholesale*. Its garment-center setting creates Jaffe's credit, *Seventh Avenue*, and even *Wholesale*'s composer-lyricist, Harold Rome, as Earl Milan, is given replicas of his work: *Destry Rides Again* turns up as *The Sheriff Was a Lady*.

Of course Fritzhand would make one of his leads a young songwriter, and of course he would be modeled on Sondheim. The character is Philip Ehrlich, more Sondheimesque in his professional life—*Company* shows up in the book as *Singles*—than in his offstage identity. For instance, Fritzhand doesn't mention the most famous personal aspect of the Sondheim life, his love of games, from anagrams and those extra-tricky British crossword puzzles to treasure hunts with all of Manhattan as the hunting field.

One thing Fritzhand did get to was Sondheim's sexuality: Philip Ehrlich is gay. Sondheim was closeted at this time, as was his most notable predecessor as Broadway composer-lyricist, Cole Porter. Indeed, Porter even married, albeit to an older woman who did not share his love of wicked fun; a hypochondriac, Linda Lee Porter was really only happy in an iron lung. Also unlike Sondheim, Porter slipped encoded double meanings into his lyrics, as when *Kiss Me, Kate*'s "Too Darn Hot" cites the attraction of "a marine for his queen." Too, Porter favored the steamier sort of musical, not just musigirl but musiboy. *Jubilee*, about a royal family off on a madcap vacation, included a Tarzan figure called Mowgli who made his entrance in a peekaboo bearskin and attended a costume party wearing little more than makeup and sandals as an oversized Cupid.

Sondheim's shows through *Merrily We Roll Along* hadn't a trace of gay in them, even if *West Side Story*'s Riff is drawn from Shakespeare's Mercutio, arguably Romeo's former adolescent crush. In truth, there were so few gay characters in the musical before, say, the 1980s that they stand out—at that, less as milestones than as newer incarnations of the ethnic stereotypes that thronged musicals of the very early 1900s. In 1941, Danny Kaye played a flaming magazine photographer in *Lady in the Dark*, openly raving over a beefcake movie star with "This one is the end—the *end*!" In his *Times* review, Brooks Atkinson daintied his way around this flamboyant exhibit by calling Kaye "infectiously exuberant," a euphemism if I ever heard one.

Fourteen years later, Ray Walston's devil in *Damn Yankees* seemed distinctly minty by the attitudes of the era: a single man living in opulent interior decoration and up to devious manipulations with the aid of a sexy woman whom he goads into seducing a vulnerable young man—an amalgam of Truman Capote and Roy Cohn. By comparison, *Applause*, in 1970, seemed liberated in letting Lee Roy Reams play Lauren Bacall's personal assistant with no more than a soupçon of swish. The tipping point arrived in 1983, with a gay honeymooning couple in *Dance a Little Closer* and, pièce de resistance, *La Cage aux Folles*, featuring gay parents who had raised a son.

Sondheim's shows have so often dealt in period tales (especially of the nineteenth century) that they defy trendy accommodations. But the vivaciously contemporary *Company* eventually had to slip a bit of gay content into one scene to avoid seeming prim, even specious. *A Little Night Music*'s libretto bears an unmistakable gay flavor (about which more later). And Sondheim's latest work, *Road Show*, has two gay principals. Still, the disparate nature of Sondheim's shows so textures his output that one doesn't think of them as "missing" a particular identity group. It's not that these titles are heterocentric: it's that they're all different from each other, and rarified in their dramatis personae. *Company* is a Zeitgeist musical, sharp and hip. But the next piece, *Follies*, is a show-biz phantasmagoria. Then *A Little Night Music* is a romance, so *Pacific Overtures* is an epic and *Sweeney Todd* a thriller.

And *Sunday in the Park with George* (1984) is a painting—or, really, a navigation through art to discover how the creator relates to the life around him. This work launched Sondheim's third period. The first covered his years writing lyrics only and composing musical comedies. The second was Sondheim-Prince. And now the third took Sondheim into physically smaller productions than heretofore, mainly with librettist and director James Lapine, pensive and measured where Hal Prince is impulsive and enthusiastic. In Sondheim's aforementioned *Look, I Made a Hat*, he recalls realizing that his and Lapine's "tastes [in art] were surprisingly alike." "Surprisingly" because Lapine's background lay in—this is Sondheim again—the "off-Broadway nonprofit theater," and those "nurtured in that protective atmosphere think differently than we Great White Way dinosaurs who were raised in commercial theater do."

Thus, Harold Bloom's Chaotic Age seizes the musical, for Sondheim's description of Lapine really means "experimental." As the Sondheim-Prince shows were already innovative, the following set was doubly so, though some of the directors (such as Jerry Zaks and Susan Stroman) usually work in conservative precincts. Nevertheless, three of the third-period shows— *Sunday*, *Into the Woods* (1987), and *Passion* (1994)—were not only directed but scripted by Lapine, making him almost as central to this group of shows as the very collaborative (though never actually libretto-writing) Prince was to the previous group.

Then, too, the Lapine aesthetic, which turns a story into a suite of variations, as if that story were a symphonic theme, appears to govern the writing style of even the non-Lapine titles. For example, *Sunday* is about George (Seurat) only at first. Then it tells of a different George altogether, one who is both like and unlike the first George. One is obsessed (about "finishing the hat": fulfilling the enchantment). The other is drifting. But doesn't obsession create a loss of place in the world? And doesn't one drift to avoid obsession, release oneself from enchantment?

Comparably, *Assassins* (1990) with a libretto by not Lapine but John Weidman, considers the differences among various president-killers to unify them: variations in search of a theme. And the theme, at last, is Lee Harvey Oswald. *Road Show* (2008), also by Weidman, is as interested in the vanished America of its two leads, the Mizner brothers, as it is in the two siblings themselves.

This was not true of *Company*, *Follies*, or *Sweeney Todd* of the Prince sequence. Nor was it true of shows written by Steve's mentor, Oscar Hammerstein. Those works expand. The Lapine-era titles concentrate. The Harold Bloomian Chaos inheres not in any confusion in how these shows play but in their transgressively nonconformist atmosphere, that "nonprofit theater" attitude that Sondheim spoke of earlier. Of these latest Sondheim shows, only *Into the Woods* observes Broadway protocols, at least in its ample dimensions. *Assassins* risks angry controversy in its subject matter; *Passion* dares the unbelievable: beauty learns to love the beast.

Ironically, the more Sondheim challenged the rules for wide commercial acceptance, the more accepted he became. He even got offers from the Coast, a certain sign that a composer has caught the American ear. Lotte Lenya once said, "If you become a legend you must have made your point somewhere," and we can revise this to "If Hollywood is calling, you're the Great Gatsby, Gandalf, and the Statue of Liberty." First it was Warren Beatty, who wanted Sondheim to score his films (though Sondheim preferred to write songs and leave the underscoring to others). Then it was Barbra Streisand, who wanted to record Sondheim songs with a certain amount of hand-crafting by Sondheim, to repurpose his lyrics to suit Streisand's ID. Thus, Sondheim had attained a position that had never existed before, that of philosopher-king of the American musical, mainly because there was so much content in his shows. Even Oscar Hammerstein was not so exclusively eminent.

So it had to be Sondheim to denounce the American Repertory Theatre's proposal, in 2011, to stage *Porgy and Bess* in a substantial revision. In a letter to the *New York Times*, Sondheim ripped the ART's plan to shreds, basing his objections on comments made by the director, Diane Paulus, and the dramaturg, Suzan Lori-Parks. Sondheim's first criticism was aimed at the billing of the production as "*The Gershwins' Porgy and Bess*," because it made no mention of co-lyricist Du Bose Heyward, who thought up the novel *Porgy* and then, with his wife, Dorothy, wrote the play *Porgy* that served Gershwin as his matrix. Heyward's was an essential *Porgy and Bess* credit; to leave him out was to leave George Bernard Shaw out of the credit for *My Fair Lady*.

In fact, the Gershwin estates have been demanding billing that eliminates Du Bose Heyward for a generation. But Sondheim's more important objection concerned the planned changes to the work itself. "I wanted to flesh out the two main characters," said Parks. "I think that's what George Gershwin wanted." Said Sondheim, "It's reassuring that Ms. Parks has a direct pipeline to Gershwin and is just carrying out his work for him." Sondheim's basic point was that, in an acknowledged masterpiece like *Porgy and Bess*, changes of emphasis (in the staging) are acceptable, but changes of kind (in the text) are not.

This is entirely appropriate behavior for someone who spent most of the 1970s as president of the Dramatists Guild of America, which protects the rights of authors in their dealings with producers and directors. But more: this is loyalty, one of Sondheim's salient personal qualities. Loyalty to his colleagues, to Hammerstein, to integrity of text, and to *Porgy and Bess*, which Sondheim regards as one of the greatest of all Broadway offerings (and which is, again, a work written for the popular stage along classical lines). And, while we're at it, do not praise Agnes de Mille to Sondheim, because he recalls a dinner party many years ago in California at which de Mille deliberately spoke ill of Oscar Hammerstein, knowing how important he had been in Steve's life. We should note, too, that it took Sondheim forever to break with the notoriously obnoxious Arthur Laurents, simply because they had worked together on shows that helped define Sondheim as an artist. And, despite his difficulties with Leonard Bernstein, Sondheim remained close to him on the personal level. Sharing the creation of *West Side Story* made the two more than colleagues: lovers, in the metaphorical sense.

Now in his eighties, Sondheim enjoys an unusual celebrity based entirely on his work, safe from tabloid gotcha!s. Many of his friends were not aware that in the 1990s, he met a young songwriter from Colorado, Peter Jones, and embarked on a romantic liaison. It was not Sondheim's first such involvement, but his first serious one, succeeded by a second affair, with Jeff Romley.

Before that, Sondheim's most important relationships were those with his collaborators, liaisons of art—those whom he has learned from and, himself, instructed. Leonard Bernstein, Jerome Robbins, Arthur Laurents, Jule Styne, Hal Prince, James Lapine, and above all Oscar Hammerstein. Shortly before he died, Hammerstein gave his photograph to Sondheim, inscribing it, "For Stevie, my friend and teacher."

Sondheim's Mentors and the
Concept Musical

W hen Stephen Sondheim first began visiting Oscar Hammerstein's farm in Doylestown, Pennsylvania, the youngster was barely a teenager and Hammerstein was in his late forties. It is hard to imagine anyone who had logged more experience in creating musicals, and very, very good ones at that. He had written or co-written over twenty-five of them, including classic titles. A Hammerstein libretto sought out above all logical opportunities for music-making while keeping its narration sensible; Hammerstein lyrics were so wedded to character that one could follow the action through the songs alone. However, for the decade preceding young Steve's more or less joining the Hammerstein household, every Hammerstein show had been either a modest success that left no reputation behind or an outright failure.

As I've said, Hammerstein was even then collaborating with Richard Rodgers on *Oklahoma!*, the work that would restart Hammerstein's career, as a master of the "musical play"—neither a fun-filled musical comedy nor a lyrically expansive operetta but a work combining elements of both forms into insightful storytelling based on powerful character interaction. By the time of the final Rodgers and Hammerstein title, *The Sound of Music* (1959), there was scarcely a musical of any kind that hadn't been influenced by musical-play reforms.

However, Hammerstein had long been engaged in filling the musical with content. For one thing, he was attracted to tales made of genuine conflict, not cute twists and contrived quarrels. For instance, out in North Africa with the French Foreign Legion: what if dashing Margot Bonvalet just isn't into that geeky Pierre? What if she secretly thrills to the studly hurly-burly of the freedom-fighting Red Shadow? What if the Red Shadow carries her off to his tent of passion? Now she fears the Red Shadow. She longs for Pierre. But what if they're *the same guy*? That's *The Desert Song* (1926), which Hammerstein co-wrote, with Otto Harbach and Frank Mandel, to Sigmund Romberg's music.

Further, Hammerstein was the musical's first writer to specify character in song lyrics. Pierre sounds prim, his alter ego the Red Shadow comes off as passionate, and Margot sounds sensible with a romantic streak that sometimes overpowers her. The first reason that the famous twenties operettas have survived (if marginally) is the music. But the second is the way Hammerstein pursues the narrative through the music: in *The Desert Song*, *Rose-Marie*, *The New Moon*, and that proto-musical play *Show Boat*. Indeed, Hammerstein is perhaps the musical's only major lyricist-librettist before *Oklahoma!* who maintained a worldview: have compassion, beware the despotic male, and trust the strong woman, a combination of themes that reached apotheosis in *The King and I*.

Hammerstein has a folksy image, painted in by "Ol' Man River" and "You'll Never Walk Alone," not to mention the "lark who is learning to pray" in *The Sound of Music's* title song. Yet the Hammerstein Sondheim knew was sophisticated, not merely intelligent but wise, and quick and sharp in retort. The difference between the man Hammerstein was and the characters Hammerstein wrote about were striking, and never more so than in the third Rodgers and Hammerstein show, *Allegro*. An experimental musical that divided its public into admirers and scoffers, *Allegro* also occasioned young Steve's first experience in the commercial theatre, when he was still in college. With the show scheduled to play its tryout in September of 1947, Steve was able to spend the latter half of his summer vacation from Williams as a "gofer" during *Allegro's* rehearsals. Along with *West Side Story* ten years later, *Allegro* was, by Steve's own admission, "the show which shaped my professional life."

Arguably the most significant musical that most people have never heard of, *Allegro* tells of a doctor, Joseph Taylor Jr., who is led to seek material success treating rich hypochondriacs. Answering a subconscious call from the small-town people he came from, he suddenly renounces his fancy practice, reclaims his ideals, and heads for home to begin his life anew.

It's a dangerously ordinary story. Other musicals of 1947 offered more picturesque tales: of a pot of leprechaun gold that grants three wishes (*Finian's Rainbow*), a ghost village in kilts (*Brigadoon*), Tchaikofsky's love life, heterosexual in this version (*Music In My Heart*), con men on a madcap rampage in bygone days (*High Button Shoes*). What made *Allegro* special was not its plot but its execution, for Rodgers and Hammerstein wrote it to defy traditional realism. The action took place on a mostly bare stage on which a group of reciter-singers in "chorus" costumes would address both the public and the protagonist as if embodying a bizarre theatrical id. People would die only to reappear, figments of someone's recollections, and other people would turn up in places they had no physical access to.

Thus, at one point in Act Two, when Joe was in deepest despair about the way he was wasting his life, his father and others of his home town materialized upstage calling to him, though geographically they were many miles apart. This was, of course, a musical number. But instead of the soliloquy one expected from Joe himself, articulating through musical-play sophistication the abstractions in his mind, the song closed in on him from outside: his mother, who died in Act One, stole in from the shadows to sing "Come Home."

Allegro wasn't a fantasy, but its staging was, as scenes tumbled into each other cinematically, one set of players leaving the stage as the next set entered, in a kind of dissolve; as back projections, black traveler curtains, and bits of furniture replaced the customary scenic package that no big musical dared go without; as Agnes de Mille's ballets kept seizing control of the action; as that chorus analyzed events for us.

This was a revolution in format. Where other musicals narrate directly, *Allegro* was stylized. Its presentation was as much a part of its relationship with the audience as its content was, and it explained its story while it was unfolding. No musical had ever attempted anything like this before, and the result was, truly, shocking. Some were baffled, irritated. Others—especially theatre people—were enthralled. Then, too, the piece was inconsistent in tone, giddy at times (as its title suggests: "lively") but sober or corny at others. As with Hammerstein's great experiment with *Show Boat*, twenty years before, parts of it didn't match.*

For example, too much of the score is distributed among minor characters (the heroine scarcely sings at all), possibly to emphasize Hammerstein's notion that when someone becomes prominent, importunate forces make demands on him. Thus, over the thirty-odd years of his life that *Allegro* covers, Joe Taylor is defined for us almost entirely by others: as though his ability to express himself in song is being compromised, crowded off the stage.

---

* Nobody realizes how incoherent *Show Boat* is, because coherence was not an issue for audiences when it was new, in 1927, and from the 1940s on it has been seen in homogenizing revisions. It now appears to be a musical play of the Rodgers and Hammerstein type, though its genre is more precisely musical comedy with the soul of a spoken play and the heart of an operetta. And then there's "Ol' Man River," a genre in itself.

Of course, this subversion of the formal etiquette—ripping open a show's "cover" to reveal its insides in operation—is exactly why *Allegro* struck its admirers as a marvel. Young Steve, assisting on the production, was one of those inspired by its meta-theatricality. "Content dictates form" is a favorite Sondheim maxim, and *Allegro*'s whirlwind staging—with sub-texts bubbling up from the unconscious amid a hubbub of ever-changing optics—was made necessary by *Allegro*'s subject matter, which can be summed up as It all goes by so fast. Too fast, really, for us to think things through and make the right decisions.

This notion haunts many of Sondheim's own shows: should I marry?—because partnering is so hazardous. Or: should we Westernize or maintain our natural Asian culture? In Sondheim's world, we define our lives by our choices: so make them carefully! Then, too, *Allegro*'s non-realistic staging* influenced the way Sondheim's mature works—from *Company* through *Roadshow*—behaved. However, in one way Sondheim's musicals are very unlike *Allegro*. They are eminently stageable, as countless productions—large and small, with stars and penny plain—have proved. But *Allegro* is very, very difficult to bring off. It has emerged as a seminal title in the mu-sical's history, yet revivals are rare and seldom enthuse the public. As the famous joke goes, the English producer Cameron Mackintosh told Sond-heim, "You've spent your life trying to fix the second act of *Allegro*."

Simply bringing Steve into his first contact with the backstage of Broad-way was mentoring in itself, but, as we know, Hammerstein then gave his unofficial ward the assignment to write his four practice musicals. The first of them, based on Kaufman and Connelly's *Beggar on Horseback* with the title *All That Glitters*,† was Sondheim's first adventure with the notion that free will, not destiny, is the animating force in life. It is the direct opposite of the theme that dominates classical tragedy from the Greeks through Corneille to Eugene O'Neill, who all picture man as not the master but the subject of his identity. This inheres in his family, his class, his race, his social caste. *Beggar on Horseback*'s composer-protagonist, on the other hand, is in a quandary of his own making, one that would prove pertinent to Sond-

---

* Agnes de Mille directed as well choreographed the show, but during the Boston tryout Hammerstein stepped in as unbilled play doctor. *She* said it was because his script revisions were too last-minute for her to function effectively. *He* said she wasn't up to the job.

† Seeking Kaufman's permission to perform the show at Williams, Sondheim sent Kaufman the script encased in a heavy binder. Kaufman gave his assent and returned the script without the binder, presumably because it didn't fit inside the envelope he used. Many years later, Sondheim amused himself by making an issue of this with Kaufman's daughter, Anne, who dutifully went shopping for the nicest binder she could find. Protecting the family name, she then sent this prize to Sondheim. By return note, he joked, "It's about time."

heim's career: should he create, as an artist, what he is drawn to create, or what is likely to gain him a public?

Clearly, the hero of Sondheim's first musical is very like the composer in *Hangover Square*. Better, he is like the doctor in *Allegro*: he can fulfill himself as a small-town healer—a nobody, although, paradoxically, one of greatness— yet he allows himself to be vacuumed up by the one per cent in the Big City.

One makes theatre out of how one feels about life, and Sondheim felt very differently than Hammerstein did. The Sondheim worldview is: free will is wasted on the young, nothing is easy, and everything is personal. Thus, while Sondheim learned from Hammerstein's use of the musical's structural elements, he borrowed nothing from his mentor's philosophy of life. *Allegro* ends as its hero sets forth—at about the age of forty, remember— to reboot his purpose on earth. In one of Sondheim's key works, *Follies*, turning forty marks one's dissolution into a space enclosed by nostalgia, regret, despair, inaction: "not going left," as a *Follies* lyric puts it, "not going right."

And yet Sondheim inherited something very personal from Hammer- stein: a sense of indebtedness to society that some public figures acquire. In an interview with me in 1990, Sondheim referenced *Allegro*'s theme of the Important Man who falls victim to social pressures that rob him of not only time but the concentration needed to bring an artistic idea to fruition. Hammerstein usually wrote about romantic subjects—exotic, tempestuous heroines like Rose-Marie, enchanted meme-arias like "Indian Love Call," uniformed adventurers from French revolutionaries to Mounties. In *Allegro*, suddenly, Hammerstein was making theatre out of not how he felt about life but how he was actually living it—not least because he was, as Sond- heim put it, a "one-worlder."* In the 1940s, his prominent name would ensure that Hammerstein would be beseeched to substantiate mastheads, commit- tees, meetings. Which is more important, musical comedy or peace on earth?

When *Allegro* was new, in 1947, this was subject matter too intellectual for a musical. As Sondheim put it, "I remember thinking at the time, 'Gee, that's an awfully special problem'... and guess what? The same thing has happened to me. Because you suddenly feel a reponsibility to give some- thing back [to society]." Thus, Sondheim became the president of the Dra- matists Guild—not a figurehead position, but a time-consuming job in which one who has Arrived tries to make it easier for others to Get There as well.

Sondheim had other mentors, though they all appeared once he was grown up and less emotionally vulnerable. Hammerstein entered Sondheim's life

---

* After presidential candidate Wendell Wilkie's bestseller of 1943, *One World*, which became the focus of a movement hoping to install a global social and legal administration— which of course ultimately took form as the United Nations.

when he was cut off from his father, whom he loved, and living with his mother, whom he disliked, so he was more than a teacher: a friend. A tricky one, too, for—as I've said already—though outwardly jovial and generous, Hammerstein could be insensitive and sarcastic with intimates, and he hid from the world a fierce competitive streak. Still, he was very, very smart, and so was Sondheim; very, very smart people tend to want to know each other. It makes life interesting, even if some of them are enraged beasts like Lillian Hellman or sneaky-Pete troublemakers like Gore Vidal. Besides, it is generally only smart people who can maintain relationships based on mutual understanding. Most of our friends, however loyal, will not understand us in the deepest sense, and, without an understanding, sympathetically comprehending friend or two, no one will know who we are. We become isolated—which, ironically, is the condition of more than a few of Sondheim's major characters.

It is worth noting that, while Sondheim is fiercely loyal to Hammerstein on the personal level, he thinks that Hammerstein's artistry was "limited," and that, after his first phenomenally influential titles with Richard Rodgers, from *Oklahoma!* to *The King and I*, Hammerstein's voice lost its urgency in his last five Rodgers shows. (In an interview with me, the word Sondheim uses is "dead," though this is presumably a colloquial exaggeration.)

Unlike Hammerstein, with whom Sondheim never wrote a show, his later mentors were all collaborators. First was Leonard Bernstein—composer, conductor, author, television eminence on *Omnibus* and the Young People's Concerts, New York cultural personality, and international workaholic gadabout. One definition of a genius is the person who sees the world differently than everyone else does and persuades you that he's right and everyone else is wrong. It's also called "thinking outside the box," but it really means "living on the strength of an intense and productive imagination"—and that was Bernstein. Though he was no more than twelve years Sondheim's senior when they wrote *West Side Story*'s score, Bernstein was already very rich in theatrical and musical experience, with hit Broadway shows, symphonic works, and a reputation as one of the world's greatest and most melodramatic conductors, emoting and stamping and gesturing on the podium as though he was as much a part of the program as Beethoven or Stravinsky.

In short, Bernstein was show biz with a classical background. So was Sondheim, and he would take command of Broadway as Bernstein never quite did. Still, at the time it was very much the relationship of the kid and his Dutch uncle; in a letter to fellow composer David Diamond, Bernstein called Sondheim "a charming gifted boy." As I've said, Bernstein's one-upmanship could be maddening, but he and Sondheim remained close on the personal (but not professional) level, and Bernstein would play guru when Sondheim needed to talk to someone who understood musical composition and theatrical expedience, a rare combination.

West Side Story was also the show on which Sondheim first worked with Hal Prince, at that time a producer but later the producer-director of Sondheim's seventies shows, from *Company* and *Follies* through *A Little Night Music* to *Pacific Overtures* and *Sweeney Todd*. If Oscar Hammerstein taught Sondheim the basics of construction in the musical, it was Prince who with Sondheim worked out the deconstruction of the musical, liquidating realism for a presentational style in which the audience is always to remember that it is in the theatre, that the action is not "real" but an assembly of performers who discuss the story while enacting it.

This is the famous "concept musical," a term that has been used so differently by so many that today it has no meaning. In the 1970s, however—and because of the Sondheim-Prince shows—the words invoked the format introduced in *Allegro* and developed in Kurt Weill and Alan Jay Lerner's *Love Life* (1948) and John Kander and Fred Ebb's *Cabaret* (1966). In the usual musical, such as *The Music Man*, a story is told straightforwardly and the characters come and go as if in life. In the concept musical, however—as I said about *Allegro*—characters can "step out of the show" to comment to the audience, or slip into a scene in which they are not actually "present," or even reappear after death. If *The Music Man* were a concept musical, some of the Iowa chorus people would infiltrate scenes with the principals or occupy the audience during set changes, gossiping in snatches of song from their unique take on things, Iowa Confidential; and the father whose early death has traumatized young Winthrop would physically haunt the story, his survivors sensing his presence without actually communicating with him. Perhaps he'd have a number essentializing the show's theme, "Listen To the Music," or something of the like.

So let us drop in on one of Sondheim's concept musicals, *A Little Night Music*. There is no chorus per se, but, along with its principals, the show uses an ensemble of five operatic vocalists, always referred to as "Liebeslieder [Love Songs] Singers," after the quartet that Brahms used in his two *Liebeslieder-Walzer* song cycles.* Sondheim's two sopranos, one mezzo, tenor, and baritone have no roles in the plot, yet they take part in its unfolding, to share with the audience what the benighted characters in the actual storyline cannot articulate themselves. Thus, a lawyer and his lovely young bride attend the theatre, she unaware that he once had an affair with the actress starring in the play that very night. Shall we make it interesting? The lawyer

---

* Brahms used a two-piano accompaniment, and the show alludes to this by starting and ending with one of the Liebeslieder men hitting a few keys on a stage piano.

is twice his wife's age, and they have never had sex. What, we wonder, holds them together?

Meanwhile, the play begins, and two of the Liebeslieder women appear in courtier costumes in what is obviously a period *comédie érotique* in the manner of Marivaux, creating a ramp-up for the actress' entrance with salacious tidbits about her proficiency in the sensual arts. Then the actress cascades onto the stage in flashy prima donna style, curtseys to accept her applause, and, "old pro that she is," the stage directions tell us, "she cases the house."

And there's the lawyer she knew years before—who happens to be the love of her life.

Instantly, the action feezes while, in their thoughts, lawyer and actress connect once again. But now the Liebeslieder group takes the stage to tell us, in effect, what these two old friends are thinking, or what they should be thinking if they were wise enough to comprehend love and its discontents. "Remember?" one of the quintet sings. "Remember?" asks another. They get a song out of it, the music caroling merrily away as lawyer and actress pensively revisit that most fatal territory in the Sondheim geography, the past.

"Remember?" is broken into sections and intercut with narrative-driving dialogue scenes as the young wife, disturbed by the actress's apparent familiarity with her husband, flees the theatre and this only technically married couple returns home. They're just in time to miss an arresting turn of plot: the lawyer's son and housemaid have just cut off a failed sexual union of their own.

The question of sexual congruity—not just who loves but who *needs*—is elemental in *A Little Night Music*, and now the Liebeslieder group buttons up the sequence with a last bit of "Remember?." The rhyme scheme runs from "through" to "flu," and now, as the actress' rooms appear, she herself holding a glass of beer and eating a sandwich, the five so to say "concept" singers finish their analysis with an ironic "I'm sure it was—you."

That last word is key, for the entire show asks us if we can ever know who "you" is. Why have the lawyer and actress, so well made for each other, been separated for fourteen years? Why is the lawyer married to a near-child who is in fact in love with the lawyer's son? Why is the actress involved with a selfish lout without an ounce of culture or intellect? In a traditional musical, the lawyer or actress might have had a nostalgic solo reviewing their affair—or perhaps a duet in which each tells a different story about the same events. It takes a concept musical to slip in a "Remember?," liquidating the very notion of romance, of our ability to comprehend it. Instead of learning only what the characters know about themselves, we learn much more: what the *authors* know about the world.

And that is the concept musical in a nutshell. It doesn't simply tell the story: it dissects the story. Thus, the public gets two Sondheim shows in one—what happened and what it means, complete with startling theatrical gestures and the characters' occasionally revealing that they know they're in a play.

This is the art of Sondheim, but also that of Prince. The key transitional show between the first concept musical, *Allegro*, and Sondheim's own *Allegros* is Kander and Ebb's aforementioned *Cabaret*, which Prince not only produced but directed. *Cabaret* takes place in two distinct worlds. One is a humdrum "real life" in Weimar Germany and the other the magical cabaret itself, which comments on the real-life story in songs comic and biting. Thus, Nazi Jew-hatred is mocked in "If They Could See Her Through My Eyes," the lament of a man in love with a socially incorrect female...a gorilla. But never fear: "She doesn't look Jewish at all," he sings at the end, for the concept musical often disturbs the average theatregoer's comfort zone, another reason why the Sondheim-Prince titles dismayed some of the public at first.

Each of *Cabaret*'s two worlds counts its own inhabitants. The cabaret offers a sycophantic court led by the mischievous Emcee, while the real-life figures are middle class and self-defining. Only one character moves freely between the two spheres—the enchantingly peculiar Sally Bowles, who takes part in a real-life romance but also entertains on the cabaret stage, where nothing is real, especially life.

Because the concept musical is mercurial as a rule, ever renovating the genre, each concept show devises new ways to tweak format, and *Cabaret*'s best innovation occurs when, near the end, Sally sings the title number. At first, we take it for her club act. But then, in the original production, a curtain of streamers fell behind her, cutting her off from the cabaret, from everywhere. "Come to the cabaret," she urged: hide from reality. The show had melted, so to say, into its message, though Sally was articulating the opposite of the evening's theme. It was a warning by irony and, at the same time, a dramatic stunt, a coup. And its communication lay as much in how it was staged as in what it was saying. That's how the concept musical works.

Here's another example, moving back to Sondheim's works. *Sweeney Todd* uses an eerie ballad as its theme song to frame the evening and supply transitions between scenes. A realistic musical might include such a piece, but it would have to be sung by a miscellaneous ensemble, representing an out-of-story guide, comparable to a novel's omniscient narrator. *Sweeney Todd*, however, gives us its theme song in concept style, mixing the leads in with the chorus and thus letting them relate data to the audience that their characters do not have access to. Using a kind of Brechtian meta-theatre, the concept musical allows its players to slip into and out of character, so the last rendition of the ballad is given by the entire company, the principals stepping forward from where they were when the storytelling ended. They're thus still in costume, yet not strictly in chime with their roles. They're "ensemble" now, a concept crew. At the ballad's last line, they turn to race offstage, except the two stars, originally Len Cariou and Angela Lansbury. One has been a deranged serial killer, the other his accomplice—and both just got killed. But now they've become actors in an epilogue.

Or have they? They appear still in character, she ambivalent in some hard to describe way and he as intense as ever. Rounding off the ballad, they, too, quit this very high-tech playing area, this reality puppet show. It's over, right? No: in a concept musical, it isn't over till the lights go out. At the last moment, they turn and, as the script indicates, "exchange a look." But, as Prince directed it, what Cariou and Lansbury shared was not just the ending of a play but the spirit of solipsistic savagery that had been guiding it almost from the first scene. Lansbury went offstage right and Cariou straight upstage through a doorway. As he disappeared, he glared at the public while slamming the door behind him. It's a promise: "I'll be back!"

As with so much of modern play production—Peter Brook's work comes to mind—that final gesture of defiance caps the show's excitement in general. It puts a final button on the style of the production: it *feels* right. Art can be studied or improvisational; Sondheim is studied, eloquent in explaining what his music is meant to accomplish in specific detail. In an interview with Eddie Shapiro for his book *Nothing Like a Dame*, Donna Murphy recalled Sondheim giving notes on *Passion*: "Rarely was something just a musical note; it was about this whole life behind . . . why it was a quarter note, or . . . the tempo would be faster because she was closer to orgasm, and then [Sondheim] was going to pull [the tempo] back.

On the other hand, Prince is more instinctive, improvisational *naïve*, in Friedrich Schiller's famous terminology, rather than *sentimental*. That is, Prince is at one with nature (or as much nature as contemporary Manhattan offers) and creates out of an unexamined urge rather than an articulated purpose. Sondheim, on the contrary, is the sentimental artist, seeking to reconnect with nature. In other words, Prince works within the world as he "feels" it. Sondheim examines the world from the outside, to claim a place in it. Prince is the smooth, Sondheim the rough.

This presents a kind of friendly antagonism, a chemistry that explodes in the rich theatricality of their shows. It may explain why the five Sondheim-Prince titles of the 1970s give us so much to think about. They have resonance and honesty but also the classic's interior contradictions that keep us enthralled. If God is love, why is *The Divine Comedy* obsessed with ghastly punishment? Is Don Quixote a lunatic or a visionary? How did the senior Karamazov end up with sons so different from each other—a prude, a hysteric, a priest? Why doesn't Wotan simply keep the Nibelung's ring?

Don't we have comparable questions about *Company*? *Follies*? The marvelous friction between Sondheim's calculated playwrighting and Prince's intuitive producing—in effect, their Harold Bloomian Chaos—certainly brought something new to the musical, for most preceding masterpieces, such as *Show Boat* and *Carousel*, were conceived and executed in harmonious circumstances.* Then, too, such shows came along at a time when everyone agreed on what a musical *was*. By the time of Sondheim-Prince, the musical had become so protean that there was disagreement on the very purposes of the form and how it should comport itself. This is why the term "concept musical" lost its meaning so quickly: today, there is no single definition even of what constitutes a musical, period.

It is only fair to note that Prince hates the whole "concept musical" thing. It seemed to paste a brag on his work that he had never intended, creating, he says, a "backlash" from those who felt uneasy at these shows and were looking for something to blame them for. Further, and to repeat, Sondheim hates the theatre of Bertolt Brecht and would not be caught dead letting anything "Brechtian" occur in his works. "The cartoonish characters and polemic dialogue," he wrote in the second volume of his collected lyrics, are "for me, insufferably simplistic."

Nevertheless, Brecht and the concept musical share qualities we think of as thrilling—moments when a play seems to crash off the stage into our imagination, creating a realism beyond theatre and, simultaneously, a theatre beyond realism.

Think of that scene in Brecht's *Mother Courage* when the protagonist's younger son is executed (offstage) because, instead of ransoming him for the demanded price, she tried to bargain. Now he is dead, and, worse, when they bring his corpse in, she must pretend that she doesn't know who he is. Brecht's stage directions say only that she shakes her head, but in the playwright's own production for the Berliner Ensemble, the Mother Courage—Brecht's wife, Helene Weigel—let out a silent scream, an O of despair so titanic it could not be given voice. This bit of, as they used to call it, "business" has achieved a bullet point in the annals of post-Stanislafsky stagecraft, a kind of stylized naturalism that takes one's breath away. There is nothing simplistic about it. Still, it is absolute Brecht, confronting the audience with his worldview while stimulating it with honesty.

Sondheim gives us something comparable in *Follies*, when the four leads have been showing off in a private Follies of their own, one gala number

---

* *Show Boat*'s producer, Florenz Ziegfeld, harried the authors with demands for more laughs but otherwise let them alone. *Carousel* saw a bit of static between its director, Rouben Mamoulian, and choreographer, Agnes de Mille, because he had a musical sensibility and she was territorial. Both wanted to lead the band.

after another . . . till the last of the four, leading a hat-and-cane strut with the chorus, blows his lines, shakes, stutters, and finally breaks down as the show retreats from him, liquidating itself as his own sense of self dissolves.

Now, for the first moments of all this, spectators new to *Follies* think it's the actor, not the character, who has lost his way, and thus are hurled into the drama, sharing his terror. Because, in the world of Sondheim-Prince, anyone who struts is a fraud: strutting is a mark of confidence, and the naturalism of Sondheim's musicals insists that everyone of talent or intelligence is either ambivalent or in denial.

Sondheim's Shows

Saturday Night

Lighthearted musical comedy on the traditional American theme of Be Yourself, unproduced, 1954. Premiere England, 1997.

Based on an unproduced play, *Front Porch in Flatbush*, by Philip G. and Julius J. Epstein.

Music and lyrics: Stephen Sondheim. Book: Julius Epstein.

After Sondheim's apprentice musicals in his college years, *Saturday Night* was the work planned to effect his entrée on Broadway. The action, set on three successive Saturday nights, tells of young Brooklynites trying out courtship tactics while one of the boys, seeking to aggrandize himself, gets into legal trouble. The Epstein brothers, known primarily for screenplays (including *Casablanca*), based their reckless protagonist on a third Epstein sibling, using a figure popular in American art, the lovable rogue. This particular one is obsessed with success as a style: getting ahead is what a smart young gentleman *does*, like knowing how to dress or when to tip.

The show's producer, Lemuel Ayers, was one of Broadway's major set and costume designers. His credits took in dazzling work on *Song of Norway*, *Bloomer Girl*, *My Darlin' Aida*, and *Kismet*, and he had produced (and designed) two Cole Porter shows, *Kiss Me, Kate* and *Out of This World*, truly spectacular-looking productions. Ayers had put on straight plays as well, but he saw *Front Porch in Flatbush* as a musical—possibly a second *Guys and Dolls* (1950), imbued with the argot and character of a lowdown New York subculture. It was an out-of-character project for Ayers, who concentrated on period shows with opportunities for high-toned vocalism; the six shows cited before *Guys and Dolls* above were virtually all operettas or operetta-related. But then, Ayers had just handled the sets and costumes for *The Pajama*

Game (1954), a contemporary working-class piece utterly lacking in show-off optics or legit singing, and it turned out a smash. Frank Loesser had written *Guys and Dolls'* songs, and Ayers wanted Loesser for *Saturday Night*. However, Loesser was busy with (immediately) Samuel Goldwyn's *Hans Christian Andersen* movie and (in the long range) *The Most Happy Fella*. So Sondheim got the job, the show to open during the 1955–56 season (which turned out a poor one for musicals, though *My Fair Lady* arrived in March).

It is tempting to speculate on how *Saturday Night* would have affected Sondheim's career if the show had been produced after all. And it's especially intriguing to meet the composer-lyricist on his first professional outing, twenty-four years old and eager to assert himself, working in a form he never returned to, traditional multi-scene musical comedy using more or less simple character motivations to drive the plot and unambiguous character songs to expand it emotionally. Later Sondheim shows aren't traditional anything, and his characters struggle with neurotic problems, just as people in the audience do.

Thus, *Saturday Night* is something of an homage to the fantasy world of musical comedies like, say, *The Gingham Girl* and *Good News!*, both from the 1920s, *Saturday Night's* time setting. Such shows inhabit an essentially carefree world. People know who they are, and their only problem is usually romantic and temporary, though *The Gingham Girl's* heroine wants to build a cookie business and the college students of *Good News!* obsess over the Big Game.

Saturday Night's anti-hero, Gene, knows who he is, but restively, unhappily. A runner on Wall Street, he has access to the world of the rich and social, yet only as an outsider. He wants in. To explain him to us, Sondheim gives him one of the most basic implements in the musical's toolbox, the Wanting Song. Gene's is "Class," set to a mildly cocky swagger and, endearingly, showing how little Gene actually knows about the usages of the great world, as when he pictures himself stylishly ordering "a large demitasse." There's a key line in this number, on that very American notion that a commoner can be king. Gene understands that there may be some alchemy involved, but he thinks it's all exterior—clothes and manners. He has contempt for "some people" who are happy buying a bit of this and that "on the installment plan." Not Gene. What he is is useless to him: "I want to be what I can!"

Interestingly, "Some People," the Wanting Song of Madam Rose, *Gypsy's* anti-heroine, expresses similar hopes. But to Rose, it isn't about style. It's about determination. Gene's worldview is materialistic: he wants to be rich. Rose's worldview is artistic: she wants to be famous.

And that's not a joke. Whether in *Saturday Night*, the much darker *Gypsy*, or the naturalistically fantastical shows of the Sondheim-Prince era, the songs are a portal into the meaning of the piece. That wasn't true of *The Gingham Girl* or *Good News!*. These two "Some people" songs drive their respective shows' plot momentum even as they observe character, especially of the pushy and selfish but all the same spectacular Rose. Her lyrics reveal that she thinks renown is synonymous with guts. If you're famous, it *is* art. *Saturday Night*'s "Class," however, gives us an unspectacular fellow, even something of a loser.

But then, *Saturday Night*'s characters are strictly from the neighborhood. Later, Sondheim will give us jazzy New Yorkers, fairy-tale folk, even John Wilkes Booth and Squeaky Fromme. *Saturday Night*'s crew, by contrast, lacks color. The show is plotty, as fifties musical comedies tended to be, but these boys and girls of Flatbush are believable to a fault: dull. Sondheim enlivens them in the opening title number, as one of them plays a ragtime piano solo to punch up a humdrum situation: four dateless guys hoping for a hook-up. And "In the Movies" allows two girls to make ironic remarks on the difference between Hollywood scenarios and real life. Hollywood is self-sacrificing mothers and Rudolph Valentino; real life is this musical.

It was daring, really: to confront sexy, zany, rowdy musical comedy—in the age of *Wonderful Town*, *Can-Can*, and *Damn Yankees*—with a taste of the ordinary. Perhaps that was why no producer offered to take over the project when Lemuel Ayers suddenly died, of leukemia. In 1960, however, after working with Sondheim on *Gypsy*, Jule Styne (a producer as well as composer, who co-presented four musicals written by others out of sheer enthusiasm for talent) decided to resuscitate *Saturday Night*. Grateful but uneasy, Sondheim went along with it till the audition stage, when, feeling that his compositional level had outstripped what he was capable of six years before, he halted the proceedings. This reveals an important aspect of Sondheim's art: his musical style ceaselessly evolves, and he finds it difficult to return creatively to ancient history.

When *Saturday Night* was finally given an airing, in 1997 at the small Bridewell Theatre in London, the score revealed Sondheim glowing with melody and as clever as one can be while justifying the characters' narrow cultural background. Chicago saw the show in 1999, and it finally reached New York in 2000 (some forty-five years late), at an off-Broadway house, the Second Stage Theatre, scored by Sondheim's usual orchestrator, Jonathan Tunick, and with a Broadway-level cast.

The work went over very well, and it's amusing to see Sondheim composing those "hummable" tunes that his detractors love to accuse him of never writing. On the other hand, *Saturday Night*'s uncomplicated characters seem to need endearing melody of a basic kind, and when a band vocalist solos on "Love's a Bond," one feels the tune could almost—mind you, I say *almost*—slip into a *Good News!* revival without vexing the soundscape. Later, when Sondheim composes for the troubled leads of *Follies* or the demented creatures of *Sweeney Todd*, the music grows more textured.

Unfortunately, this air of all too ordinary lives having a bit of adventure handicaps *Saturday Night* and keeps it from taking a major place in the Sondheim oeuvre. And, as for speculation about how it might have fared on Broadway in the mid-1950s, I don't believe it would have succeeded, because it was so unlike the other musicals of that time. They were big, with singing and dancing choruses, lots of scenery, and a rota of big-deal production numbers. *Saturday Night* has no chorus, its decor is modest, and there is little opportunity for exhibition dancing. Today, we are used to offbeat musicals—even those that, like *Saturday Night*, are unconventionally conventional, doing the usual things in a unique way. But critics and the public of the 1950s would have been skeptical. It might have harmed Sondheim's career, so it is just as well that it didn't turn up till much later: because, with no *Saturday Night* in the counting, Sondheim's first three Broadway shows were all hits.

West Side Story

Gesamtkunstwerk on gang violence, 1957.

Suggested by Shakespeare's *Romeo and Juliet*.

Music: Leonard Bernstein. Lyrics: Stephen Sondheim. Book: Arthur Laurents.

Original Leads: Larry Kert, Carol Lawrence, Chita Rivera. Director: Jerome Robbins.

Experimental artwork doesn't usually attract a mass audience, but *West Side Story* is one of the most popular American musicals, even if it took the movie adaptation (1961) to win the piece its national public. All the same, Sondheim at first wanted no part of it: a composer doesn't write lyrics to someone else's music. As I've said, Oscar Hammerstein urged him to take advantage of this opportunity to work with top talent, for besides composer Bernstein and librettist Laurents there was director-choreographer Jerome Robbins (working with co-choreographer Peter Gennaro). Designers Oliver Smith (for the sets) and Irene Sharaff (for the costumes) were high on the go-to list themselves, though one wonders how important clothing design was in a show about kids who run around in jeans and T-shirts. Further, this was Sondheim's first professional union with Hal Prince, the show's co-producer with his usual partner, Robert E. Griffith. The credits thus bulged with talent to an embarrassing degree, and daddy knows best, so Sondheim signed on.

West Side Story was originally to have treated hostilities between Roman Catholic and Jewish gangs, as *East Side Story*—but had there ever been organized tribal violence of that kind? A Catholic-Jewish gang war? It sounds imaginary, and the authors gave up on it till the news started to tell of antagonism between natives and immigrant Hispanics in Los Angeles.

Suddenly, a modern retelling of the war between Shakespeare's Capulet and Montague clans seemed naturalistic.

Yet the show took on a dreamlike quality, a very romanticized naturalism. One reason was its heavy reliance on dance. Granted, the era's musicals were saturated with choreography. Yet somehow the way Robbins and Gennaro laid out the routines united movement and narrative as seldom before. Perhaps it was because this above all youthful story kept erupting in the extroverted energy of the young, whether in the joyous "Dance at the Gym" or "The Rumble," when the Jets and Sharks met in combat and the first-act curtain fell on a stage decorated with two corpses—the most shocking curtain to that point in the musical's history.

Then, too, musicals of the day juggled a succession of sets alternating from full-stage views to forestage views with sometimes cumbersome mechanical transitions, while *West Side Story* moved almost cinematically from view to view. The full stage was almost always in use, with smaller sets rolled on for the alleys, a bridal shop, a bedroom. Thus, there were none of the stop-and-start hiccups of the usual production; this gave *West Side Story* a unique air of suspense and inevitability as it charged from event to event.

Further affirming the show's unique appeal was its resetting and updating of *Romeo and Juliet*, with just enough correspondence to give the audience the sense of a new reading of an old story, rather as with the theatre festivals of Ancient Greece. Better, *West Side Story* was *Romeo and Juliet* put into music, as Romeo wonders what marvelous adventure is on its way (in "Something's Coming"), as the lovers take vows in secret (in "One Hand, One Heart"), as Juliet brings up the second-act curtain on a never-fail theatrical irony: the carefree moment before the bad news, in this case of the two deaths in the rumble (in "I Feel Pretty").

Finally, *West Side Story* was the first *Gesamtkunstwerk* among musicals. The term is Richard Wagner's, meaning, roughly, "all the arts combined in a single organism." The fusion of script and score dated back to *The Beggar's Opera* (1728), in the English genre called "ballad opera." Dance was integrated in various ways in *The Band Wagon* (1931), *Oklahoma!* (1943), *On the Town* (1944), and *The Golden Apple* (1954). But *West Side Story* pioneered a seamless visual flow using a full-scale scenic design (as opposed to *Allegro's* "bare stage with bits and pieces" approach).

Even the cast's résumés were integrated. The usual musical hired performers strong in acting, or in singing, or in dancing, then tried to blend them, more or less, into a unit. For *West Side Story*, however, Jerome Robbins wanted people who could do everything. So heroine Maria (Carol Lawrence) and her confidante, Anita (Chita Rivera), could act, sing, and dance. The leader of the Jets, Riff (Mickey Calin), urged transcendence upon his hyper cohort in "Cool"—but he did not then leave the stage to the ensemble for the dance, as he would have in many another musical: he dominated the choreography as he dominated the gang.

Again, *West Side Story* was a naturalized fantasy. True, the Sharks' leader, Bernardo (Ken LeRoy), had been dancing since *Oklahoma!*, which made him far too old for the part. And the hero, Tony (Larry Kert), was a wonderful singer who could neither act nor dance. Still, Kert embodied the ardor that is the salient quality of Shakespeare's text, that youthful wonder that makes the tragedy all the more harrowing. A song cut during the tryout, "Like Everybody Else," sung by three of the Jets, emphasizes how the score takes its point of view from not society but its children. "I been to Night Court and I been rolled," Baby John complains. "Why can't I be old?" Here we see how much Shakespeare inheres in *West Side Story*, for *Romeo and Juliet* is all but overrun with the extravagant self-dramatizations of the young.

The parallels between play and musical are well observed, for Romeo meets Juliet at a ball, gets his close friend Mercutio killed through interference in a duel, and avenges him by killing Tybalt—and this is all in the musical. It does end differently: Maria survives. The authors were considering killing her as well, but Richard Rodgers advised them not to. "She's dead already," he told them.

Here are the musical's characters next to their source counterparts:

In Shakespeare	In the musical
Montagues	Jets
Capulets	Sharks
Romeo	Tony
Juliet	Maria
Mercutio	Riff*
Tybalt	Bernardo
Juliet's Nurse	Anita
Paris	Chino
Friar Laurence	Doc (proprietor of the local drug store)
The Prince of Verona	A combination of Lieutenant Schrank (a police detective) and Officer Krupke (a beat cop)

---

* *West Side Story*'s Mercutio is, as gang leader, the chief Montague, but in Shakespeare he is of neither feuding family. Though Romeo's buddy and ultimately a victim of Capulet belligerence, Mercutio is actually aligned with the ruling house of Verona. Benvolio, Romeo's other closest friend (who has no counterpart in *West Side Story*, having been absorbed by Riff) makes this clear in addressing the Prince in Act Three. When describing Shakespeare's anticipatory equivalent of the musical's rumble, he refers to "thy kinsman, brave Mercutio."

It's worth noting that Arthur Laurents' libretto doesn't simply echo Shakespeare. Laurents *adapts* him, retaining compelling character information to give the musical color. Consider: Shakespeare's Mercutio is a professional cynosure, witty and ribald, using words in endless stream-of-consciousness riddles:

> O Romeo, that she were, O that she were
> An open et cetera, thou a pop'rin pear!

So Laurents' Riff is the equivalent in high middle bop: "Unwind" and "Easy, freezy" and "I say I want the Jets to be Number One, to sail, to hold the sky!"

Further, Laurents' use of the Nurse in his invention of Anita is fascinating, for both characters have, at once, a lot of power and no power at all. The Nurse is in charge of Juliet yet remains a nobody in the Capulet hierarchy; Anita dominates Maria yet is nobody in the "man's world" of Latin culture. A sharp actress can steal the show in either role. Chita Rivera's Anita was thought imposing enough for her to replay the part in the first London production, in 1958, and, to look at it from another angle, Edna May Oliver turned down her chance to preserve her Broadway Parthy Ann in the 1936 *Show Boat* film in order to have a go at the Nurse for MGM's *Romeo*, with Leslie Howard and Norma Shearer.

This coming together of Shakespeare and the musical—however artistically ambitious a musical it was—is something of a creative oxymoron, as the performers needed for Elizabethan drama are vastly different from those who populated fifties musicals. Of course, *West Side Story* is not Elizabethan—but it would not have worked if the cast had not been able to find some modern equivalent of the original's passion and poetry. The challenge lies in the score as well as the script—in the ecstasy of "Maria," the helpless tenderness of "Tonight."

Thus, Jerome Robbins demanded twice the usual rehearsal time—an unprecedented eight weeks—in order to match the performances to his vision. He broke the actors apart—Jets here, Sharks there, grownups elsewhere altogether—and forbade intermingling. You *hate* each other. Don't present it. *Live* it! Tony Mordente, the original A-Rab, one of the Jets, told Robbins' biographer Amanda Vail that the notoriously sadistic Robbins was especially abusive with the good-natured Mickey Calin: "It was hard to think of [Calin] as our chief, our button guy, who if he would say, 'Go kill somebody,' we'd do it." So Robbins "pounded [Calin] into dust and molded him back into clay. . . . And you could see the change happening. More and more, Mickey became the leader of the Jets." Chita Rivera told Vail that Robbins' somewhat improvisational staging of the scene in which the Jets attack Anita—again, a development of a much less violent episode in *Romeo and Juliet*—set loose something rough and primitive in what till then had been guy-next-door chorus boys. Vail thought Rivera was "still shaken" talking about it many years later. Said Rivera, "We were getting in touch with feelings we never knew we had."

The posters for the first performances, out of town, billed Sondheim and Bernstein as co-lyricists. But Bernstein, master of so many trades, was adept at only comic verses. He had written some of the words to *On the Town*'s "I Can Cook, Too," a list song made of erotic double meanings ("My gravies just ooze"). And, on *Candide*, he gave verse to "I Am Easily Assimilated," a sardonic spoof of the "When in Rome" immigrant. At romantic numbers, however, Bernstein could not tell attar from deodorant, and Sondheim ended up writing so much of *West Side Story*'s lyrics that Bernstein let his partner take full billing credit for them. As Steve loves to tell us, Bernstein even offered to give up his royalty percentage, but a grateful Sondheim thought that might be too much to want. One thing Sondheim has never been intent on is money; rather, he navigates around loyalty and talent. So Sondheim took the credit without the bank, and thus gave up ninety-five years' (under the pre-1978 copyright law and the so-called "Sonny Bono amendment") worth of extra revenue.

Strange to say, Sondheim looks back on this first set of Sondheim lyrics to be heard on Broadway with rue. He likes "Something's Coming" because its images reflect the interests of a teenager. He likes the "Jet Song" and "Gee, Officer Krupke," the latter of which Robbins set on its feet in three hours—"one of the most brilliantly inventive [stagings] in one number I've ever seen."

Sondheim said this at a Dramatists Guild panel some thirty years later, when he noted that the "more contemplative lyrics" now struck him as self-conscious and even pretentious, as though he were dictating to characters rather than letting them express themselves. "Very 'written'" is how he put it. He felt this in particular about "I Feel Pretty," because the emphasis on rhyme must suggest sophistication, and Maria, who sings it, is a very sheltered young woman. I think something's wrong here. Everyone responds to rhyme, if only the "Roses are red, violets are blue" sort, and much of "I Feel Pretty" deals in obvious matches, like "pretty" and "witty." Other lines perfectly capture a young girl jumping for joy—"Such a pretty me," for instance.

Then, too, that number always goes over wonderfully. If there were a discord between who Maria is and what Sondheim gave her to sing, the audience would be confused and resistant. Sondheim even said that, after run-throughs before the tryout, he changed the lyrics, the better to respect character. But his collaborators preferred the first version, and it stayed in.

Jerome Robbins hated the number. He left it to the assistant choreographer, Peter Gennaro, to stage.* According to Carol Lawrence, Gennaro allowed her to make up her own idea of an "I Feel Pretty" dance, sporting a mantilla, faking a bullfight, then flopping on the bed for the blackout. Oscar Hammerstein particularly loved the number—did *he* ever tell Sondheim that the lyrics weren't apt?—and later congratulated Robbins on its spontaneity, never dreaming that Robbins had nothing to do with it. Robbins took credit for it all the same.

As so often with breakaway projects, *West Side Story* had trouble getting its capitalization. As Bernstein put it at that Guild panel, "There was tremendous animosity to the whole idea." The production was about to go into rehearsal when its co-producer (and primary money-raiser) Cheryl Crawford abruptly pulled out on spurious grounds. "Cheryl," said Laurents, "you are an immoral woman." But this does show how strange *West Side Story* appeared to the "angels" (as they used to be called: those who backed Broadway productions), because Crawford in fact liked taking chances on unusual material. Amazingly, Columbia Records, Bernstein's own label, is supposed, at first, to have passed on making the cast album.

What? This after the firm's President and artistic guru, Goddard Lieberson, had just masterminded Columbia's financing of *My Fair Lady*, the most profitable musical (and biggest-selling LP) of its era? One year later, Lieberson, with all his power, wouldn't record Bernstein's Broadway show? With that score—which Lieberson must have heard? This is unbelievable; indeed, Columbia did in fact tape the *West Side Story* score in the end.

The show opened on September 26, 1957, at the Winter Garden Theatre after very successful tryouts in Washington, D.C., and Philadelphia. It was an electric event, the first big show of the season. Angry Young Man John Osborne's *Look Back in Anger*; Lena Horne; Helen Hayes and Richard Burton in Jean Anouilh; Noël Coward; Julie Harris; William Inge; and *The Music Man* were all to come, but only later in the year, and *West Side Story* won mostly raves. The *Times'* Brooks Atkinson caught the aspect of the *Gesamtkunstwerk*, noting, "Everything in *West Side Story* blends—the scenery...the costumes...the lighting. For this is one of those occasions when theatre people, engrossed in an original project, are all in top form." Only Walter Kerr, who specialized in hating any music more complex than "Three Blind Mice," gave it a mixed review: "Apart from the spinetingling velocity of the dances, [it is] almost never emotionally affecting."

---

* Robbins made a specialty of hating outstanding numbers in various shows. On *Gypsy*, he wanted the spectacular overture cut. Was it because the (of course unstaged) overture was the only part of the production that he couldn't take credit for?

At least Kerr mentioned Sondheim. He felt wonderful finally to have a show on Broadway, though that heady mix of big-wheel Names overwhelmed his credit. However, *West Side Story*'s true lost author was Peter Gennaro, who choreographed "America" and all of the Sharks' steps in the "Dance at the Gym." Jerome Robbins, apparently foreseeing how long the show's art would prove, made Gennaro sign a contract including the line "You hereby assign to me any and all rights in, and to any and all choreographic material created or suggested by you in connection with, the play." And when *West Side Story* won the Tony Award for Best Choreography, Jerome Robbins was the only recipient—and he didn't even thank Gennaro in his acceptance speech. (Compare that with Bernstein's giving Sondheim sole credit for the show's lyrics.)

And this came to light in a panel in the series *Dancers Over Forty*, in which Chita Rivera eulogized Gennaro. They worked on several shows together, with backgrounds ranging from Parisian to gypsy, and while Gennaro was, unlike Robbins, genuinely well liked by his dancers, Rivera emphasized how adept he was in ethnic styles. "Every nationality," she said. "Every color. He was the rainbow." And, finally: "My rhythm of life is Peter."

All this reminds us how much collaboration goes into the making of musicals—how much that doesn't get credited, whether from a co-choreographer, a dance arranger, an orchestrator, an assistant director. Once, especially in the 1920s and 1930s, musicals were assembled out of separate parts, script and score written off a treatment with little or no consultation between book writers and songwriters. Directors and choreographers also worked apart from each other, then everything would be shoved together. But *West Side Story* in particular marked a break from such practices, as when Robbins cast a single ensemble to act, sing, and dance together, or when all the creators contributed all the time in everyone else's department. This fluid collaboration had been evolving since *Oklahoma!*, fourteen years before. But *West Side Story* instituted it most completely. It really was the first all-talking, all-singing, all-dancing integrated musical.

After 734 performances, the production went out on tour—prematurely, for once the closing notice went up, the house started selling out. After ten months on the road, it returned to Broadway for 249 further repetitions. In London, rapturously received, it lasted longer than the combined New York runs. As I've said, the film expanded the show's reputation considerably, and we discern in this very formative Sondheim work the beginning of a pattern: a Sondheim musical achieves a qualified success made of intense admiration from some, mixed with ambivalence from others, only to grow in popularity till it reaches classic status.

Gypsy

Backstager drawn from Gypsy Rose Lee's autobiography, 1959.

Music: Jule Styne. Lyrics: Stephen Sondheim. Book: Arthur Laurents.

Original Leads: Ethel Merman, Jack Klugman, Sandra Church. Director: Jerome Robbins.

Billed as "a musical fable" (presumably because it tells a true story with fanciful alterations), *Gypsy* marked Sondheim's only experience working with an old-fashioned Broadway star who wore her roles like tailoring, made to measure. Ethel Merman was, most famously, the revivalist singer Reno Sweeney, the spy-foiling Canal Zone good-time gal Panama Hattie, and Annie Oakley, but she was born to play Rose,* the mother of stripper Gypsy Rose Lee and actress June Havoc (from Hovick, the family name). Merman did have to expand her normal playing space from a face-front, stand-and-deliver caricature to accommodate a more organic participation in the action, but Rose was the part of a lifetime, worth the trouble. Besides, the story gave her something really arresting to play: she pushes her two daughters into vaudeville, promoting first the cute one and, when she flees, then the other one. But vaudeville is dead, and somehow the act ends up in burlesque, so Rose now pushes the other one into stripping. Rose's vis-à-vis, Herbie, is so disgusted he walks out on her, and at length she realizes that she threw her life away chasing a lie:

ROSE: I guess I did do it for me.... Just wanted to be noticed.

---

* Often referred to as "Momma Rose," she is never called that in the show. A few characters address her as "Madam Rose," and librettist Arthur Laurents popularized it; bit by bit, it has been catching on.

Jule Styne composed Merman's hullaballoo of a voice into the music, and Laurents and Sondheim wrote book and lyrics around her aggressive self-confidence. And these three and Merman made the show, for while Jerome Robbins was directing, there actually was little for him to do in his unique way. *Gypsy* is not a choreographer's show. There is some modest vaudeville hoofing and one exhibition dance (in "All I Need Is the Girl") for a supporting player. But *Gypsy* is really a very tight little tale about three people—Rose, Herbie, and Louise (Gypsy Rose Lee herself). There is no Second Couple, no local-color chorus, no title song.

And no Robbins "production." He had envisioned a panorama of bygone show business, a very vaudeville in itself. Laurents, in his memoir *Original Story By*, thought Robbins "listless" in rehearsal: because he was "directing a *Gypsy* that wasn't the *Gypsy* that he had conceived." *West Side Story* was a staging triumph. But *Gypsy* was a writing triumph.

Sondheim's definition of his work as "playwrighting" is much more fulfilled here than in *West Side Story*. The script tells us how the world sees Rose, from her disapproving father to the boys in the act, who might like her but don't trust her. *Gypsy*'s songs, however, tell us how Rose sees the world. "Some People," her establishing number, is, as I've said, a cousin of *Saturday Night*'s "Class": a statement of purpose that scorns those who don't get it. But Jule Styne gave "Some People" an emphatic vocal line, and Sondheim's lyrics fold themselves around the unique sense of self that Merman always brought to her raveups. So Oscar Hammerstein was right to guide his protégé into creating for a star: it centers the art on not just character and theme but on how that character will present that theme. "Playing bingo and paying rent," Rose sings: that's the ninety-nine per cent. Rose is going to join her own one per cent: not in money and power but in the self-esteem that show-biz success inspires.

It's the American dream—starring in the *Follies*, as Marilyn Miller did at the end of *Sally* (1920) and Barbra Streisand did halfway through Act One of *Funny Girl* (1964). Or becoming the greatest showman in the land, as Jim Dale did in *Barnum* (1980). Does Rose harbor comparable ambitions? All we see her attain, really, is low-rent vaudeville. One reason "Some People" never loses its fascination is its paradoxical flavor of flop confidence. It sounds like the start of a great career (like another Jule Styne number, *Funny Girl*'s "I'm the Greatest Star," to Bob Merrill's lyrics), yet it leads to nowhere.

Pursuing their stimulation of the Merman persona, Styne and Sondheim followed "Some People" with softer spots—the ballad "Small World," the comic number "Mr. Goldstone," the fox trot "You'll Never Get Away From Me." Thus, Rose can be loving (or is it opportunistic?), amusing (or is it overkill?), or at ease in romance (or is it fatally lacking in perspective?). To close Act One, when the cute daughter has abandoned her and the other one is all that's left, the authors provisioned the titanic Merman again, in "Everything's Coming Up Roses." The script describes the number as "violently joyous," and, once more, Sondheim fills the air with the images that Rose thinks of as exciting, though to us they're clichés—"curtain up" and "Santa Claus." It's the Little Golden Book version of success, or, for a later time, Barney the Dinosaur's version. We'll make popcorn and stay up till seven o'clock! The odd confluence of Rose's name and the use of "roses" in the lyric confused Jerome Robbins when he first heard it. "Everything's coming up Rose's *what*?" he famously asked.

These five character songs limn Rose so brilliantly that *Gypsy* got away with giving her relatively little more to sing in Act Two—a trio with Herbie and Louise ("Together Wherever We Go"), nine vocal bars of a reprise of part of "Small World," and a final solo, "Rose's Turn." For a short while during the tryout, Merman had another comedy spot, "Smile, Girls," a tango to open the second act, when Rose is rehearsing the new act, the Toreadorables. It's a droll spot, with a running gag, for Rose twice peps the team up, addressing each girl individually except the one who gets "Smile, Whateveryournameis." However, the show had already made it plain that Rose thinks she can make art with literally anyone, and the number was dropped as redundant. Besides, as an audiotape of Merman's final New York Rose attests, no later Rose got more laughs out of the script than Merman; the last thing she needed was more comedy. At that, "Together," which directly succeeded "Smile, Girls," boasted a great joke on a rhyme to match "By threes": as two go off left in a show-biz exit, one goes off right—and Merman sang, "No, this way, Louise!" Sondheim habitually wrote stage business into his songs after Jerome Robbins scalded him with the usual Robbins acid when *West Side Story*'s "Maria" gave him nothing to play with visually. It's a love song. A guy met a girl. He's radiant with tenderness and hope, so he stands there and sings.

He stands there and sings *for three minutes*?

So Robbins says, "*You* stage it."

"Rose's Turn" was the opposite: staged before it was written. It was Rose's moment of *anagnorisis*, the ancient Greek "recognition," when the protagonist is shattered by a catastrophic discovery, and Rose, reviewing her life, realizes that all her conniving and cheating and hoping and planning created one victim above all: herself. The scene was dreamed up during rehearsals, when, mapping it out in improvisation, Robbins "played" Rose while Sondheim, at the keyboard, hammered out reminiscences of the show's score. "Rose's Turn"—her own personal act, after the years of devising acts for others—was to be the ultimate eleven o'clock song. Not just the greatest yet, but one to land with an intensity this exhibition genre had never known before.

"It's sorta more an aria than a song," Merman told Sondheim—"doubtfully," he recalls—when he and Styne played the finished number for her.

Exactly—and it took Merman's conservative outlook to pinpoint Sondheim's modernist renovations in how a score works. Yes, Sondheim writes songs. But he writes, as well, "arias": musical scenes that are more encompassing, more dramatically kinetic, than songs. Of course, the musical scene has been around for a long time, but mainly in operettas. The musical comedies that Merman specialized in used the building blocks of simple song structures. For the public to see Madam Rose having a nervous breakdown of *anagnorisis* in an "aria" was an illuminating shock—not least when Rose stumbled over the word "Momma," repeating it over and over in panic.

One might have expected Merman to balk at such personal loss of command—as a character, of course, not as a performer. But on Merman's Broadway, the star *was* the character.

Furthermore, *Gypsy* had been rehearsing very well. It ran too long and had too many old vaudevillians in it, left over from Robbins' original plan that had been abandoned long before. (Almost all the extra players were gone before the Philadelphia tryout, and the last few were dropped before New York.) Still, *Gypsy* had the one thing Merman knew a Merman show had to have, a Great Merman Score. After all, this was why she had been unwilling to take a chance on the as yet unknown music of Sondheim in the first place. Styne, Merman thought, was a little nutty, but what composer wasn't? And Sondheim was a bit too sure of himself for a kid. But they had come through for her—Laurents, too. Rose, she declared in *Merman: An Autobiography*, was "the most memorable character ever portrayed in any musical, with all due respect to Nellie Forbush [in *South Pacific*], Liza Doolittle [in *My Fair Lady*], and any of the rest." So Merman sang that Mad Scene of a "Rose's Turn," complete with the embarrassing "Momma"s, and no one else has ever brought them off as well.

Opening on May 21, 1959, at the Broadway Theatre, *Gypsy* was a smash, lasting 702 performances and an eight-month tour. When it turned classic, some called it the greatest musical of all—not least, surely, because the central role calls for a dense and demanding power. It is more than memorable, as Merman said: it is The Challenge. No diva is complete without a Rose in her repertory.

Oddly, *Gypsy* lost every Tony Award to *The Sound of Music* or *Fiorello!* (both of which tied for Best Musical). Merman, her Herbie (Jack Klugman), and her Louise (Sandra Church) lost in their nominations, Merman to

Mary Martin. Jerome Robbins lost to *Fiorello!*'s George Abbott. Even *The Sound of Music*'s conductor, Frederick Dvonch, won over *Gypsy*'s Milton Rosenstock. But then, *The Sound of Music* is a feelgood show, while *Gypsy*, for all its humor, is dark—even, ultimately, dismissive. It says that your mother doesn't love you. She loves what she thinks you can do for her.

A Funny Thing Happened On the Way To the Forum

Whirlwind farce utilizing iconic characters of ancient Roman comedy, 1962.

Music and lyrics: Stephen Sondheim. Book: Burt Shevelove and Larry Gelbart.

Original lead: Zero Mostel. Director: George Abbott.

This was Sondheim's third hit in a row, and the first time Broadway heard an all-Sondheim score. The title derives from the standup comic's traditional ramp-up to a joke:

> COMIC: A funny thing happened on the way to the show tonight. Fella stopped me on the street and asked for a buck. Said he hadn't had a bite in three days. So I bit him.

Thus, for the title alone, the public was supposed to understand that *Forum* was a comic's craze-'em-up, a hellzapoppin. Stereotypes—sweethearts, arrogant military man, randy old husband and termagant wife, et al.—get into non-stop scheming and disguises, taking twists and double-twists till you couldn't recount the plot for a million dollars.

The driveline follows the slave Pseudolus (Zero Mostel) as he tries to win his freedom by bringing his young master (Brian Davies) together with the girl (Preshy Marker) he loves. Who happens to be the latest acquisition of the procurer Marcus Lycus (John Carradine), promised to an army captain, Miles Gloriosus (literally "Braggart Soldier," Ron Holgate). Who turns out later to be the girl's long-lost sibling, separated when they were stolen in infancy by pirates. And so on, in what is possibly the funniest libretto of all time. A sample: Pseudolus attempts to pry the girl, a Cretan, from Lycus. How to play it, how to ... Ah! This'll work: Crete has been ravaged by a plague:

> LYCUS: Is it contagious?
>
> PSEUDOLUS: Did you ever see a plague that wasn't?

Or consider the henpecked husband, Senex (David Burns), on his mother-in-law:

> SENEX: A hundred and four [years old] and not one organ in working condition.

Oddly, the book has few jokes as such, mainly given to Pseudolus; the script is an interlock of character lines that derive fun not from what is said but from who says it—how the words reflect a worldview. Thus, the captain amuses because he sees himself as perfection. The shrewish wife (Ruth Kobart) regards her husband as a ninny, the captain as socially thrilling, and everyone else as exasperating—probably on purpose, just to spoil her day. Every statement they and the rest of the cast make leaps out of their individual personalities, so the common view that *Forum* is a reunion of old vaudevillians is a bit misleading. Vaudeville's humor was nothing but jokes. *Forum* is cleverer than that. Its style was old and hokey—"vaudevillish," we might say—but its content was new.

Directed by George Abbott, *Forum* played entirely in one piece of scenery. Not a unit set capable of modifying its views: a single, fixed location. It represented the facades of three houses in a Roman street, backed by a cyclorama onto which mood-defining projections were thrown, to underline the plot's ever-shifting attitudes, from romance to mayhem.* Further, there was virtually no dancing, just some gleeful pacing along the stage during "Everybody Ought To Have a Maid" and gyrations from the bordello girls when Lycus showed off his inventory. *Forum* was a musical cut down to an essence of zany fun.

The score matches it well. The early 1960s saw a number of extremely comic musicals in which nearly every number was a jest of some kind—*How To Succeed In Business Without Really Trying* (1961) and *Little Me* (1962) are two such—and *Forum* is funny even in its ballads. It is well known that, in this one show, Sondheim defied the standard practice of the Hammerstein score and its emotional expansion (as with *Oklahoma!*'s "People Will Say We're In Love")

---

* Nowadays, the multi-function unit set or the single-location set are common. However, they were all but unheard of in *Forum*'s 1962, though the English musical *Stop the World—I Want To Get Off* unfolded entirely in a circus ring in 1961 (and was seen here the next year, five months after *Forum*).

or thematic development (in the testosterone territorialism of "The Farmer and the Cowman"). Instead, Sondheim's *Forum* songs give the audience relaxation zones between each next sequence of bumper-cars madness.

Even so, *Forum*'s score does embrace the action at times, characterizing the boy in "Love, I Hear" and the girl in "(I'm) Lovely," slipping into the plot in "Impossible," as the boy and his father vie for bragging rights over the girl, and capturing the show's lopsided delight in the perky discords of "Pretty Little Picture." Such numbers may seem dramatically virginal next to the way later Sondheim scores marry their librettos, but *Forum*'s music sweetens the show, fleshes it out. That may be why the songs bunch up in the first half of Act One—to endear the characters to us while we're getting used to them. After all, *Forum* is essentially a gathering of the inhabitants of late burlesque—strippers and clowns—in the format of situation comedy using the dialogue of a Restoration wit dreaming he has been reincarnated as Groucho Marx. Once the musical tone has been set, the songs appear less frequently. Having humanized the high jinks, they can let the plot run its course.

One song did not work at all. It even threatened to sabotage the show. Out of town, *Forum* began with "Love Is in the Air," a gentle ballad with a hippety-hop vocal line. Sondheim thought enough of it to include it among the *Forum* titles he published, under his own imprint, Burthen Music Comp., Inc.* It apparently led audiences into anticipating a light comedy, and, when they didn't get one, they froze on the show. The reviews were hostile and ticket sales so poor that, at one matinée in Washington, D.C., *Forum* played to some fifty people. Even the show's director, George Abbott, so often the fixer of musicals suffering tryout confusion, had no idea what had gone wrong. "I guess we'll have to call in George Abbott," he said.

They called in Jerome Robbins, who immediately isolated that sweet-toned First Number as the culprit. He told Sondheim to write a new piece

---

* Through the twentieth century into the 1960s, a show's first song sheets appeared simultaneously with its first performances, in New Haven, Boston, or the like (which is why some titles that were cut before New York, like "Love Is in the Air," ended up, however briefly, in print). The plan was to take advantage of sheet-music sales if a title should suddenly soar into hit status—"Night and Day," "If I Loved You," "Hey, There." The 1950s was the last decade in which such hits were common, for rock and the garage band were to sweep away show tunes and the home piano. Sondheim took "burthen" from Jerome Kern, the last composer to refer to the refrain of a song by that term. *The Oxford Companion To Music*, Ninth Edition, tells us that it was originally "Burden," as in "faburden," in use from the tenth century and a term of changing meanings. It denotes, mainly, the harmonization of a choral piece, then only the bass line, and at last the main strain of a song. That is, following the verse (e.g., "Dere's an ol' man...") comes the burthen ("Ol' man river...") The word is more often encountered as the French *faux-bourdon* and the Italian *falsobordone*.

to match *Forum*'s high-pitched craziness, and Sondheim came up with "Comedy Tonight." The show opened in New York to rave reviews and gave Sondheim his longest Broadway run.

Everyone involved with the show tells the tale the same way, so it must have happened, yet it's still a strange story. Some hit musicals have opened perfectly. *Hello, Dolly!*: curtain up, chorus people ranged in "little old New York" poses hymn Dolly's praises, trolley trundles on with passengers, lady in purple dress lowers her newspaper—it's Dolly; we cheer—and sings a great establishing number, "I Put My Hand In."

But some hit musicals have opened oddly. *My Fair Lady*: Covent Garden operagoers look on as buskers run through a pointless dance. It does take an Instagram of the show's analysis of class: the haughty, dressy elite versus the ragamuffins. But it gives no hint of the wit and wisdom to come.

Forum's tryout turnaround is possibly the most famous backstage story in the book of Sondheim lore. But why this show suffered when others don't is a mystery. Is it possible that *Forum*'s difficulty lay not in the sweet nature of "Love Is in the Air" but rather because the lyrics emphasize romance? *Forum* has nothing to do with romance. Its love plot is a generic formality used to kick the plot into motion (Pseudolus gets his freedom if Boy Gets Girl). Anyway, farce is not a romantic form generally. *The Man Who Came To Dinner* is about egomania. *Noises Off* is about how art attempts (and fails) to order the chaos of life.

Another famous Sondheim story concerns *Forum*'s star, Zero Mostel, who was a gifted but selfish performer. "You don't give awards to the show," he cried, when *Fiddler on the Roof*, Mostel's next Broadway job after *Forum*, won a trophy. "You give the awards to *me*!" It was Mostel's habit to decorate over the course of a run, changing lines and business, so toying with his role that he would break out of character. When reproached, Mostel defended his ad libs, even stating that playing a show's run in its opening-night conformation was performing in "monotone."

As it happens, ad libbing was once very much a part of a star clown's performing etiquette. If Eddie Cantor, the Marx Brothers, or their colleagues saw an opportunity for an unscheduled laugh, they would grab it. It kept the art lively, and the public didn't expect a performance that had been "frozen" on opening night. However, this tradition began to die out in the 1930s; by Mostel's day it was over. Further, Mostel's inventions were often vulgar. In *Sondheim & Co.*, *Forum*'s co-librettist Burt Shevelove recalled his outrage in hearing Mostel, in a summer tour in the 1970s, spicing up *Forum* with childish violations of taste. Thus, when the plot demanded the use of a corpse, Shevelove and Gelbart played along with:

PSEUDOLUS: Gusto! Gusto, the body snatcher! He owes me a favor!

It's funny because the notion of someone running around ancient Rome with the name Gusto and the profession of body snatcher *is* funny. But Mostel changed it to:

PSEUDOLUS: Gusto, the body snatcher! He owes me a snatch!

And that's cheap and stupid.

Anyone Can Whistle

Satire on conformism, 1964

Music and lyrics: Stephen Sondheim. Book: Arthur Laurents.

Original Leads: Lee Remick, Angela Lansbury, Harry Guardino. Director: Arthur Laurents.

Billed variously as "a wild new musical," "a musical fable" (like the authors' *Gypsy*), and simply as "a new musical," *Anyone Can Whistle* was originally to be called *The Natives Are Restless*, the title of its (later cut) opening number. The natives inhabit an impoverished town ruled by a venal Mayoress and her three officials. When a fake "miracle" rock gushes saintly water, attracting pilgrims, the town stands to become profitable—but at this point the plot veers into that of a different show altogether. In this new storyline, the inmates of the Cookie Jar—the local insane asylum—mingle with the pilgrims and must be identified and isolated. Why? Because. But they aren't insane. They're nonconformists.

That's why they were locked up: individuals are dangerous to repressive regimes. But now their rebellious Nurse has taken charge of the storyline. She's not a Cookie, but she doesn't Fit In any more than her charges do. If the world is corrupt, why accommodate it?

Clearly designed as the show's heroine, the Nurse warns us that some sort of savior is on his way. But, in another cut number, "There Won't Be Trumpets," she assures us that he won't arrive in a heroic commotion. He'll just arrive. And about ten seconds later, he does—to a burst of trumpets.

Thus the work presents its central principals: the Mayoress, the Nurse, the Hero. The last two, who have the love plot, were supposed to have been Barbra Streisand (who took *Funny Girl* instead) and the Australian Keith

Michell, known on Broadway in the early 1960s as the comic-romantic lead of *Irma la Douce* and for one of the two key roles in Jean Anouilh's *The Rehearsal*: French pieces, a silly-sexy musical and a very dark comedy. It suggests Michell's versatility, and he was not only an ingratiating performer but, like Streisand, a singer of impact.

One wonders what might have happened had these two headed the cast, for in the end all three of *Whistle*'s leads went to Novelty Stars, unknown for work in musicals: Angela Lansbury,* Lee Remick, and Harry Guardino. They fielded what we can call "Broadway voices," with more personality than vocal tone (and Guardino got hoarse during the tryout and never recovered). But then, musical comedy has always got away with non-singing singers. It is operetta and the musical play—*The Student Prince, Carousel, Titanic*—that demand quasi-operatic voices.

And *Anyone Can Whistle* was pure musical comedy, pursuing a more or less nonsensical premise with the devil-may-care plotting favored in the 1920s and 1930s, in which crazy events lead on to more crazy events, filled with disguise and coincidence. *Whistle* has none of the archetypal beauty of *West Side Story* or *Gypsy*'s strict naturalism. It's a loony show, filled with reckless shenanigans. If *Hair* (1967) was the hippy of musicals, *Whistle* was the *Saturday Night Live*.

The show did have a point of view. Arthur Laurents, the author of *Whistle*'s script (as well as those to *West Side Story* and *Gypsy*), never wrote about nothing. Still, he failed to anchor *Whistle* clearly. Its villains are cartoons while the heroine is shaded nicely but the hero is a mystery. He is smart and magnetic if nothing else, but he *is* nothing else. Keeping to musical comedy, think of "pal" Joey, *The Pajama Game*'s Sid Sorokin, the music man Harold Hill: men we understand. At one point, *Whistle*'s hero tells the Mayoress, "You've got the wrong man." It's the truest line in the show: everyone's the wrong man, one way or another.

Bizarrely enough, that's Laurents' point. Society needs us all to be "right," because then we're easier to manage. To control. Historically, however, the American musical has always sided with the wrong men, from rogues to underdogs. It's an essentially subversive form. So *Whistle* should have succeeded—but it lacked clarity. If we don't know what the hero is for, at least tell us what he's against. Ultimately, *Anyone Can Whistle* confused critics and public alike. After a ghastly three weeks before hostile tryout audiences

---

* *Whistle* gave Lansbury her Big Break after twenty years in film. Jerry Herman saw *Whistle*, and he kept Lansbury in mind when, two years later, *Mame* was casting and Dolores Gray heavily favored for the lead. Herman held out for Lansbury, who made a sensation and remained one of the biggest of headliners—though it was *Murder, She Wrote*, on television, that made Lansbury a household name.

in Philadelphia, the show opened in New York (on April 4, 1964) to extremely mixed notices, from keen praise ("A happy escapist evening"— *Journal-American*; "Breathtaking surprises"—*World Telegram & Sun*) to scathing rejection ("It's unconstitutional to omit imagination and wit"— *New York Times*; "Forget it"—*Herald Tribune*). The run lasted 9 performances.

The worst problem was perhaps not the gnomic libretto but the terrible director: Arthur Laurents. He had directed on Broadway only twice before, first his own straight play *Invitation To a March* (with incidental music by Sondheim), then the Harold Rome musical *I Can Get It For You Wholesale*. On neither show was Laurents' work distinguished—*Wholesale*'s excitement was generated by Barbra Streisand's Broadway debut and by Herbert Ross' staging of the numbers. It is worth noting that *Wholesale*'s producer, David Merrick, was willing to present *Anyone Can Whistle* but not if Laurents directed it. Sondheim says that Merrick was wary of the "egoistic self-indulgence" of playwright-directors, but Merrick occasionally let writers stage their own works, play (*Cactus Flower*) and musical (*Do Re Mi*) alike. Rather, it would appear that Merrick didn't trust Laurents as a director, period. He never hired him after *Wholesale*—and among *Whistle*'s admirers it was once more Herbert Ross' choreography (including the arrestingly fantastical "Cookie Chase" ballet) that justified the production. Indeed, *Whistle*'s dancing was a positive talking point for reviewers, even those who didn't like the show as a whole.

Another problem lay in using Philadelphia as the tryout platform, for its public was notoriously resistant to offbeat material. With theatregoers bound to hate the show from the start, Sondheim and Laurents never got a fair assessment of where they might be erring. Still, the ending of *Whistle*'s first act, in those days almost invariably an amusing cliffhanger, to draw the public back after the intermission with a sense of anticipation, was, in this case, unfriendly. As the lights darkened on everyone but Guardino, he told the audience, "You are all mad." Whereupon the rest of the cast appeared in theatre seats as if they were the audience, clapping and laughing hysterically—uncomprehendingly, really. It came off exactly as the authors had imagined it, which thrilled them—such special effects often don't quite equal what the artists had envisioned. *Whistle*'s public, however, was not thrilled. They probably had the feeling that if they got this obscure joke they wouldn't like it.

Well, that's the price of leadership. *Anyone Can Whistle* was truly "ahead of its time," in the familiar phrase. True, it honored musical-comedy tradition, as I've said, in its prankish plot; those old George Gershwin and Cole Porter shows are just as silly. However, *Whistle* did treat serious matters in a gladsome way—repressive authority, intolerance of anyone "different."

These were concerns of the day, yes, but they hadn't yet found a secure place in musical comedy.

While tending these themes, however, the authors failed to define their two romantic leads, Remick and Guardino, with the traditional establishing number and character song. From, say, *Naughty Marietta* (1910) to *Thoroughly Modern Millie* (2002), the heroine needs to tell us who she is. Marietta's first solo, the title song, reveals her rebellious nature in music of expansive charm; instantly, after her first few lines of dialogue, she has come to life. And Millie's opener, "Not For the Life of Me," goes into its refrain in, the score demands, "Hot Dixieland," because this girl is sexy, ambitious, and surprising.

Unfortunately, *Anyone Can Whistle* skipped these field expedients. In *Sondheim & Co.*, Herbert Ross caught exactly why the show was so innovative but so difficult: "It had no musical comedy symbols, which left the audience with few recognizable things, very few anchors...to hold on to." Lee Remick did have a "what I'm like" solo—but it wasn't a song. Rather, it was a ferocious speech with musical underscoring. If it had a title, it would be "NOT—THAT—WORD!," and it was a marvelous flood of defiant statements about the Cookies and the "miracle" waters. But the public just wanted to know if the Nurse was waitin' for her dearie or contemplating what might make her life loverly. The speech had such impact that it dwarfed Remick's establishing song a few minutes later, the aforementioned "There Won't Be Trumpets," which is why it was cut. It's a terrific number (revivals tend to reinstate it, and it was recorded for and released on the cast album) but, following "NOT—THAT—WORD!," it felt like a second song in the same slot. It did give the audience an anchor—but only after the show had taken the audience out to sea in a storm.*

Of course, now that musicals in general are more sophisticated, *Whistle* poses no challenges. The book remains smug and cocksure, but the score carefully separates the lovers from the liars. Still, much of *Whistle* treats the difficulty in categorizing people, especially regarding who is sane and who insane. When Guardino, an alleged "doctor," drew such distinctions among the townspeople, he divided them into Group A...and Group One. A villain on the Mayoress' team asked, "But which group is what?," and then warned Guardino, "Doctor, you're not doing what we want you to!" Well, of course he isn't: *you've got the wrong man.* And all of this occurs in a

---

* The word she bans is "loonies." It's an attack word; her charges, remember, are called "Cookies," probably from the fifties term meaning "eccentric," *kook* and its adjective, *kookie*. Edd Byrnes played a character named Kookie on the television detective series *77 Sunset Strip*, though his Kookie was less eccentric than hip, with an opaque vocabulary. "Baby," he would say—and it's praise—"you're the ginchiest!"

fifteen-minute musical scene, "Simple," using dialogue, orchestral punctuation, and song in a sort of mini-opera, something unusual, to suit the unusual "doctor."

Conversely, the Mayoress' numbers are pastiche recollections of various genres. Sondheim had written two of *Saturday Night's* songs in the style of twenties ballads, but they were band-vocalist inserts, not character pieces. In *Whistle*, Sondheim limned the Mayoress to emphasize the politician's artificiality through the very artifice of her song spots—specialty numbers that strike poses using show-biz clues. The show's First Number, "Me and My Town," presented Lansbury in a Diva and Her Boys act complete with a fast middle section made of hand claps and call-and-response outcries. This format probably reached its apex in Judy Garland's spot in MGM's 1946 revue film *The Ziegfeld Follies*, "A Great Lady Has an Interview" (remember, Sondheim logged his most impressionable moviegoing in the 1940s), and was still entertainment lingua franca in 1964. It may have contributed to the feeling that *Whistle* was arch and precious, but it spoke to the public in terms it could readily absorb, and explains why the only thing the Philadelphians seemed to like about the show was Lansbury.

Similarly, the "Miracle Song," on the revelation of the town's "healing" waters, suggested a Frank Loesser gospel raveup, in the manner of *Guys and Dolls'* "Sit Down, You're Rockin' the Boat" and *How To Succeed's* "The Brotherhood Of Man." Most creative of all in *Whistle* is "I've Got You To Lean On," for the Mayoress and her three henchmen and something like Jule Styne writing in the Cole Porter manner. Feeling limited by all this referencing of song tropes, Lansbury asked Sondheim to give the Mayoress something personal, with feeling. Doesn't our Steve want his show to ring with human truth, with a core of frailty, honesty, need? Besides, Lansbury concluded, "[Lee] has five songs and [I] have only four."

It's "as good a reason to write a song as any," Sondheim dryly observes, recalling the moment in *Finishing the Hat*. He provided "A Parade in Town," which does indeed expand the Mayoress' ID beyond her membership in the one per cent. The song is intercut with an actual parade, as Guardino is carried aloft by an exuberant crowd, and the Mayoress' forlorn solo leaves us uncertain whether she's envious of his popularity or simply lonely, for her music stalks the celebrants with a heavy heart. It's a curious moment in an already extremely curious show; perhaps *Whistle's* trouble lies in its trying to do too much in one evening.

It certainly did texture Remick's and Guardino's parts. The Boy Meets Girl is supposed to be the easiest element in a musical, but *Whistle's* "doctor" and Nurse are puzzles. Authors can't get through an entire show on "You've got the wrong man"—we have to know *something* about him or we can't connect the dots. Remick's Nurse, too, was elusive. She and Guardino had a flirtation duet, "Come Play Wiz Me," in which the Nurse was disguised as the Lady from Lourdes (another town boasting of miracle healings). A few lines were in French—translated by a subtitle screen that sometimes didn't work properly—and Remick then went into an erotic dance with the Mayoress' four boys. It was an intriguing idea, playing on the notion that the inhibited Nurse—she's the one who, unlike anyone else, can't whistle—gets comfortable with sex (in other words, well adjusted in general) only when she's pretending to be somebody else. Still, it must have confused spectators.

Even Sondheim fans are confused by *Whistle*'s title song, a tender lament by one who can't "lower my guard." They fondly think of this as Sondheim's most personal number, a revelation he inadvertently affirmed by singling it out as his performance piece in one of the first Sondheim tribute concerts, in 1973. However, writing a theme song for an introvert doesn't mean you are one.

Do I Hear a Waltz?

An American in Venice, 1965.

Based on Arthur Laurents' play *The Time of the Cuckoo*.

Music: Richard Rodgers. Lyrics: Stephen Sondheim. Book: Arthur Laurents.

Original Leads: Elizabeth Allen, Sergio Franchi. Director: John Dexter.

This show shares something crucial with *Anyone Can Whistle*—a lamed heroine who believes she can redeem herself through music. *Whistle*'s Nurse wants to whistle, and *Waltz*'s Leona Samish needs to hear a romantic strain in three-quarter time. Otherwise, these two works are each other's opposite. *Whistle* was one of the sixties breakaway shows, while *Waltz*, just a year later, was conservative.

Its source, *The Time of the Cuckoo* (1952), was typical of its day: one set and a cast of ten. Shirley Booth played an American spinster in Venice, a thirty-something (though Booth was forty-five) hoping to spark her humdrum life with European romance. She got a taste of it with a suave but untrustworthy local, but could not finally open up and embrace it and took out her frustration on her fellow pensione guests at a party. Alone, she hurled a martini glass to shatter against a wall—a shocking moment in what had at first seemed like a boulevard comedy. One scene later, heartbroken, she returned to America.

Audiences at the play had already heard that its theatre, the Empire, was to be demolished when *Cuckoo* had closed. As the sixty-year-old house's red-and-gold interior had hosted many a beloved title (including *Life With Father*, to our own day the longest-running music-less play in Broadway history), *Cuckoo* remained a sentimental memory for many. Further, *Do I*

Hear a Waltz? arrived a mere eleven years after its antecedent had closed, so the recollection was vivid, not least of Shirley Booth's superb performance in her trademark blend of baby-doll sarcasm and self-deprecating whimsey. Booth created a character that women in the audience, however ruefully, recognized as a very American type, playful but on the needy side. Katharine Hepburn left her mark on the role in the film version, retitled *Summertime* (1955), the story beautifully opened up with location shooting in Venice itself. Most tourists arrive by train, and, upon exiting the station, find themselves staring at the western end of the Grand Canal, to realize—for the first time—that this city *really is built on water*. The movie caught this famous traveler's epiphany very precisely, later showing Hepburn falling into a canal when she backs up to take a photograph, which, in *Cuckoo*, of course occurred offstage.

No stage musical could challenge such filming, but the project had potential musical personalities in minor characters—two troubled newlyweds; the seen-it-all pensione proprietor, Signora Fioria...and of course the Venetian Leona becomes involved with someone who could be an Ezio Pinza sort, as in *South Pacific*. An opera guy—perhaps Cesare Siepi, trim and handsome, with a Don Giovanni air about him.

Still, who could equal in a musical *Cuckoo* what Shirley Booth (not to mention Hepburn) had made of Leona? This is not a multi-lead story, like *Guys and Dolls*, nor a triangle tale, like *Camelot*, nor even a two-person piece like *The Music Man*. Leona *is* the story: was there someone in the mid-sixties musical who could encompass the paradoxes of Leona's friendly and open yet suspicious and even angrily resentful character?

There was one: Shirley Booth herself, a marvelous singer in her own very strange way but now in her late fifties, too old to consider more than momentarily. So was Mary Martin—or so said Richard Rodgers, not only the show's composer but its producer; his calls were final. And yet. Martin was, above all, an enchanting gamine, with a youthful quality that might have borne her along wonderfully. In the right part—and Leona was perfect for her, though she would have had to finesse the anger—Martin was matchless.

Barbara Cook, one of Broadway's greatest vocalists, could have justified Leona's eccentricities as well. But no one would have accepted her as a love-starved spinster; having just come off of *The Gay Life* and *She Loves Me*, she was still in the cute-ingenue stage.

Then Rodgers decided to hire Sergio Franchi, an Italian matinée idol with a phenomenal tenor voice and, after just a few years in America, a huge following. Though not an accomplished actor, Franchi was a life-loving soul with a good heart and a willingness to try anything. The Leona should probably have been someone as big as Franchi, but not too grand a singer, because an extroverted delivery would overwhelm the needed wounded-bird portrayal. (At one point, it was even thought that Leona shouldn't sing at all, or only after she "heard" her waltz and opened up characterologically.) So Leona would be someone who reads as about thirty-eight, capable of a rich and nuanced portrayal, and just singer enough to interlock with the tonally abundant Franchi.

There was nobody like that anywhere. Rodgers hired Elizabeth Allen, an excellent performer in every respect, but simply too self-assured and attractive for Leona. Even Allen's singing voice gave her away: a confident, friendly belt with sharp diction, perfect for a glamor role like Mame but wrong for Leona.

So that was Problem One. Problem Two was Rodgers himself, because, after *The Sound of Music* (1959) and the death of Oscar Hammerstein, in 1960, Rodgers had failed to produce a single hit tune. His generation of composers—which took in Irving Berlin, Jerome Kern, George Gershwin, and Cole Porter, among others—tended to measure success by the number of hit songs they achieved rather than by the overall quality of a given score. Yes, that counted, too. But a certain commercial analysis, let us say, was hardwired into their worldview: if you're good at songwriting, you have hit songs. And note that Rodgers' biggest hit shows—*Oklahoma!*, *Carousel*, *South Pacific*, *The King and I*, and *The Sound of Music*, all with Hammerstein—each produced hits by the bunch. Let's rephrase: if you're good at songwriting, you have hit *scores*.

But Rodgers' recent work, on *No Strings* (1962) and the new numbers for the *State Fair* movie remake (1962), produced no genuine hits; the *State Fair* inserts were especially feeble. So Rodgers was in a cranky mood. Then, too, he felt crowded by all the gays on the scene, for, besides Sondheim and Laurents, the director, John Dexter, was gay, and Dexter's assistant, Wakefield Poole, was gay. And the doctor called in to cure the show's ailments in Boston, our old friend Herbert Ross, was gay-friendly. Rodgers definitely was not, though he had collaborated for over twenty years with Lorenz Hart, not only gay but of that mischievous and ironic spirit that we nowadays recognize as the gay style in art.

At least *Waltz* would enjoy a unique look. Beni Montresor (yet another gay artist) designed shimmering backdrops depicting views of Venice, with mobile pieces—bridges, the pensione furnishings—in front of them and lighting creating cinematic "dissolves." The plan was to capture the beauty of the city by suggestion, anticipating techniques Julie Taymor uses to create reality through unreal devices. Further, there was to be no dancing, in order to emphasize the dramatic core of the story. There was a chorus, but it was used as little more than the equivalent of LEGO mini-figs or Hollywood extras: window dressing.

Thus, *The Time of the Cuckoo* would not be musical-comedyized, as other plays were, in the manner of *Hello, Dolly!* (1964), *Mame* (1966), and *Cabaret* (1966). Instead, the original text would be deepened with the addition of songs but not inflated with production numbers. It was actually a somewhat daring notion, likely to frustrate a public now used to splashy play-into-musical adaptations. Why is there a chorus if not to sing? And if the principals don't dance, isn't *somebody* going to?

As well, there was Problem Number Three, the director. John Dexter, an Englishman, was a very difficult man, intense and bitter. He was also not a seasoned director of musicals. Dexter forged his career largely in the progressive social drama that seized the British stage from Noël Coward and Terence Rattigan. You know . . . fluff. True, Dexter directed Peter Shaffer's *Black Comedy*. (The "black" denotes not the macabre but a lighting stunt: the electricity goes off and the characters fumble about in the darkness, though the audience sees everything in blinding light.) Incredibly, Dexter directed also the most old-fashioned of English musicals, the light-as-lace *Half a Sixpence*, just a year before he did *Waltz*. (Dexter and his crew staged the London *Sixpence* only; the New York production was completely repurposed by others.) Later, as Director of Production at the Metropolitan Opera, Dexter was to revolutionize the house presentational style, emphasizing modest optics but genuine acting from the singers. So Dexter must have had sound instincts in music theatre. Yet on *Waltz* he seemed unable to deal with the form and heedless of its effect on the company.

Then, too, Dexter can't have been glad when Herbert Ross came in during the Boston tryout, in effect to bring *Waltz* more in line with audience expectations for a sixties musical. One of Ross' best improvements invigorated the title number, the heroine's exuberant celebration of her love—requited love—for the Venetian. At first alone on stage, she was gradually joined by more and more of the locals—two young girls, carabinieri in their very colorful uniforms topped by plumed headgear, a sailor, a nun, a balloon seller. Rodgers of course cast the music as a waltz, a form he was particularly adept in, and the irresistible three-quarter time captivated everyone on stage. Allen began to move to the beat, then the sailor and one of the girls danced separately on either side of Allen. Two Alpine tourists appeared, to take turns sweeping along the floor with Allen as now, suddenly, the whole place—the city, the world—began dancing to share Allen's joy. It was a moment basic to the musical since the 1920s, portraying the thrill of loving and being loved back. The number became a high point, and it was at this time, apparently, that Dexter stopped coming to rehearsals almost as a rule.

So perhaps what hurt *Waltz*—the show opened on March 18, 1965, to play for 220 performances in an atmosphere of disappointment from which it has never recovered—was its conception as a drama punctuated by song, modest and limited. The play would be the thing—but *The Time of the Cuckoo* isn't all that interesting in itself. Shirley Booth made it compelling. Without that performance, or something comparable, the piece seemed flat.

Rodgers didn't get a hit tune out of it, but he and Sondheim wote a solid story score, tuneful and clever. Carol Bruce, as the worldly Signora Fioria, had an amusing turn in "This Week Americans," excoriating the other nationalities she had to host; near the show's end, a reprise, "Last Week Americans," now welcomed the British. Bruce took part also in a trio, "Moon In My Window," as she, the young American wife, and Leona each took a chorus of a beguiling melody, the lyrics changing to reflect three different views of love.

Sondheim buffs especially admire the Second Couple's ironic "We're Gonna Be All Right," as Stuart Damon and Julienne Marie anticipated *Company*'s fears of the difficulties of marriage. As originally written, the song included one strophe with commentary so scathing that, after first appreciating its break-the-rules honesty, Rodgers later became enraged at it. Sondheim told me that, at dinner at the Chambord restaurant, Rodgers rolled up the lyric sheet and repeatedly banged it on the table in scorn—possibly because Mrs. Rodgers had detected in it a summation of her less than Happily Ever After with Dick. Sondheim had to rewrite that verse, though revivals reinstate the original.

With Franchi's smashing tenor at their disposal, Rodgers and Sondheim dreamed up an exhibition piece for him, "Bargaining," in which he gives Allen a lesson in shopping for the best price—not simply haggling but winning a contest of wills. The song was a "duet for one," Franchi voicing the seller in his natural tones and then the buyer in a pinging falsetto, switching back and forth with flashy dexterity till he capped the number with a gigantic high A flat.

As with the title song and its dancing villagers, "Bargaining" suggested what *Waltz* might have been like with a more adventurous score. It's a fine one: but it generally lacks the surprise we get when Sondheim writes the score by himself—the truly unexpected numbers like *Company*'s "The Little Things You Do Together" or *Pacific Overtures*' "Someone In a Tree." And after all the devilry of *Forum* and *Whistle*, *Do I Hear a Waltz?*'s lyrics sounded as if, almost, someone else could have written them. It's Sondheim's only set that isn't truly characteristic of what he does.

Sondheim did the show out of generosity rather than out of creative need: as a favor to Mary Rodgers, the composer's daughter and a longtime Sondheim intimate, and to Arthur Laurents. That was bad enough; worse was the barren partnership with the unyielding and by this time old-fashioned Rodgers, devoid of the inspiration Sondheim would get from people like

Jerome Robbins and Hal Prince. In the end, *Waltz* was ordinary by Sondheim standards: "No passion, no blood, and no reason to be" is how he put it in the recent television documentary *Six By Sondheim*. *Waltz* was rich in charm, but charm shows were fading in the 1960s—*The Gay Life*, *She Loves Me*, and *Flora, the Red Menace* were all lovely charm shows, and all failed.

Sondheim moved on, but that's putting it mildly. *Waltz* was the last show in what we might call his first period, when he at times wrote musicals he didn't compose himself. No more: and the second period further keynoted Sondheim as the musical's resident intellectual, writing shows with passion and blood but, even more, ideas. Again, Sondheim calls his scores "playwrighting" because they further action and character development. However, they are also playwrighting because they operate without the "charm" tag once so basic to the musical. Like Shaw or Giraudoux, Sondheim grapples with the human condition and its discontents.

Company

Stream-of-consciousness cross-section of marriage, 1970.

Music and lyrics: Stephen Sondheim. Book: George Furth.

Original Lead: Dean Jones. Director: Hal Prince.

A paradox: Sondheim is the disciple of Oscar Hammerstein, and he grew up in the Rodgers and Hammerstein era. Yet *Company*, arguably the most Sondheim of shows, is the musical that, more than any other, definitively ended the Rodgers and Hammerstein regime, with its straightforward structure made of dialogue scenes that build in power till they burst into song, emotionalizing the characters. *Company* offers songs interfering with dialogue scenes, commenting on them. Sometimes the songs emotionalize an idea rather than a character, and sometimes the songs get mischievous rather than emotional.

Company is: bachelor Robert, the five couples he pals around with, and his three girl friends—but we can't anticipate from that simple breakdown where the songs will fall or what they'll express. More than most musicals, *Company* is a surprise. Three husbands introduce "Sorry-Grateful," a touching ballad about one's ambivalence in sharing life, and Robert himself sings "Someone Is Waiting," another touching ballad. You could have guessed as much. But "The Little Things You Do Together" springs out at us as if from nowhere; its cue is a husband and wife physically fighting. (They're actually trying out her karate moves. But still.) This number doesn't specify anyone or guide narrative. It observes. And "The Ladies Who Lunch" is yet more removed from the action. A titanic "je ne regrette rien" from one of the wives, it's really a specialty spot that momentarily turns *Company* into a revue instead of a story show.

But *Company* isn't a story show. It isn't a revue, either. It has a book, and, to complete the paradox, it is very much under the influence of *Allegro*. So *Company* doesn't end the Rodgers and Hammerstein era? Indeed it does: because *Allegro* was Rodgers and Hammerstein's UFO, as the French put it.*
In their canon, *Allegro* itself defied the Rodgers and Hammerstein genre. That format demands "fourth wall" realism (even in *Carousel's* closing fantasy scenes), while *Allegro* is gestural theatre, using performers in deliberately unreal ways. Somehow, Hammerstein never could fit all the *Allegro* pieces together successfully, but Sondheim, Furth, producer-director Hal Prince, choreographer Michael Bennett, and set designer Boris Aronson "fixed *Allegro's* second act" in *Company*. For here was a show that combined all the elements of the musical—in both writing and staging—into a whole as smooth as a pane of glass.

What is *Company*? It's fast and trim yet something of a saga, a sweeping look at Robert's life among his dates and coterie, continually asking him, Why are you alone? Now, who exactly is the "company"? Is it Robert's friends, the couples? Is it his girl friends? Is it the troupe putting on this very show, so unlike the usual ensemble in a musical? Where are the cute boys and girls of the chorus, some superb singers and some superb dancers, cleverly blended together to look like singer-dancers? Prince cast the couples to *look* like couples—lived-in and "real," not confident show-biz pros or singer-dancers. Or is the company Robert himself, the permanent third wheel in a succession of scenes, the guy who comes over for drinks and chat: *your* company?

It's an easy role to cast, Robert, but difficult to play. He's in his thirties, handsome, fit, magnetic: one of the most basic types in the casting pool. However, he is passive in his scenes with the couples while they variously support, provoke, resent, and understand each other. They're the colorful figures, the energy that drives the show forward. Robert is, by comparison, a mystery. One character likens him to the Seagram Building—impenetrable without x-ray vision—and another says she sometimes catches him "just looking and looking." They love him, they depend on him, they crowd him, they urge him. In certain ways, Robert is a direct descendant of *Allegro's* protagonist, Joseph Taylor Jr.—a fine fellow who lets life happen to him instead of creating one for himself.

That is, until *Allegro's* climax, when, for the first time, Joe Taylor breaks out and chooses the way he wants to live. This moment is likened to a little

---

* As "objet volant non identifié," literally "unidentified flying object" but, idiomatically, the work unlike the other works in a creator's oeuvre.

boy's learning to walk—his late mother and grandmother appear as they did early in Act One, when little Joey took the first steps of his life. Similarly, Sondheim sees Robert as a youngster, goofing around in life till, at the end of *Company*, in the song "Being Alive," he attains maturity. In an interview with Robert Sokol in *The Sondheim Review*, Neil Patrick Harris (who played Robert in a New York Philharmonic staging in 2011) said Sondheim told him that *Company* is about "a boy becoming a man."

In other words, Robert isn't afraid of commitment: he's simply enjoying himself in a state of total freedom. Many Sondheim characters live in a form of slavery—frustrated wives in *Follies* and *A Little Night Music*, much of the population of Japan in *Pacific Overtures*, the working class in *Sweeney Todd*, the artist heroes of *Sunday in the Park With George*, Seurat a slave to his art and his great-grandson a slave to the politics and commercialization of art. And *Forum*'s Pseudolus is literally a slave. So Robert is unique, moving with absolute liberty through his world, helping out, refereeing, superintending the recreations. As Harris put it, "He's sort of a talk-show host."

Right. But then, as all of *Company*'s information clicks in, Robert realizes that his freedom is compromised by a worrisome solitude. Liberty has become a prison. In "Being Alive," he asserts a new attitude: now he wants to be half of a union, difficulties be damned. Another of those eleven o'clock songs that, in Sondheim shows, is less a star turn than a moment in which the entire work revolves on its axis and reverses its energy (as in *Gypsy*'s "Rose's Turn," *Anyone Can Whistle*'s "With So Little To Be Sure Of," and *A Little Night Music*'s "Send in the Clowns"), "Being Alive" moves Robert, step by step, with encouragements from his "company" (Joanne's "You're not a kid any more"; Amy's "*Want* something! Want *something!*"), to the realization that he can't live on friends. He needs romance, a *best* friend…marriage. In John Doyle's 2006 Cincinnati staging (later seen on Broadway), the performers played the instruments of the reduced orchestration themselves. Robert was the exception—to this moment. For now Raúl Esparza, the Robert, sat at the piano to accompany his own "Being Alive": a compelling objective-correlative for what is happening in the action. Music is love. Robert plays music for the first time: Robert learns to love.

That may sound a bit fanciful, but then *Company* itself is an almost imaginary piece, a sort of "realism-but." To return to Neil Patrick Harris' interview with Robert Sokol: Sondheim told Harris that, on one level, *Company* takes place entirely in Robert's mind. He sings, in the title number, about "All those photos up on the wall," and *Company* shows us what he's thinking as he looks at those photos. This musical is a dream, a collage of impressions. Thus, the other characters can irrupt into the action any time they want to: none of it is really happening. All we know for certain is that Robert is this amazing guy and everyone wants to know him.

So it's all the more ironic that, just after the show opened—on April 26, 1970, at the Alvin Theatre—the Robert, Dean Jones, wanted to quit the company (that word again, taking on many extra meanings) because of personal problems. He was going through a divorce, which made the material dangerously real to him, and Hal Prince replaced him with Larry Kert. The original Tony in *West Side Story*, Kert had worked for Prince again in *A Family Affair* (which Prince directed, taking over during the tryout) and as a replacement Cliff in *Cabaret*. So Prince knew that Kert, though a wonderful singer, was a less than compelling actor. With more time at his disposal, Prince might have looked harder for a new Robert. But Jones was very unhappy and anxious to leave. So Prince made a deal with him, which ran something like: Give me an opening night so that the critics see the show at its best, and I'll let you go within two weeks.

Then Kert took over, leaving something of a blank spot in the center of the work. Even so, the notion of an attractive and sophisticated bachelor, so utterly reconstructed from the Curlys (in *Oklahoma!*) and Sky Mastersons (in *Guys and Dolls*), only emphasized how new *Company* was, how fresh its attitudes. I single out Curly and Sky precisely because they, like Robert, are seen as very active in their respective communities, Curly's cowboys in a "cold" range war against the farmers and Sky's gamblers and touts of Damon Runyonland. Robert, too, claims a community, but it's the fractured world of knowitall New Yorkers, one that—you'd think—wouldn't "sing" as easily as Curly's wild west or Sky's cartoon outlawry. Again, that only made *Company* all the more special: intense and persuasive. If Dean Jones had been appearing as Curly or Sky, he might easily have played out his contract, for those roles are, however interesting, utterly untroubled. Curly and Sky know who they are; Robert only thinks he does.

As it was, Larry Kert was glad to play such a charismatic character, and he certainly looked the part. I knew a bunch of gay men who developed crushes on Kert at least partly because George Furth had given him a remarkably charming persona to fit into. I even knew one man who waited outside the stage door and knocked out an affair with Kert starting that night. *Company* was, all told, extremely glamorous, for all its "real" people in plain clothes. It was Manhattan, smart talk, wisecracks, and *now!* sex rolled into one.

Many people who are not professional writers used to take up writing as a hobby, or to articulate feelings about their lives, or just for relaxation. Being an actor, George Furth took up writing plays, and that's how *Company* got started, as a series of one-acts in which various third parties would interact with various married couples. Most of Sondheim's shows in his Prince era began life in a form different from the one they ultimately attained.

Follies was a murder mystery (actually a who'lldoit rather than a whodunit), with none of the Ziegfeldian pageantry. *Pacific Overtures* was a straight play. *Sweeney Todd* was going to be through-sung.

And *Company*, also a straight play, lacked Robert. Having trouble with his script, Furth turned to Sondheim, who showed it to Prince, who heard a musical in it. Somebody then came up with the idea of making the third parties a single individual—a thirty-something bachelor who is taken on a voyage of discovery in the world of heterosexual bonding. But Sondheim and Furth retained Furth's original structure of serial sketches rather than invent a linear narrative—though that wouldn't have been difficult. You start with Robert in his place of work, making plans to see one of the couples, and they reveal something that clicks on the plot-starter tab, leading to more scenes with more couples. Add in a designated sweetheart, making Robert half of a First Couple in the manner of the King and Mrs. Anna, or perhaps Candide and Cunegonde...

But why not originate a format? *Company* has no First Couple, no official Robert romance beyond, it appears, a one-night stand with a stewardess. Of his two other girl friends, one does little more than break up with him, and the other simply meets him on a park bench and then accompanies him on one of his couples visits. *Company*'s ending isn't wedding bells: instead, it's Robert's reaching the maturity of wanting to—as they used to call it—Settle Down.

This is a surprisingly gooey conclusion to the most innovative of shows; all it needs is a Neil Simon father thundering that Robert is a "bum" because he isn't married. There are no fathers in *Company*; there aren't even any children, though there are references to them. And Robert has no place of work. We don't even know how he makes his living. Furth's libretto strips away all the earmarks that particularize a story, because there isn't a story. *Company* disintegrated the musical's habitual framework that tells us who everybody is: a student prince in Heidelberg amid glee-singing classmates, the waitress he loves, and the class system that separates them. A crippled beggar, his woman, her brutal ex, a crafty dope peddler, and the rest of the ghetto of prayer and jubilation in *Porgy and Bess*. A matchmaker and the "well-known half-a-millionaire" she's after, along with a Second and even Third Couple, in *Hello, Dolly!*.

Not in *Company*. We don't know who anyone is, and no sets slip in and out to tell us where we are. All we saw (in the original production) was a high-rise apartment building, complete with elevator, that functioned as a kind of ant farm of high-end Manhattan life. Most interesting, Furth's dialogue is more playful than informative, pointed yet mysterious. It doesn't explain anything—for instance, how does Robert know these people?

Where did they meet? Is he on gala terms with all of them equally, or is there one husband, one wife, that he simply puts up with?

He does seem particularly drawn to Amy, the bride who, in "Getting Married Today," gives way to genuinely frantic jitters at the thought of being legally involved with the man she has been living with in—we imagine—bliss. It's a key scene, because Robert impulsively proposes to Amy himself—and that appears to soothe her anxiety. "You have to want to marry *some*body," she tells him, "not some*body*." And she hurries off to meet her other half at the church, and the first act ends almost immediately thereafter, pointing up this lesson in love: the marriage thing is scary, contagious, pervasive. Couples saying, "I do" are ubiquitous, and not only because of social pressures or economic benefits.

But why did Robert propose to Amy and not the unattached women he knows? What's the history of Robert and Amy? Furth gives no clues, and that's no accident, because *Company* cuts to the chase in every scene. This explains why the show's every revival plays like a new piece: it has no baggage.

Then there's Furth's oddly skewed dialogue, redolent of Manhattan smarties reveling in their bons mots. Some might call it mannered, but it's the opposite: purified. Robert's friends are always blurting out what most people think but don't say. This is in contrast with Robert, who's an open-sesame of feelgood clichés. It's as if he keeps trying to grab hold of the show, to twist it into a more typical musical, one that doesn't confront you with your demons. Then, in the work's most telling scene, the last of the "couples" sketches, it is Robert who suddenly does the blurting out, sitting in a night spot with the worldly Joanne. He is finally completing his voyage from carefree child to grownup, with a sense of responsibility and, by marriage contract to come, officially giving and being given to in turn. It sounds nice. And he's scared.

Before we quote him, let's consider whether or not Furth was influenced by the Broadway airings, in the 1960s, of Harold Pinter's plays, for, like Furth in *Company*, Pinter leaves out the explanatory details that reassure an audience but defy realism of character. Many playwrights, even today, puppet their players into delivering contrived expository lines, little synopses of what they're up to. It's akin to one character's telling another, in scene one, "Oh, I'm so resentful of my job at the pickle factory that pays for my younger brother's education but is certain to provision guilt and antagonism in the style of Arthur Miller directed by Elia Kazan, with Tonys for all of us."

But some of the interaction in *Company* does bear a Pinteresque feeling, as characters talk *around* the apparent subject rather than within it. In Pinter's *The Homecoming* (1965), a Canadian university professor visits his London family with his wife, who, at the play's end, stays to become the family's prostitute while her husband departs for home. No, *really*? In fact, she *is* a prostitute. He has just hired her off the street to *impersonate* his wife in order to express his contempt for his seedy relatives, coaching her in a couple of facts—they have three kids and they've just been in Venice—to give her credibility.

Of course, Pinter never states this in so many words because the professor and his "wife" wouldn't state it, either. But a careful reading of their first scene, when the two are alone in the family house, makes it unmistakable that they don't know each other:

> RUTH: Can I sit down?
> TEDDY: Of course.
> RUTH: I'm tired.
>   (Pause)
> TEDDY: Then sit down.
>   (She does not move.)

This hardly sounds like two people who have been living with each other for years. On the contrary, it sounds like two strangers, she so uncertain about this odd gig that she has no idea what she is allowed to do. And would the wife of an academic with career and standing—a doctor of philosophy, no less—want to prostitute herself for anyone, much less her husband's degenerate bloodline?

There's just enough of this in *Company* to make us wonder, comparably, how well Robert really knows these wonderful friends of his. Let's go back to his scene with Joanne—and, remember, she's the really edgy member of the "company." With a drink in one hand and a cigarette in the other, she fixes Robert with a look as sharp as the butterfly collector's needle, and Robert goes into a tensely rambling monologue, which ends:

> ROBERT: Whew! It's very drunk out tonight. What are you looking at, Joanne? It's my charisma, huh? Well, stop looking at my charisma!
> JOANNE: (still staring; no change in position or voice) When are we gonna make it?

Or consider *Company*'s opening scene, when Robert comes into his apartment to be met by a surprise party. He starts verbally overcompensating while his friends answer "lifelessly," intoning in ghostly chorus:

> ROBERT: Thank you for including me in your thoughts, your lives, your families. Yes, thank you for remembering. Thank you.
> THE COUPLES: You don't look it.

A double meaning: he states his age and they respond with the indicated cliché. But he *hasn't* stated his age. He has expressed gratitude for their being in his life *and they say he isn't really grateful at all.* So what kind of relationships are these, anyway? Is this Furth's revelation that the intimacy available in urban American civilization is fragile and elusive, even unattainable? We think *Company* says that marriage is difficult, but it says also that friendship is difficult as well.

As a seasoned actor,* Furth knew instinctively how written dialogue would play. Limiting this discussion to American writers of the twentieth century, let us observe that the playwrights who outlast their era, such as Clifford Odets or Tennessee Williams, create dialogue that plays. S. N. Behrman wrote dialogue that doesn't, which is why he is seldom revived, despite his great success in the 1930s and 1940s. Just to confuse the issue, Eugene O'Neill's early expressionist works (like *The Hairy Ape* and *The Great God Brown*) play well, but the grander yet still expressionist *Strange Interlude* does not. Later, *The Iceman Cometh* plays well even with some awkwardly self-conscious writing, but the following *A Long Day's Journey Into Night* plays magnificently from start to finish.

And so does *Company*, partly because the score does not blend into the book any more than the book "blends" into the lives it presents to us. The entire show is skewed, brilliant, lopsided in the way Furth and Sondheim approach the material. For instance, how does Robert know Larry and Joanne? They're an older couple, Larry a successful businessman (I guess), affable and easygoing and Joanne the typical Elaine Stritch role: a mean-girl sophisticate. And of course Stritch was the original New York Joanne—but that puzzles us all the more. Elaine Stritch and Robert are an extremely unlikely mix. Robert might have met Larry in some professional connection, but would they have become buddies? And, given that Robert doesn't appear to enjoy being analyzed, wouldn't he have been put off very early on by Joanne, who is as invasive as a colonoscopy? She rips into him in that aforementioned nightclub scene with "Jesus, you are lifted right out of a Krafft-Ebing case history" and then hits him with that "When are we going to make it?" line, throwing Robert and *Company* itself off its pins.

But is Joanne really coming on to Robert? She gives him a potential passion slot—two o'clock at her place, when Larry is at the gym—but we're not sure exactly what is happening in that transaction, except that it leads directly to the climax of the show, when Robert "makes it" to his moment

---

* Furth's acting career never reached breakout, but he did achieve a limited immortality in *Butch Cassidy and the Sundance Kid*, as Woodcock, who stands up to Paul Newman and Robert Redford when they rob a train. Twice. FURTH: "I work for Mr. E. H. Harriman of the Union Pacific Railroad, and he entrusted me . . ."

of self-discovery and more or less walks out of the forest of apartments and "extra man" socializing and becomes, at last, himself, setting aside the toys of youth to reach the most old-fashioned possibility in musical comedy, the solo in which someone we like pours out his heart to us. Being alive, losing my mind, what's the use of wond'rin'?. Messages that essentialize with such illumination that entertainment becomes enlightenment.

Robert has a few of these numbers—"Someone Is Waiting" and (added to the 1995 Roundabout revival and now a part of the show) "Marry Me a Little." They stand apart from the other songs, which tend to jut into rather than materialize out of the action. In *Contradictions*, Hal Prince specifically cites as the inspiration for this odd use of the music the English director Joan Littlewood's staging of Brendan Behan's *The Hostage* (1958), an indescribable farrago set in a Dublin boardinghouse. Seen in New York in 1960 in the Littlewood production, *The Hostage*, says Prince, "maneuvered currents of realism and fantasy compatibly in one play," which makes it sound a bit like *Company*. (Even if Behan's raucous farce-melodrama includes very disparate character elements, from flaming queens and prostitutes to outright crazies, and, further, deals with Irish Republican Army terrorism, while *Company*'s milieu is that of the serenely middle class.) *The Hostage*'s musical numbers, Prince continues, "erupted from rather than grew out of moments. They had the abrasive effect of attacking when you least expected, creating such life."

We've already remarked on this aspect of *Company* regarding "The Little Things You Do Together," and it is one of *Company*'s salient features. Some might think of this as Brechtian, despite Sondheim's distaste for Brecht's style. In fact, the songs in Brecht's plays are usually performance pieces— specialty numbers, like those in Kander and Ebb's *Chicago*. But that's not how *Company* uses its songs. The *Company* score is, for the most part, naturalistically integrated with the *Company* continuity. The trick is that you never know just who is going to sing about what till he or she has already started the number—creating, as Prince said of *The Hostage*, "such life."

In fact, *Company* is the show that introduced the mature Sondheim style in song. There is, for example:

One: The "playwrighting" plot number, in "Barcelona." This is in effect a dialogue scene turned into music, on the morning after Robert has enjoyed a sexual encounter with a stewardess. Made almost entirely of an exchange of very short lines, the song catches his sleepy trance and her wistful regret with an eerie realism. A much more elaborate version of this type of composition is the opening of *Into the Woods*, a vast rondo in which a number of plotlines are initiated, united by the refrain of the title melody, the whole thing taking up fifty pages of vocal score.

Two: The pastiche number, in "You Could Drive a Person Crazy." This one brings us back to the days of close-harmony "girl groups," as they were termed. Usually sister threesomes—the Boswells, the Andrewses—they sang everything from slow-dance ballads to raveups but were often best known for novelty songs with a unique hook in the lyrics, as with the German tang of the Andrews Sisters' "Bei Mir Bist Du Schoen" or the combination of war and jitterbug in "Boogie Woogie Bugle Boy [of Company B]." *Company*'s equivalent offers Robert's three girl friends—Kathy, the would-be homebody; April, the stewardess, a bit of an air-head; and Marta, the hipster ("The pulse of this city, kiddo, is me")—in a jump blues, given as a performance piece complete with a bow at the end. Sondheim's scores often delve into pastiche, perhaps most dazzlingly in the opening of *Pacific Overtures'* second act, "Please Hello." A playwrighting number as well, it treats the diplomacy of international emissaries engaging with a Japanese official: an American, to a Sousaesque march; a Brit, in Gilbert and Sullivan patter style; a Dutchman, in a waltz clog to the clacking of wooden shoes (on Japanese temple blocks); a Russian, in a wail of the steppes in f minor; and at last a Frenchman, in an Offenbachian cancan.

Three: The showstopper solo, in "The Ladies Who Lunch." Perhaps it was inevitable that Joanne would have something special to sing, as Elaine Stritch was known as much for her voice as for her expertise in tart badinage. But her number stands apart from the rest of the *Company* score; it almost doesn't even belong in the show. An ironic eulogy for the kind of woman Joanne might have been were she not utterly nonconformist, it does not relate to the show's theme, as the other songs do. It's simply great music-making, though it does demand a top-notch singer, confounding Hal Prince's wish to cast realistically rather than theatrically. Later Sondheim showstoppers are rooted in a work's scenario—*Follies'* "I'm Still Here" and "Could I Leave You?," for instance. *Sunday in the Park With George* offers, in "Finishing the Hat," an artist's credo that encapsulates not only the show but, arguably, Sondheim's canon as a whole: in the artist's life, the art comes first.

Four: The ingeniously verbal comic number, in "Getting Married Today." Sung by Amy, frantic at the thought of graduating her love affair to marriage, this one puts the singer through several verses of lines jammed together, feverishly hurtling forth with scarcely a second's breath break. There are funny lines within it, but the central jest is watching Amy zooming along while trying to keep her diction apt and her air intake indiscernible. Typically for Sondheim, this is also another playwrighting number, for Amy's hysteria is packaged with a church-choir soloist backed by choral Amens and snatches of dialogue from Paul and Robert and Paul's own rather clueless vocals. Interestingly, Amy's lines in this musical scene are her only real solo opportunities in the *Company* score, yet we infer that she is the only woman of the couples whom Robert could love as a husband. (His proposal comes later in this scene, and a cut number, "Multitudes of Amys," emphasizes his attraction to her.) Thus, an important character never gets her Wanting Song. She would in a conventional show, but *Company* is so unconventional that we don't know how important Amy really is: because Robert doesn't, despite his proposal. This is another reason why *Company* gives the director and his troupe so much to play: the piece is deliberately left blank or ambiguous here and there, leaving the actors to choose what to project, how to specify.

Indeed, *Company* truly is an actors' musical; few other musicals give the crew so much to explore. Take Sarah and Harry, the dieter and the drinker who end up in a karate fight. Is this a Strindbergian war of the genders, or just edgy play in the James Thurber manner? Or David and Jenny, who spend their scene smoking toke with Robert until...well, is it until David makes her stop against her will or until he senses that she *wants* him to stop her?

Again, all this interpretive room links *Company* to the postwar spoken drama, to, say, Sam Shepard or Edward Albee. But it also looks back to Oscar Hammerstein, for many of his characters can be tilted by actor's choices. Why is *Oklahoma!*'s Laurey so ambivalent about Curly? Is *The King and I*'s Mrs. Anna a progressive or a scold? *Company* marked a breakaway from the musical As It Was, but also from Sondheim's work before it. This title initiated Serious Sondheim, when he—as I've said—intellectualized the musical. It already was art, but from now on it would be controversial.

Follies

Gloomy pageant on disenchantment after the Expulsion From Eden, 1971.

Music and Lyrics: Stephen Sondheim. Book: James Goldman.

Original Leads: Alexis Smith, Gene Nelson, Dorothy Collins, John McMartin, Yvonne De Carlo. Directors: Hal Prince and Michael Bennett.

O
n April 4, 1971, Sondheim returned to the Winter Garden—the site of his first Broadway outing, *West Side Story*—for a show billed, in the manner of the day, as "a new musical." This is the greatest understatement in the history of new musicals, for *Follies* is an epic in miniature, a review of the past while examining the present, the most intimate of spectacles in its confidential outpourings, and, like *Allegro*, a work that divided theatregoers' reactions, from "fabulous" to "depressing."

But then, *Follies* is fabulous and depressing. It's also a very textured and deceptively complex piece, so let's deconstruct its layers one at a time. First the four leads:

BEN: an imposing public figure. His profession is never stated, but he seems to be a cross between Henry Kissinger and Gore Vidal.

PHYLLIS: Ben's wife. Chic, smart, and fearless.

BUDDY: a traveling salesman. A good guy, but corny. Forever in love with

SALLY: whom he married. Sally is dumb and frustrated, because she didn't want Buddy. She wanted Ben. But Ben and Buddy were close, or seemed to be—no one is close to Ben except Phyllis—so Sally may have married Buddy to be close to Ben.

There are four other leads: the same four people, except we see them as they were some twenty years before:

YOUNG BEN: suave, ambitious, opportunistic.

YOUNG PHYLLIS: nice, open, unformed.

YOUNG BUDDY: the same guy he'll become, but unaware of how miserable he'll be with

YOUNG SALLY: because when they married she was cute and amusingly unpredictable.

Now the scenario. *Follies* takes place at a show-biz reunion in a theatre that once housed a series of revues comparable to the *Ziegfeld Follies*. On the eve of its demolition, the Ziegfeld—here called Dimitri Weismann—throws a party for his former players. There is no story per se, no beginning, middle, and end. As the guests parade before us, reminiscing and bragging, we learn about Phyllis and Sally, who were members of Weismann's corps, and about Ben and Buddy, who courted them.

But let's be more precise. Buddy courted Sally. Ben's courting ranged more widely, because, while he was interested in Sally, she was too simple to serve as the consort of the grandee Ben planned to become. But Phyllis, intelligent and adaptable, could educate herself. When Elaine Stritch first heard *Company*'s "The Ladies Who Lunch," she thought a reference to "a piece of Mahler's" concerned something from a bakery. Phyllis *was* like that: culturally limited. However, to live up to Ben's expectations, she learned who Gustav Mahler was, and what concerts are about, and why people listen to—and, better, write—symphonies. She's a game girl; that might even be her salient quality.

Meanwhile, as the evening wears on, the central quartet's problems rise up and engulf them, especially Ben's self-hatred, Phyllis' anger at his neglect of her, Buddy's deflated marriage, and Sally's belief that Ben is her white knight. Finally, their misery and ire erupt in a *Follies* to end the follies: a revue that is set, ironically, in a place called Loveland. Each of the four gets his or her specialty, but Ben, as an "Is everybody happy?" vaudeville sybarite in top hat with cane, falls apart during his turn. Loveland dissolves, and the quartet finds itself alone in the empty theatre, alone in life. Now they leave, Ben and Phyllis perhaps to make the best of a vexed but suitable marriage and Buddy and Sally to endure an even worse one. The party—the very idea of a *Follies* itself—is over.

And the score? About half consists of character numbers for the four leads. The other half is pastiche numbers revisiting the show biz that the Weismann *Follies* would have thrived on—the tenor in tails' "bring on the dollies" anthem, "Beautiful Girls"; the De Sylva, Brown, and Henderson salute to the starry-eyed grunt, "Broadway Baby"; the Ziegfeldian spot, in which the lyrics of a song dictate the theme of the following dance, here a

Mirror Number, "Who's That Woman?," in which the movements of aged, former showgirls are haunted (that is, *mirrored*) by the ghosts of the kicky little tricks they used to be; the ode to an exotic address, "Ah, Paris!"; and so on. Thus *Follies'* songs keep the ear accustomed to shifts in the timescape from the present to the past and back again, for the entire show is built upon the juxtaposition of what we were and what we are, asking, How did we become so unsatisfied?

This confrontation of past and present adds yet another layer to *Follies'* pile-up of memes. The present is haunted, the four leads are haunted, show biz is haunted, America is haunted, and *Follies* is haunted: by the recollection of bygone days. Days before—depending on which level of the *Follies* dig one excavates—the Vietnam War soured us on the American mission to democratize the world. Or before the entertainment platform of Ziegfeld and his beautiful girls was compromised by rock and gay. Or before Ben realized that free will doesn't necessarily make you happy.

So Hal Prince and his co-director, Michael Bennett, filled their stage with ghosts. A choice collection of spooks owned the show's first five minutes, to the accompaniment of Sondheim's use of classical pastiche, to match the hommages to old pop music. In the style of (but more richly harmonized than) Erik Satie's delicate *gymnopédies*,* the ectoplasmic population of the Weismann Theater (*sic*) materialized alone, in pairs, in groups: the dead, made up in black and white, as if silent film was whispering in Technicolor, so much a part of what was once thought of as American life that they haven't quite departed just yet.

Preparing for the party, Weismann's service staff bustled about, utterly unaware of the secret *Follies* the ghosts were putting on: first the Butterfly Girl, a replica of Ziegfeld's resplendent (and mononymous) Dolores in her fabulous winged gown by (the similarly mononymous) Lucile, gliding as serenely as time across the stage. Then other models appeared, then six dancing girls in top hats, silently mouthing some old lyric—Gene Buck? Ira Gershwin?—as they moved toward us in formation. Bennett's dancers were under strict orders to keep to a count in their head, ignoring the orchestra and the tense rhythms of the party wait staff or they'd be thrown off, for the ghosts weren't in sync with what was happening at the party. That was *now*. The ghosts were *then*.

---

* These were three short piano pieces in antique style, written in 1888. In three-quarter time, they are marked "Slow and Sorrowful," "Slow and Sad," and "Slow and Serious." (Sondheim's is marked "Slowly—in 3.") All three resemble one another closely, with a simple, flowing melody in the right hand and a halting alternation of bass note and chord in each measure in the left. Satie's design, apparently, was to revive ancient Greek ritual dances, the sort of thing Isadora Duncan would use.

And the first guest has arrived: Sally, the one with the most to gain, or lose, this night. Either she will claim her knight and trade now for then, or he will reject her, trapping her in her wretched now. Phyllis, by contrast, has the ability to adapt, to fashion a now that suits her. But Sally is forever the little bundle of wounded feelings that she was at twenty, and that's her salient quality.

As Sally nervously chatted with a party official, one of the six dancing girls broke out of line and came up to look at Sally. It was *then* staring at *now*: Sally's ghost, marveling at what happens when time makes the choices. You lose the Vietnam War. You lose Jerome Kern and Cole Porter. You lose your way.

Follies ran giddy with ghosts. Some of the pastiche performing spots featured then and now actors, as when an operetta waltz maven was followed by her younger self, in so much better voice; or in that Mirror Number, choreographed for an intricate interlacing of old and young. Of course, the musical as a form was ontologically centered on the young, and *Follies* is secretly, deceptively, filled with youth. It is *Young* Ben who really starts the story when he makes his life's choice, setting off on the Smart Career with the Correct Partner. Will it be Sally? Typical man, he loved what she was: sweet and pretty. Typical woman, she loved what he represented: strength and authority. Halfway through the show, the older Ben sings the love song "Too Many Mornings" to her—both of her, Sally and her ghost. Because it's really the Young Sally that he wants, even now. The older Sally is as ruined as he is. Yet she's the only Sally there "is."

The quandaries of *Follies*. It's a very difficult show for some, because, despite the high-powered show biz that guides it, it is indeed depressing. Further, James Goldman's book is completely unlike all other books, not only concise but gnomic and allusive. It often suggests that characters are somehow or other voicing unspoken thoughts. Or they utter extremely important statements in passing.

Thus, Ben and Sally are chatting about the fascinating world of the bigwigs Ben hobnobs with. "Your life must be so glamorous," she tells him. Yes, it looks that way from a distance. And now he's going to explain to her, in "The Road You Didn't Take," about free will. Cut into the music are two flashback vignettes pivoting around Young Buddy lending Young Ben his jalopy for a date with Phyllis. A few lines fix the two boys for us: Buddy takes life as it comes ("It's only money"), while Ben needs to arrange it ("Some day I'm going to have the biggest goddamn limousine").

But a satisfying arrangement is elusive, so be careful what you wish for. Just before launching "The Road You Didn't Take," Ben observes, "It's knowing what you want, that's the secret"—and this might be the script's essential line. However, it typifies Goldman's wily writing that these words slither past us as a song cue, so we don't realize how telling they are. And Sally isn't listening: she's drinking him in, her daddy and redeemer. In fact, knowing what you want—even getting it—isn't enough. Time takes it all away, so nothing's enough. And that's *Follies*.

Music emphasizes everything, so *Follies'* score adds to *Follies'* disenchantment. There are plenty of key numbers, built around *Follies'* various themes, but "Waiting For the Girls Upstairs" stands out for its odd conflation of youth and age, joy and regret—and those contrary feelings inhere in the music as well as the words. The four young people are off on a night on the town while their older selves look back with inexpressible sadness. It was wonderful, but it was nothing: like being homesick when you were raised in an orphanage. The kids thought they lived in Loveland, but Loveland is a Ziegfeldian fantasy, pure show biz. There is no Loveland.

But why is American life so saturated with this fantasy? Boy Meets (or Re-meets) Girl creates our art, from *The Great Gatsby* to *Porgy and Bess*, from *Casablanca* to *Cabaret*. "Waiting For the Girls Upstairs" starts and ends with a melody associated with the four young people, a jumpy five-note pattern repeated four times, the musical equivalent of flickering light. Ghost music. "Hey, up there," Young Buddy calls out, to the girls in their dressing room. It's Boy ready to Get Girl.

Or, later, Phyllis tears into Ben with "Could I Leave You?," the enraged waltz of a would-be gay divorcée. The music bears the same breathless calm that we hear in the lyrics, that of a wife trying to fight with a husband who apparently doesn't care any more. Could she leave him? Will she? She answers her own question with a deeply helpless "Guess!"—because she won't. Girl got Boy, and she's keeping him.

Follies is an ambivalent work, though Americans like finality in their musicals. They don't ask it of *Long Day's Journey Into Night* or *Cat on a Hot Tin Roof*, but, as I've said, the musical is still struggling to escape from its antique mandate to divert with essentially carefree art—the very sort of thing that *Follies* reveals to be a sham. Yes, Loveland is a nice place to visit. But they don't let you live there. Or they do but your stay leads to the blues, the torch song, the split personality, the fraud: the four *Follies* numbers that close the score in defeat.

Many of the other *Follies* numbers are guiltless evocations of the great old defunct entertainment world that *Follies* explodes. "I'm Still Here," an autobiography (which Sondheim says he modeled on the life of Joan Crawford) has become an unofficial anthem to go with "There's No Business Like Show Business" and "That's Entertainment." Another *Follies* solo, "Broadway Baby," crackles with ambition, and "Who's That Woman?," for all its misgivings about the hedonistic lifestyle, is exuberant, reveling in our right to mess up our lives with wicked fun.

Besides *Follies* itself, there is as well the original Broadway staging, which has become a thing-in-itself, perhaps the most famous Original Production in the musical's history. Ask a younger musical buff what title he or she would like to go back in time to see and, believe me, it won't be *Show Boat* or *Guys and Dolls*. It's this one. One of the most costly mountings in Broadway history at something like $750,000, *Follies* rehearsed for two weeks longer than the usual four, to work out the intricate deployment of partygoers and ghosts and the elaborate musical numbers. Designers Boris Aronson (for the sets) and Florence Klotz (for costumes) toyed intriguingly with the show's driveline, for, until Loveland took over in the "dream" *Follies*, the stage looked as barren as you'd expect of a building about to be torn down. Yet the ghosts kept wandering through the action in their gala outfits, contextual signifiers of the opulence of show biz. *Follies* was a rare case of a musical "wearing" its themes; it really looked like a comparison of now and then.

The original four leads were so well cast that *Follies* buffs declare them *hors concours*, though many distinguished performers have graced the roles in revivals and concerts: Lee Remick and Barbara Cook with the New York Philharmonic; Donna McKechnie, Ron Moody (creator of Fagin in *Oliver!*), Julia McKenzie, and Denis Quilley for BBC radio. McKechnie switched from Phyllis to Sally at Paper Mill Playhouse in New Jersey, then went on to the "I'm Still Here" character (rather like an opera soprano tackling Sophie, then Octavian, then the Marschallin in *Der Rosenkavalier*) in a Reprise! concert, in Los Angeles. The party-guest minor roles, originally played by such professional has-beens as Ethel Shutta (pronounced Shut-*tay*), a singer and dancer who actually worked for Ziegfeld; Fifi D'Orsay; and Mary McCarty, who had played leads on Broadway around 1950 and who later created the amiably corrupt prison Matron in *Chicago*, have become star cameos. At times, these supplementary functionaries out-headline the leads: Dolores Gray, Ann Miller, or Polly Bergen for "I'm Still Here"; Elaine Stritch; Grover Dale and Carol Lawrence as Vincent and Vanessa, who lead the "Bolero d'Amour," a recreation of the ballroom specialty and composed by not Sondheim but John Berkman; Edie Adams (as, improbably, the old operetta star; one would have anticipated her "I'm Still Here," though she was strongly considered for Cunegonde in the original production of *Candide*, Leonard Bernstein's "comic operetta"); Elizabeth Seal; and eerie-Incangoddess-with-four-octave-range Yma Sumac.

Still, when speaking of *Follies* performers, one has to start with the moviestar radiance of Alexis Smith's Phyllis; the startlingly down-to-earth, and so friendly, and so bitter Gene Nelson as Buddy; Dorothy Collins' pert little mouse of a Sally; and John McMartin's Ben, McMartin having been all but unknown at the time and thus the surprise of the quartet, so serene at first but later so anguished, the essential figure in this show-biz version of the Fall of Man.

Aren't these characters well named? They're almost comparable to the Lady Wishfort (in *The Way of the World*) and Snake (in *The School for Scandal*) of old English comedy, for Ben Stone is hard (at least on the surface), a ruthless achiever in the world of ruthless achievers—the Nixons and Kennedys. Buddy Plummer, his opposite, is everybody's pal and a "plumber," a low man in the order of things. Phyllis, a name common in the 1940s to writers and actresses, is glamorous—or she will be, once she learns the art of giving dinner parties that will be the talk of those in the halls of power. And Sally is simple, nothing but happy and cute. And note that when she first spots Ben at the reunion party, she calls herself by her maiden name, Sally Durant. She discards the "Plummer" as she intends to discard Buddy. It's knowing what you want, that's the secret.

Came the premiere, and *Follies'* reviews were mixed, for it's not an easy show to take in cold; those layers of meaning are hard to absorb amid the pageantry, and, as I've said, Goldman's book is deliberately downsized from the explanatory texts most musicals work within. Rodgers and Hammerstein deconstructed the staging of musicals in *Allegro*, but its book is lengthy and character motivations are underlined. *Follies* is the opposite, with a complex staging plot but a deconstructed libretto.

Nevertheless, *Follies* was a New York town topic—even a national one, as Alexis Smith got the cover of both *Time* and *Newsweek* in the smashing red number she wore for her *Follies* spot, "The Story of Lucy and Jessie": the young, lively Phyllis versus the older, elegant Phyllis, with all the fun kicked out of her. Musicals didn't get a lot of magazine covers by 1971, so there was an air of smash hit to *Follies'* talkabout. And, yes, "Everyone thought it was a success," Hal Prince said in *Six By Sondheim*, "until it closed one day. And then they suddenly realized, 'My God, it never was a success.'" The show lost most of its investment, but it did run 522 performances and won most of the important Tony Awards, losing Best Musical, amazingly, to the near-amateurish *Two Gentlemen of Verona*.

Michael Bennett, among many others, blamed *Follies'* mixed reception on its secretive, evasive book, especially its downbeat ending. But then, Bennett didn't like intellectual material in musicals. To him, song and dance were visceral pleasures, even within a sad narrative. The musical by definition required zip and dazzle, especially at the evening's end. All three of the shows Bennett had complete control of at the height of his power, *A Chorus Line*

(1975), *Ballroom* (1978), and *Dreamgirls* (1981), conclude their storytelling in something less than euphoria. (Respectively: some are Chosen and some Denied; the Girl gets the Boy only on the back street; and the act breaks up.) Still, even if he had to shunt it into the curtain call, with his cast in evening clothes, Bennett made sure to top off the entertainment on a high note.

This failure to understand why James Goldman wrote an above all ambiguous libretto has led to constant revision of the script and even the music. In 1987, Cameron Mackintosh "tried to fix the second act of *Follies*" (to redeploy his own comment), giving London a tamed version. Sondheim and Goldman prepared this revisal themselves, so it presumably represented how they felt the show should go, though the uncomfortably blatant dialogue made the book seem like a schoolboy sitting in the corner under a dunce cap. Still, the show played very well and ran for a year and a half in a big house, the Shaftesbury Theatre. Further, it boasted a great cast, with Diana Rigg and Daniel Massey as the Stones and David Healy and Julia McKenzie as the Plummers, with Dolores Gray (later replaced by Eartha Kitt) for "I'm Still Here."

Nevertheless, book modifications cannot disguise the essentially dejected nature of *Follies*, its After the Fall. The scenery for the closing Follies sequence of Mackintosh's production was more elaborate than in the original, created by Maria Björnson (who had as well designed Mackintosh's stupendous *Phantom of the Opera* set constructions), but these are optics, not content. Nor did the new songs alter anything, though the new "Loveland" was, strange to say, even more beautiful than the one used in New York. There was one miscalculation, in a rare—perhaps the only—Sondheim song that lacks melody, "[How about a] Country House," for Ben and Phyllis. It seems designed to give their cold war of a marriage a touch of warmth, but it doesn't sound like the rest of the score. Worse, it replaced Ben's "The Road You Didn't Take." This is like omitting "I Could Have Danced All Night" from *My Fair Lady*: a number that instantly connects the public to what is happening under the show's surface. Eliza is falling in love with Higgins; Ben is rationalizing his opportunism. Or: Ben is wondering if he should have married Sally after all (because she wouldn't see through him the way that terrifying Phyllis does). Or: Ben was never going to be happy because some people are too smart to be content.

So one can't "smiley face" what happens in *Follies*, even if every revival does delete worrisome lines—about Sally's suicide attempts ("I should of [sic] died the last time," she ruefully admits) or the moment when one of the old showgirls says hello to Phyllis, who cuts her in half ("I never liked you, either"). They keep changing *Show Boat*, too. But in that case they're trying to unify an epic that sprawls from musical comedy through musical play to operetta. In *Follies'* case they're trying to cheer up a woeful tale. What a nifty plan. Next, let's do *Long Day's Journey Into Night* with Adam Sandler.

Anyway, *Follies* already maintains a "cheer up" in its score, which is filled with irresistible up tunes. That's why the show keeps coming back: the subject is dire but the music is in love with the audience. So, for example, the young versions of the four leads get "You're Gonna Love Tomorrow" and "Love Will See Us Through," duets sung separately, then together, in what is called a quodlibet. Sondheim doesn't usually write such pieces, because they reiterate rather than develop. Still, the two numbers dovetail beautifully. They as well provide a bit of dramatic dead giveaway, because directors love to slip a warning into the end, finding some way to indicate that, even as Ben pairs with Phyllis and Buddy with Sally, sparks still fly between Ben and Sally. They almost—just almost—end the number hand in hand.

Phyllis is red-hot and Buddy is sympathetic, but there's something about that Ben and Sally thing. The "haunting" music that launches the show in the evocation of Erik Satie derives from a cut number, "All Things Bright and Beautiful," a duet for Ben and Sally that, again, captures youth in its spring of wonder and delight. The eternal Girl says, You won't desert me, right? And the eternal Boy says, We'll be together for all time.

Does he mean it? Does she believe him? Yes. Because that is the joy of the magical place they're in, the show-biz place, where kids are certain of the future and full of hope. They call it Loveland.

A Little Night Music

Aristocratic-romantic-erotic operetta, 1973

Based on Ingmar Bergman's film *Smiles of a Summer Night*.

Music and Lyrics: Stephen Sondheim. Book: Hugh Wheeler.

Original Leads: Glynis Johns, Len Cariou, Hermione Gingold. Director: Hal Prince.

T he French playwright Jean Anouilh categorized his works as *pièces noires* (dark plays), *roses* (sweet plays), *brillantes* (witty plays), *grin-çantes* (grating plays), and *costumées* (plays set in the historical past). Anouilh's *L'Invitation au Château* is a *brillante*, set in the winter garden of a mansion presided over by a sarcastic old baroness in a wheelchair as various characters pine for apparently unavailable lovers. The baroness, Madame Desmortes (translation: "of the dead"), is a typical Anouilh figure, somewhat like Oscar Wilde's Lady Bracknell but intimate rather than grandiose. She constantly reminisces about her affairs with various magnificoes, and overflows with wisdom about looks and courtship:

> CAPULET (The baroness' companion): I was a girl of twenty, you know, once upon a time.
> MADAME DESMORTES: (looking at her) When, for goodness' sake?... You're a nice girl, Capulet, but...you're plain. No one who is plain can ever have been twenty.

To add to the fun, the play features in its cast identical twin brothers, played by the same actor with the aid of doubles in shadow when he has to make a quick costume change.

After *Company*'s super-contemporary urban ant farm and *Follies*' pastiche dazzle, *Ring Round the Moon* (*Château*'s English title, in Christopher Fry's adaptation, which I just quoted) seemed a delightful novelty. In fact, in *Contradictions*, Hal Prince states that "right after" *West Side Story*, he and Sondheim discussed "doing a kind of court masque, a chamber opera...a gavotte in which couples interchange, suffering mightily in elegant country homes, wearing elegant clothes."

The Anouilh was ideal source material, and Prince says he made an appointment to see Anouilh himself in Paris and pitch the project to him. Unfortunately, the musical as a form occupied a very low echelon in France. Intellectuals dismissed it as meretricious spectacle, both imported and homegrown—though at least, they might grudgingly admit, French musicals had wit and a sly charm. This may be why Anouilh stood Prince up: when the producer arrived for their rendezvous, he was told that Anouilh had merrily gone off to Switzerland. Outraged, Prince returned to America determined to find another piece to source the masque.

Two films came to mind: Jean Renoir's *The Rules of the Game* (1939) and Ingmar Bergman's *Smiles of a Summer Night* (1955). The Renoir is rather dark, but the Bergman is enticingly bittersweet. Sondheim must have alerted to the music heard over the credits, as a soprano and chorus sing "Bort Med Sorg och Bitterhet" (Away With Care and Bitterness), written by Bergman himself to the music of Erik Nordgren, who scored the rest of the film as well. The number arrests the ear with its inconclusive tone; like the story it precedes, it is densely light, anxiously joyful—and that sounds like a Sondheim musical to me.

Better, *Smiles*, with a stronger story than *Ring Round the Moon*, offered some of the elements that had attracted Prince and Sondheim to the French play. It lacked the twins, but it had the acerbic beldam in the wheelchair, the gavotting, interchanging couples, and the country house. And, lo, Bergman said yes—as long as the musical bore a title different from that of the movie. (Even the poster credits did not name the source, giving the line as "Suggested by a film by Ingmar Bergman.") *Eine Kleine Nachtmusik* ("A Short Serenade" but, literally, "A Little Night Music"), one of Mozart's most popular pieces, gave the musical its name, suggesting the light-classical nature of the work. This is Sondheim's operetta, his chamber opera, his hommage to some of his favorite composers. Aside from the aforementioned Liebeslieder Singers and their echo of Brahms, the vamp to a song called "In Praise of Women" sounds very like Rachmaninof, though Ravel's *Valses Nobles et Sentimentales* casts a spell over everything in this "waltz musical," particularly Ravel's fourth number, marked "Assez animé" (Rather lively). In fact, *A Little Night Music* itself could easily have been called *Noble and Sentimental Waltzes*, for it treats of fine feelings and grand occasions and revels in dance forms, naturally the waltz but also the sarabande (in "Liaisons") and mazurka (in the introduction to "The Glamorous Life"). It really is the court masque that Prince and Sondheim envisioned in the 1950s.

But who could write the libretto for a piece so...classy? Witty? Sophisticated? Or elegant, perhaps? This was clearly to be a musical that the American stage had not seen before. The setting alone—turn-of-the-century Sweden—was a novelty; operetta favored globe-trotting, but only to places known for picturesque attire: old New Orleans, François Villon's or D'Artagnan's Paris, the East, the West, the New Moon. Not, surely, the frosty North. And as for the class and wit, that really suggested *My Fair Lady*, whose book was written (more or less) by George Bernard Shaw. The waltz musical did not sound like a job for George Furth or James Goldman, or any of Sondheim's collaborators so far.

And here librettist Hugh Wheeler enters the Sondheim scene. An Englishman who emigrated to the United States in the mid-1930s at the age of twenty-two, Wheeler was a mystery novelist who became a playwright, claiming three Broadway titles in the 1960s. *A Little Night Music* was his first try at writing a musical, but he then became a regular in the field, working with Hal Prince in particular—on later Sondheim shows; on the aforementioned *Candide* revisal; adapting Kurt Weill and Georg Kaiser's *Der Silbersee* (as *Silverlake*) for the New York City Opera; even for Prince's non-musical film, *Something For Everyone* (1970).

That last title turns a key into Wheeler's art, for it is one of the gayest creations ever, and it is so entirely because of Wheeler. The film claims to be based on Harry Kressing's novel *The Cook*, but it isn't. Wheeler simply used Kressing's premise of an employee gaining power over a family, and built upon it a campy black comedy in which servant Michael York uses bisexual charm to seduce, destroy, or kill everyone in his way as he takes over a noble but impoverished Austrian family. In the first reel, he encounters daughter Jane Carr with two dogs who take to York immediately.

"They only like thieves and murderers," she tells him. "Which are you?"

"Both," York replies, with an engaging smile.

Add to this the gay parish favorite Angela Lansbury as the head of the family, and the playing area is set for a kind of thief's carnival in the Noël Coward manner, erected around a beautiful young man who uses sex as a weapon, a classic gay trope.

A Little Night Music, for all its erotic undercurrents, has no real homosexual content. But there's a heavy dose of gay in Wheeler's treatment of the Old Woman figure, Madame Armfeldt, who is a lot closer to Jean Anouilh's bitchy Klingon in a tiara than to Bergman's character. Many of her lines echo the minty sarcasm popularized in Mart Crowley's *The Boys in the Band*:

MADAME ARMFELDT: To lose a lover or even a husband or two in the course of one's life can be vexing. But to lose one's teeth is a catastrophe.

Otherwise, *A Little Night Music* follows Bergman's script quite closely, so the leads are generally paired off incorrectly at first. The narrative energy lies in correcting the distressed partnerships. Leaving out Madame Armfeldt, who is by seniority above the dance of lovers and liars, here is a précis:

CHARACTER	INVOLVED WITH	BUT LOVES
The Lawyer	His virginal wife.	The actress, though he somehow doesn't know it yet.
The Virginal Wife	The lawyer, her husband.	The lawyer's son.
The Lawyer's Son	God, in study for the Church.	The lawyer's wife, his stepmother.
The Actress	Her boy friend, the Count.	The lawyer.
The Count	The actress, his mistress.	Himself.
The Countess	Her husband, the Count.	The Count, not only deeply but masochistically.
The Maid	No one, though she messes around several times, including full-out sex with Frid, Madame Armfeldt's groom.	"The miller's son," an abstraction for financial security through a sensible marriage.

Wheeler's fidelity to Bergman was almost absolute; there are differences of emphasis but not of kind. For instance, in the film, the actress, Désirée Armfeldt, Madame Armfeldt's daughter, has a little boy about four years old named Fredrik (presumably after the lawyer, Fredrik Egerman, and surely his child), who is little more than an extra. In the musical, Désirée has a daughter aged thirteen, named Fredrika, who takes an active role in the proceedings.

Or: in the film, the lawyer's son, Henrik Egerman, plays piano and guitar; in the musical, he plays the 'cello—whose deep-toned elegy makes a better fit with the lachrymose divinity student. Then, too, in the film the Count forces lawyer Egerman to play Russian roulette, but has filled the revolver with soot, while in the musical the gun is loaded. When Egerman dislodges the bullet, however, it only grazes his temple.

There is one major change, in the theme of the night's three smiles. In the film, it is introduced by Frid: philosophy from the most basic of characters, close to the earth and the elements, so unlike the airy folk with their rarefied manners. But in the musical, the theory of the three smiles is given to Madame Armfeldt, again the most jaded and worldly of characters, who unlike Frid views life from a great distance, with perspective. Thus, Wheeler simplified Bergman's dialogue about these three smiles. When Frid explains the concept, it is improvised and wordy. But Madame Armfeldt has had many years in which to gather her thoughts. She is epigrammatic, fanciful but precise:

> MADAME ARMFELDT: The first smile smiles at the young, who know nothing. The second at the fools, who know too little....And the third at the old, who know too much—like me.

The concept of the smiles was too rich for Sondheim to resist, and he gave his Frid a song on the matter, "Silly People." It was an excellent way to remind the audience of this central idea, and the music is almost menacing, creating an arresting dissonance within the score—within the entire show, even. To a growling accompaniment that seems to uncoil from the lowest instruments, Frid states the theme of the smiles in a kind of ecstatic contempt. "Silly People" could be called the work's essential number, but it occurred very late in the running time, when the plot was nearing its resolution and the audience is thinking, Cut to the chase, already. The song was dropped in Boston.

In all, Hugh Wheeler wrote a truly funny libretto, giving all his characters a chance to amuse the house (though all the "gay" observations belong to Madame Armfeldt and the Countess). In traditional operetta, a format codified in the 1920s, the comedy was always relegated to one or two jesters of marginal importance in the action; everyone else is a lover, an official, or a villain. But *A Little Night Music*, operetta though it be, uses its cast as an ensemble, interlocked in versatility. And of course there is no chorus, only the five Liebeslieder Singers, whose burnished vocal tone supports the varied vocal abilities of the principals. Désirée and Egerman (and sometimes the Countess) are often given to actors with "Broadway" voices, smooth enough but short of operetta's silk. The maid, Petra, is a Broadway belter, also not silken but a fierce competitor, while the Count, young Henrik, and the lawyer's wife, Anne, are usually a baritone, a tenor, and a soprano. In fact, the original Anne, Victoria Mallory, shadows the role, because she was such an irresistible charmer *and* so accomplished a singer that Sondheim wrote the role around her high-flying soprano, leaving some of her successors boxing above their weight.

Lawyer Egerman was Len Cariou, primarily a speaking actor on the Shake-spearean level but Lauren Bacall's vis-à-vis in the musical *Applause* (1970), and Hermione Gingold made a marvelous Madame Armfeldt, hurling her juicy Wheelerisms at the public as if each next one must top the last.* But Désirée occupies the pivotal role, though she has relatively little to sing, even in a form, operetta, that was always known above all for vocal splendor. Egerman at first seems to be the work's protagonist, for the action starts by concentrating on his odd little household of the wife who won't sleep with him and the son seething with unspoken frustrations. However, once Egerman and his old flame Désirée meet up, she takes over the show's driveline. From a quiet domestic drama the play turns into an adventure: will she succeed in winning Egerman back? In this, she reminds us of *Fol-lies'* Sally and, still to come, *Sweeney Todd's* Mrs. Lovett, who both recon-vene with men they loved and have been separated from, Sally for a single evening and Mrs. Lovett till death do them part. But those are sad tales, while *Night Music* is a comedy. Girl will Get Boy.

Désirée has become a choice diva role for, among others, Jean Simmons, Dorothy Tutin, Sally Ann Howes, Judi Dench, Frederica Von Stade, Catherine Zeta-Jones, Bernadette Peters, and even Elizabeth Taylor (in the film ver-sion): everyone from opera singers to movie stars. Originally, however, the part was hard to cast. Prince wanted someone at once worldly, vulnerable, somewhat European in flavor, and in possession of a good sense of the irony that lives at the heart of light comedy. It came down to Glynis Johns and Tammy Grimes; I wonder if Prince considered Leslie Caron (who, much later, played Madame Armfeldt in Paris). Prince ended in choosing Johns, apparently because she projected a "softness-inside-a-hard-shell" feeling that Prince thought perfect for Désirée: and Johns was. That feeling, pre-sumably, is what Sondheim tapped into when he wrote "Send in the Clowns" for her during rehearsals.

This is famously Sondheim's outstanding song hit. Mark Eden Horow-itz's *Sondheim On Music* lists some four hundred separate recordings, by Rosemary Clooney, the Lettermen, Liberace (as a piano solo), and the Uni-versity of Utah A Capella Choir, for starters. Of them all, Sondheim prefers Johns' rendition. I still remember, the first time I saw the show, when Johns got to the first interesting chord—it's G Flat with a major seventh—on "You in mid-*air*," an appreciative little gasp ran through the house. There

---

* Ingmar Bergman, who loved the show, told Sondheim, "She really does tend to fuck the audience, doesn't she?" Sondheim, delighted at this touch of High Art talking Low Show Biz, couldn't wait to call up Mary Rodgers and share the tale.

was, too, that so very operetta-esque bittersweet moment, for Désirée has failed to land her lawyer, and the song expresses the exquisite pain of having one's valentine returned unopened. Yet its melody, so apt at that moment, expands spectacularly into bliss when the lawyer at last comes to his senses for the happy ending and takes Désirée into his arms. And note that the number's imagery is theatrical, as befits an actress—"entrance," "farce," "timing," and of course "clowns."

Sondheim wrote not only "Send in the Clowns" during the five-week rehearsal period but a substantial fraction of the score, including one of his most playwrighting numbers, "A Weekend in the Country." There was nothing like it in his previous work: a small epic of song and dialogue moving from place to place, all musically motivated by a ritornello—a recurring tune—suggesting suspense and travel. This is Désirée's scheme to "reset" her relationship with the lawyer, at her mother's country house. An invitation is delivered at the lawyer's home, the Count and Countess get involved, expectations are raised, then all the principals and the Liebeslieder group join together, each individual with his own agenda;* when suddenly the façade of Madame Armfeldt's mansion was revealed, orchestrator Jonathan Tunick stowed a quotation of the first seven notes of Richard Strauss' *Der Rosenkavalier* into the texture—it's a horn call, suitable for what in effect is a hunt—and the curtain falls.

Interestingly, "A Weekend in the Country" was created very much like "Rose's Turn," plotted out point by point in rehearsal and then written. Prince showed Sondheim how Boris Aronson's sliding screens would fashion "set changes" as the story moved from place to place, giving the number extraordinary flexibility in what it could show. Thus, Anne and Petra discuss the invitation and, seconds later, Désirée and Fredrika preview their future as a completed family. Fredrika guesses that the lawyer is her father-to-be (Désirée: "Dear child, you're uncanny."), instantly we're back at the Egermans' house, and so on. One wonders what would have happened if *Night Music*'s scenery had been of the old-fashioned kind, with backdrops and mini-sets moved in on bulky wagons in the *Gypsy* manner— because in that case "A Weekend in the Country" could not have been realized.

---

* Madame Armfeldt cues the number in with "[Your guests] will not be served my best champagne. I am saving that for my funeral." Then she disappears—but, with the movie camera giving him extra narrative mobility, Sondheim wrote some lyrics for her for the film, in which Hermione Gingold repeated her stage role. As she gleefully anticipates hiding from the guests for most of the weekend, she looks exactly like ventriloquist Wayland Flowers' puppet Madame.

We should note as well that Sondheim planned a subtle emphasis on the "three smiles" theme in a unique relationship between "Liaisons" and "Silly People"—that is, between Madame Armfeldt and Frid. She owns the theme in the musical but he owns it in the movie—and, of course, they are the only adult principals who represent the Armfeldt country estate. Thus, they create a "class partnership" of high and low that reflects *Night Music*'s interaction of social classes generally. (Petra, the Egermans' maid, is of course Frid's vis-à-vis, and she elaborates on the show's junction of classes in "The Miller's Son," giving a verse each to iconic figures of the settled bourgeoisie, the upstart entrepreneurial group, and the nobility.) Then, too, "Liaisons" and "Silly People" are both in $\frac{3}{2}$, an unusual movement for music heard on Broadway, and Jonathan Tunick's orchestration further bonded the two numbers in rhythmic undercurrents in the bass and splashes of harp.* This makes the loss of "Silly People" all the more regrettable.

In all, *A Little Night Music* is the first Sondheim show that brings the musical organization of opera to Broadway in an overt way, and thus marks a break within the Sondheim-Prince canon. Bit by bit, the show is creeping into the opera-house repertory, but the point is not that opera singers can take all the parts. Rather, it is that the music acts as the work's sole animating force. Listen to the numbers alone and you can follow the plot; this is not true of *Company* or *Follies*.

One might categorize *Night Music* as a Singspiel, the German term for works in the time of Mozart and Beethoven that we call opera but which navigate between the numbers through spoken dialogue, as do *The Magic Flute* and *Fidelio*. It is all the more astonishing, then, that Sondheim felt Hugh Wheeler never quite understood how the music fits into music theatre. Sondheim told me that Wheeler was musically inclined in general, but that Sondheim's other librettists seemed to comprehend far more naturally than Wheeler how song would devour first-draft dialogue, or how melodies would recur for dramatic reasons.

All the same, Wheeler's book is one reason *Night Music* continues to play well today. Much of it comes more or less straight from Ingmar Bergman's movie script, including the key passage that tells us exactly what the story is about. It occurs during the aforementioned play-within-a-play sequence. Désirée is just getting to what, in the stage directions, Wheeler calls "her first-act

* The only other *Night Music* number in $\frac{3}{2}$ is Henrik's "Later," which sounds vastly different from "Liaisons" and "Silly People" and, in yet more distancing from them, is suffused with Henrik's 'cello playing.

set speech," meaning the lines toward which the entire act of this old blunderbuss of a French comedy has been heading. Something else is going on at the same time: Désirée has spotted Egerman in his box. In Bergman's film, she lets off a millisecond's smile. In *Night Music*, she does a take, a bigger piece of business, easier for an audience to catch in a Broadway house. In any case, Anne takes note. Though sexually closed to her husband, she is jealous all the same, and now she throws a distracting scene, when suddenly, in lines all but straight from Bergman, Wheeler gives Désirée her big moment, the credo of the show and something not unlike the equivalent of a close-up:

> DÉSIRÉE: Dignity. We women have the right to commit any crime toward our husbands, our lovers, our sons, as long as we do not hurt their dignity. We should make men's dignity our best ally and caress it, cradle it, speak tenderly to it, and handle it as our most delightful toy.

Of course! Because Egerman's dignity as a man is hurt by his frigid wife. The Count's dignity is hurt by finding Désirée and Egerman together in sly circumstances. Henrik's dignity is hurt because everyone patronizes him and—the mortal blow—the woman he so guiltily loves (again: she's his stepmother; how many Commandments does that break?) teases him incessantly. In a tragedy, someone would have to pay with his life, but, in this comedy, all dignity is restored by the final curtain.

Opening on February 25, 1973, *A Little Night Music* was the third show in the post-*Forum* Sondheim-Prince era but the first smash hit in its reception. All five of the Sondheim-Prince titles of the 1970s are now classics, but only *Night Music* opened as one of New York's favorite things, a hot ticket of a show that everyone is talking of in glowing terms. Even the *New York Times'* idiot Clive Barnes—who so misunderstood how Sondheim innovates in his pastiche numbers that Barnes suggested the *Follies* cast album be issued on 78s—raved. And there was this: days before the premiere, during previews, Glynis Johns was struck with hypoglycemia and rushed to the hospital during previews. Prince, to protect the production, contacted Tammy Grimes. It was a notable opportunity for her, as her career, peaking early on when she carried a smash, *The Unsinkable Molly Brown* (1960), at the age of twenty-six, seemed to sink somewhat thereafter. However, as actors sometimes will, Grimes "made demands" (as Prince tells us in *Contradictions*), which slowed negotiations, and, meanwhile, Johns made a fast recovery.

Night Music's rich character interplay allowed director Trevor Nunn to stage it on the small scale, for London's Menier Chocolate Factory, in 2008.

Along with the comparably intimate Donmar Warehouse, this is the chic venue for what we might call "reinstructed" revivals, in which subtlety of portrayal replaces the musical's traditional rhetoric of lavish sets and costumes, production numbers, and so on. Londoners eat it up, including those who habitually attend nothing but Shakespeare, Chekhof, and Brecht, and the Nunn *Night Music*, seen on Broadway, did make a strong argument in favor of this approach, especially as Angela Lansbury gave Madame Armfeldt a lift with a genuinely touching portrayal instead of the usual snarky riffing. Lansbury was especially compelling when speaking of the wooden ring she was offered by an admirer. It was an heirloom, apparently something very special in his family, but, her courtesan pride thus offended, she sent him packing:

MADAME ARMFELDT: And now—who knows? He might have been the love of my life.

Lansbury delivered the words as though they were a very renunciation of all that she had lived for, even a requiem for the end of all love. In rejecting the ring because it lacked splendor, she had failed in the thing that matters most: style. It's the middle-class pieties that are the true vanities—the belief that an expensive ring betokens a wealth of love. No: the man free of conformist piety creates life and love. Others' acts are clichés; his acts are unique.

Nunn's *Night Music* was filled with such revisionist readings. Catherine Zeta-Jones's Désirée gave an elaborated spoof of diva dos and don'ts on her play-within-a-play entrance, and her Egerman, Alexander Hanson, threw away many lines that other lawyers emphasize. Hanson, who had originated the role for Nunn in London, had played Henrik years before, at Chichester in 1989—the best Sondheim had seen to that point, he told me, though he did think young Hanson's toned physique, unshirted for a spell in Act Two, suggested a heavy program at the Malmö Crunch outlet. Now in his seniority, Hanson's individualized delivery repositioned the lawyer as the show's protagonist, thus realigning the part with its use in the film, wherein Bergman clearly sees him and not Désirée as the actuating force.

Incidentally, near the end of *Night Music*'s Boston tryout, Jean Anouilh's agent contacted Hal Prince with the exciting news that the rights to *Ring Round the Moon* were now available for negotiation. In reply, Prince simply said he was no longer interested.

Ha!

Pacific Overtures

Kabuki Broadway on events in Japanese history, 1976.

Music and Lyrics: Stephen Sondheim. Book: John Weidman (with "additional material" by Hugh Wheeler).

Original Leads: Mako, Soon-Teck Oh, Yuki Shimoda, Sab Shimono, Isao Sato. Director: Hal Prince.

Richard Storry, in *A History of Modern Japan*, explains three intentions behind Admiral Matthew Calbraith Perry's delivery of a letter from President Millard Fillmore to the Japanese authorities, requesting the opening of relations between their two countries. One purpose was simple trade, another the need to secure decent treatment for American seamen who, through shipwreck or other hazards, became stranded in Japan. And the third purpose was the need for steamships to pick up supplies (especially coal) in mid-journey when crossing the Pacific from California to Canton, for the United States was doing business with China.

This was gunboat diplomacy; Japan had no choice but to assent. And so it joined perforce the global community. But what *is* Japan? Storry, reflecting upon such anomalies as "*hara-kiri*" and "the tea ceremony" and upon "Kamikaze planes" and "the delicacy of Japanese paintings," concludes, "There may be stranger nations than Japan. But none... has been so praised and so reviled, so much discussed and so little understood."

Pacific Overtures is an attempt to understand the Japanese, using their own form, Kabuki theatre, as a jumping-off place. In a way, Kabuki was a concept musical before there even were musicals; it shares some of the presentational elements of the genre. *Pacific Overtures* makes much of the most formalistic qualities of Kabuki—the *hanamichi* ("flowery path") that runs from the back of the house to the stage; the all-male cast; the reciter, who narrates and plays certain roles; the flamboyant poses and gestures and broad accents on key words; the stagehands who bustle about, technically "unseen." Sondheim has described *Pacific Overtures* as what happens when "a Japanese playwright exposed to American musical theatre" writes one. But one what? Is this an American show with Kabuki flavoring or a work in Kabuki style with facets of the musical tucked in?

It's both, because the treatment varies. And a peculiar development governs the show's tone: as the action progresses and Japan becomes more and more Westernized, the score grows less and less "Asian" and more and more "Broadway" in music and lyrics.

Thus, the second number, "There Is No Other Way," is composed very sparely, as the rough soprano of a recorder outlines the melody, two vocalists repeat it, the violins echo it, and the harp adds a melody of its own. One of Sondheim's most beautiful creations, it is made of just a few strands of music sorrowfully teasing each other, quite without the rich harmony the composer utilizes elsewhere. The farewell of a husband and wife in perilous times, it is all the more notable for its lean, deceptively self-effacing presentation, a classic instance of Less is More. "Should I fail," the husband tells his wife, "you know what we must do." And, as he leaves, the wife takes out the sword with which she will commit ritual suicide.

"A scene of absorbing interest!" Thus John Weidman's version of the Kabuki Reciter might put it, in typical Japanese understatement. Yet the emotions are not dramatized in the American style, whereby the pair would sing directly to each other, in the manner of, say, *West Side Story*'s Tony and Maria. Instead, the husband is silent, the wife dances to express what she is feeling, and two Observers handle the singing, one describing the event in haiku and the other interpreting what the wife is "saying."

It is an exotic and stylized number, truly imported to Broadway from another form of drama. Yet, partway through the first act, a comic number for a bordello madam and her geishas, "Welcome To Kanagawa," has the tiniest tang of Cole Porter or Alan Jay Lerner in its lyrics about the erotic life. Thus Broadway invades the show's tone as American foreign policy will invade Japan. By the end of the act, the traditional Kabuki Lion Dance— the lion here being how the Japanese view Commodore Perry, in a flowing version of a Navy officer's blue-and-gold tunic over red-striped white trousers but with a lion's mane of white bristles down to the knees—is performed to a combination of John Philip Sousa and drums along the Mohawk.

Then, after the intermission, comes "Please Hello," made entirely of the pastiche style that the American musical can't get enough of. Finally, by *Pacific Overtures*' last number, "Next," the transformation of Japan is complete:

the women of the company are now part of the performing troupe instead of stagehands in black, and the song itself casts away all traces of Asian music.

In subject matter and approach, this show is an epic, so, to humanize it, the authors give us two individuals, good friends whose story unfolds in precise relation to how Japan is changing. One of the two Westernizes himself. The other becomes immersed in tradition and xenophobic hatred, till these two comrades end as bitter enemies.

Considering all this in terms of the ancient Greek stage, the various duties of the Chorus are embodied in the Reciter, who serves as emcee, guide, and commentator. The protagonist—there can only be one, speaking purely—is Kayama (the husband of "There Is No Other Way"), who helps Japan in dealing with the Americans. The Greek so-called Second Actor is Manjiro, who assists Kayama, but later grows conservative and unyielding. Again, referring back to Richard Storry: which one represents the real Japan, so contradictory in its culture and policies? The realist or the idealist? The political man or the cultural man? And what is the Reciter's opinion? Here we have the Chorus, the First Actor, and the Second Actor—a complete drama, at least at the time of Aeschylus. Around them, a host of minor characters—who of course could not be included in the old Greek plays, limited to the Chorus and (after Aeschylus) at most four speaking characters at a time—fill out the historical scenario. There are samurai warriors, lords and their households, common people, Perry's American crew, and three British sailors who accost a shy Japanese maid and enrage her father, who cuts them down, creating an international incident.

Colorful events require colorful representation, and *Pacific Overtures'* original production, in the Bicentennial year, was one of the musical's outstanding spectacles. It happens that the set designer, Boris Aronson (in his fourth Sondheim-Prince assignment), was already an enthusiast of Japanese art, and he planned *Pacific Overtures'* scenery to duplicate its strangely weightless quality, even in an optics-rich design plot that seemed at times to fill the stage with imposing constructions.

Consider for example the "Four Black Dragons" sequence (immediately dubbed "Four Black Drag Queens" by Broadway wags). The American warships have arrived off the coast, and the Japanese, though gravely reluctant, must take some action in response. Aronson saw this as an opportunity to "paint" the playing area with a depiction of this clash of civilizations that would read as stylized, realistic, and symbolic all at once. As Frank Rich and Aronson's widow, Lisa, recount it in *The Theatre Art of Boris Aronson*, the designer took over the costume department from Florence Klotz to dress each of four choristers as a machine, to move in automated fashion.

These four, all women, were attired in nineteenth-century business suits topped by derbies and smoking cigars, but their machine outfits combined clockwork wheels and a smokestack. Thus, they were steamships, but also icons of industrial-age capitalism, as well as menacing contraptions of mysterious power. In effect, they represented, respectively, American ingenuity, the relentless force of history, and Japanese helplessness. Surging onto the scene along the *hanamichi*, these four "machines" baffled the public at the Boston tryout. The costuming was Aronson at his most imaginative, but it may have made too arcane a leap for the audience to follow, and the machines had to be dropped.

Aronson's second idea for the same scene was far more successful. Setting aside the "four black dragons," Aronson created just Commodore Perry's flagship, the USS *Powhatan*, deliberately built to seem grotesquely ponderous in contrast to the delicacy of the Japanese structures. In an effect that often provoked cheers in the house, the boat came forward in two huge pieces from the rear of the stage in semi-darkness, accompanied by Sondheim's "Four Black Dragons" leitmotif, eerie string harmonics sustained over an ominous six-note theme in the brass, with pounding drums and squealing woodwinds. Arriving downstage, the two halves of the ship spread out and joined together as the lights came up enough for the audience to discern the grandiose *Powhatan*, with its sailors and officers and, dominating all, Commodore Perry, stylized as the Kabuki lion. Arrestingly, the *Powhatan*'s prow suggested a monster's face, its wide, fire-orange eyes glowing with elated menace. It seemed all the more devastating in that the Japanese emissary sent to meet the Americans was ensconced in a dinky little craft maneuvered by a stagehand—that is, pre-industrially. The visual message thus compared the energy the Americans had harnessed with the primitive locomotion of the Japanese.

Sondheim's musicals are unique generally, but *Pacific Overtures* stands out in the Sondheim-Prince canon for its blending of such contrary styles as Broadway and Kabuki, and its score, too, is one of a kind. Nowhere is Sondheim's "playwrighting" music more overt than in the First Number, "The Advantages of Floating in the Middle of the Sea," in which the Reciter and the ensemble establish the work's perspective, its long view of things. The number is roughly comparable to countless First Numbers before it, from *Naughty Marietta* (1910) to *Li'l Abner* (1956), but they evoke only a location—colonial New Orleans; a squonky hillbilly village—while "Advantages" actually analyzes a society. Japan, the company explains, exists as a stagnant culture where time stands still and history is banned. Nothing happens there—no *St. Matthew Passion*, no Enlightenment, no *Uncle Tom's Cabin*. And nothing is going to happen, they tell us, to a belligerent vamp in the most unusual chord of $e^{5}_{4}{}_{2}$. As the song proceeds, the cast counts off the interlocking systems of self-control: in "the arrangement of the screens" (art), "the arrangement of the rice" (economics), and "the arrangement of the bows" (the sociopolitical structure). At the end, as the Japanese slowly quit the stage, looking out at us as if daring us to disapprove in our typical Western impatience, the Reciter remains impassive in his position down-stage center. We hear a tone cluster on strings and celesta, almost asking a question. And the Reciter answers it: "We float!" End of story, it seems. But the concluding tonic chord contains a stray pitch on the fourth of the scale, creating an air of doubt. History is about to happen to Japan.

As I've said, the *Pacific Overtures* score, at first very Eastern in intonation, grows progressively more Western as Japan is opened up to foreign influence. Halfway through Act One, "Chrysanthemum Tea" is still resolutely in a Japanese mode—or so it sounds to American ears—as we look in on the Shogun and his court, all a-dither over the looming presence of Commodore Perry's warships (seen far upstage in a miniature replica of the evil-eyed *Powhatan*). The number is led by the Shogun's mother, placidly fanning herself as group by group, courtiers try to exorcise the American demons: first a soothsayer; then two Confucians offering a quaintly implausible syllogism built around the moon's reflection stirred in watery ripples; then a general supplication to the wind of kamikaze to destroy the foreigners; and nothing works. So the Shogun's mother offers her own solution, in the very tea the Shogun has been drinking, cup after cup of it: poison. After all, with the Shogun dead, Perry will have no one of rank to deal with and might sail away.

This black-comic number is something of a celebration of the Sondheim touch in rhyme, uniting "herb," "[su]perb," and "[dis]turb[ances]," along with deft expressions suitable for a lady of standing: she describes the venomous tea as "an informal variation on the normal recipe." Then, too, Kabuki practice took stage for one brief but intriguing moment when, at a report of rain, one of the black-clad stage-crew women suddenly appeared at stage right wrestling with an umbrella, turned completely around, and vanished, all within the space of a few seconds.

"Welcome To Kanagawa," as I've mentioned, points toward a transformation of the musical style, but by the end of the act, just after the Americans in fact break land and sign treaties, the score more overtly Americanizes itself in the number that Sondheim singles out as his own favorite Sondheim song, "Someone In a Tree." Its subject is history, so weighty and evident at a remove but, while it is happening, impenetrable, even invisible.

Well, fine—but how to express that in song? "What a shame," the Reciter observes, "that there is no authentic account of what took place on that historic day" when the treaties were executed. As if in response, an old man appears, as the music begins. He saw the whole thing, he says, perched in a tree. His younger self then shows up to texture the discussion, as does a samurai who was hidden beneath the floorboards of the Treaty House, poised to spring up and slaughter the foreigners if trouble broke out. So he heard it all but saw nothing; and the boy saw it all but heard nothing—and that's as close as you can get to matters of state, just as Japanese poetry often turns on tiny images that, by synechdoche, reflect patterns of vast human design. And all this is set to a beguiling five-note melodic cell over one of Sondheim's outright toe-tapping rhythmic pulses, finding joy of the moment by stealing behind the Grand Affair to isolate something personable and intimate. The bigwigs are in the Treaty House, but outside in a tree is a nameless young boy enjoying a beautiful day. And that of course has long been one of the practices of the American musical—looking at people on a show boat while, around them, life undergoes its periodic cultural transformations; or democratizing the romance of a farmer and her cowboy suitor so their land can become the state of Oklahoma; or seeking faces to put on the AIDS crisis, in *Rent*.

Casting *Pacific Overtures* can't have been easy, because the days when, say, the Swedish Warner Oland could merrily Asian his way through sixteen feature films as the Chinese-American detective Charlie Chan (and two Americans made seventeen more *Chans*) were long over. Besides, *Pacific Overtures* makes its effect as an above all *authentic* Kabuki treatment of the American musical; it had to have an all-Asian cast. At least there was now a healthy supply of race-sympathetic performers available. When Rodgers and Hammerstein cast their Chinese-American musical, *Flower Drum Song* (1958), they resorted, of necessity, to a United Nations of color-blind hires; the principals took in only one Chinese actor (coincidentally enough, the second lead in Warner Oland's *Charlie Chans*, Keye Luke, as Number One Son), along with two Japanese, one Hawaiian, one black, and one white American, who left the show during tryouts to be replaced by...another white American.

Not quite a generation later, *Pacific Overtures* claimed an accurate cast, though some theatregoers may have been baffled about who was playing what. First billed was Mako Iwamatsu (appearing, as always, under his first name only), who was at least somewhat familiar after having been hideously murdered onscreen during the Steve McQueen adventure film *The Sand Pebbles*. But the second-billed Soon-Teck (also spelled Tek) Oh was a mystery, because, after the Reciter, the most important parts were the political functionary Lord Abe and the pair from "A Bowler Hat," the assimilating Kayama and the xenophobic Manjiro. These three roles were played by, respectively, Yuki Shimoda, Isao Sato, and Sab Shimono, known to Broadway for having played Ito, the houseboy of *Mame* (1966).

So who was Soon-Teck Oh? Korean-born but raised in America, Oh played four roles: Kayama's wife, who "dances" her "lines" in "There Is No Other Way"; two bits as a samurai; and a Storyteller who, in an elaborately ritualized sequence, narrates a parable about a ruler who slays the "barbarian" foreigners till even the lordly tiger makes kowtow before this king of kings. Throughout this episode, the Storyteller uses his fan to simulate the air of a sunny day in the forest, a butterfly, the sight and even sound of an approaching enemy, and other physical elements of his tale, in an extended tour de force.

As it happens, Oh was so skilled in becoming one with his characters that he virtually disappeared into the production. Worse, the intricate interlacing of Asian and American theatrical styles confused audience members who like their art pre-digested. In 1976, most of the public still expected musicals to be "easy"—what the television comic Milton Berle termed "lappy." Berle liked jokes so obvious they so to say fell into the spectator's lap. Most musicals in the 1950s, when Sondheim got started, were like that, even the smart ones. And we remember the man who walked out of *West Side Story* during the opening number—"Don't ask," he said—because it clearly wasn't going to be a leggs-and-laffs show.

But Sondheim demanded more from the public, and parts of *Pacific Overtures* really are difficult to absorb at first viewing. Opening on January 11, 1976, at the Winter Garden, the show lasted 193 performances and has only gradually asserted its place in the calendar of classics. The 1984 off-Broadway revival greatly helped, if only because it was a second viewing, easier to absorb. This version was modest in scope, tempting some to declare that the original Broadway staging had been "overproduced," which is another way of saying that the show's conceptual complexity filled them with cognitive panic at first viewing but now sits comfortably within their reception zone.

Even then, some of the work's unique features can bemuse—for instance the Reciter's multi-tasking, as he veers from impartial emcee to fervent advocate. Here he's intense, there he's playfully irreverent. This is purely anecdotal, but Americans generally don't seem to like the use of narrators on stage; their direct address of the audience profanes the romance of theatre. Narrators are so...Brechtian. Americans prefer a narrator like the Stage Manager in *Our Town*—folksy and nonjudgmental, unlike those hectoring narrators of the modern style who think they know everything. The Reciter is one of those—and he comes from an alien folk and he's full of judgments. "We float!" he cries. But some in the house are thinking, Okay, but when does Boy meet Girl?

Sweeney Todd, the Demon Barber
Of Fleet Street

Operatic serial-killer melodrama, 1979.

Based on the eponymous play by Christopher Bond.

Music and Lyrics: Stephen Sondheim. Book: Hugh Wheeler.

Original Leads: Len Cariou, Angela Lansbury. Director: Hal Prince.

Sweeney Todd made his professional debut in a novel published in serial form in 1846–47 and entitled *The String of Pearls*. Thomas Peckett Prest is the presumed (and uncredited) author. This first Todd is a basic nineteenth-century villain, a savage who murders men for their valuables. In a business arrangement with a neighbor, Mrs. Lovett, Todd butchers the corpses, and a hired man, locked in Mrs. Lovett's basement, combines the meat and breading into pies. When this employee tires of his solitary confinement, he is killed, and the next unwary hire replaces him.

Meanwhile, the romantic lead, Mark Ingestrie, and his fiancée, Johanna Oakley, become involved in the tale; the rank odor of the butchered flesh pervades a local church, creating public alarm; and justice finally catches up with Todd, who is hanged, though not before poisoning Mrs. Lovett. She collapses just after her latest prisoner—Mark Ingestrie, who was thought murdered for most of the novel—explodes into Mrs. Lovett's shop through a secret passageway, telling her customers, "I fear that what I am going to say will spoil your appetites." The anonymous author helpfully describes the scene: "How the throng of persons recoiled." The titular string of pearls, though crucial evidence in the case against Todd, appears but here and there in the narrative.

Was there a Sweeney Todd? He is at least a venerable urban legend in London, and *The String of Pearls* had not completed its serial publication when George Dibdin Pitt offered the first of the tale's many theatrical adaptations. In 1973, Sondheim, in London for its first *Gypsy*, with Angela Lansbury, happened to see Christopher Bond's new version of the play. Almost all of Sondheim's musicals originated with someone other than himself: Leonard Bernstein and Jerome Robbins conceived *West Side Story* (though Robbins hogged the credit), David Merrick got the idea for *Gypsy*, George Furth launched the *Company* project, Hal Prince dreamed of an elegant European *je ne sais quoi* that ended as *A Little Night Music*, and so on. But *Sweeney Todd* the musical was Sondheim's inspiration, and it was going to be his *Porgy and Bess*: an opera.

Sondheim doesn't use that term for his works—he billed *Sweeney Todd* as "a musical thriller"—because opera is over *there* and Broadway is over *here*. Still, the espressivo level of the *Sweeney Todd* music is nothing like what Broadway normally hears. Further, it was Sondheim's intention to set Bond's text as a series of numbers separated by underscored dialogue. Music would thus haunt the show, as in the kind of symphonic commentary pioneered in Hollywood soundtrack accompaniment by Erich Wolfgang Korngold in the 1930s. Sondheim's model would, however, have been Korngold's younger contemporary Bernard Herrmann, a specialist in thrillers from *The Devil and Daniel Webster* (1941) through *Psycho* (1960) and *The Birds* (1963) to *Taxi Driver* (1976). We might recall that Herrmann made an important contribution to a film that vastly impressed the young Sondheim, *Hangover Square*—especially its *Concerto Macabre*, which could almost be a subtitle for *Sweeney Todd*.

No wonder this was the project that Sondheim initiated himself: it was a chance to write his own *Hangover Square*. He started work without a librettist, simply putting Bond to music. However, this meant prolonging every scene's running time. As the composer says, in *Sondheim & Co.*, "I did the first twenty minutes and . . . I was only on page five of Bond's script."

So, rather than marinate Bond in music, Sondheim invited Hugh Wheeler to effect a script out of Bond for Sondheim to work from. Wheeler may seem an odd choice, given his aforementioned lack of sympathy for the way music coordinates action and emotion in music theatre. But Wheeler was English, and *Sweeney Todd* is an extremely English piece, a typical product of that culture's strange love of lurid crime stories. And, indeed, the *Sweeney Todd* book, though slim next to the huge score, is adroit in keeping the tale in motion, for *Sweeney Todd* is plot-heavy, as a thriller needs to be.

True, the original novel is busier. But Bond's retelling complicates while it simplifies, for, while dropping numerous subsidiary characters, Bond gives Todd and Mrs. Lovett motivations they utterly lack in all earlier versions of the tale. For one thing, the barber is no longer a mercenary evildoer but a revolutionary, striking out at a corrupt system that empowers cruelty and scorns the helpless. Mrs. Lovett, formerly a mere opportunist, is now Todd's romantic vis-à-vis, not that he cares. In truth, one of the humanizing elements in this Guignol of torn throats and eaten flesh is Mrs. Lovett's abiding love for Todd, which has sustained her for the fifteen years of his absence and which has kept her from pawning his set of chased-silver* razors. Anyone else as poor as she would have given them up for money. But she had a dream, a kind of ghoulish version of Sally's dream in *Follies*: someday we will be together. Thus Bond transformed a mere page turner into a study in how people behave when living on the brink.

In Bond's repurposing, the string of pearls is gone. But it was Bond's fond game to utilize much of the original story, including Fogg (the manager of an insane asylum where inconvenient innocents are incarcerated, tortured, and murdered), the boy Tobias (Todd's assistant, who realizes that something unsavory is afoot and is bundled off to Fogg's house of despair, though he escapes), and even the notion of a plucky young woman disguising herself as a boy.

Bond's masterstroke is the new, improved Todd, tragedy's favorite kind of hero: a good man wronged. Transported to Australia on false charges, the victim of a vicious judge and his accommodating beadle (both Bond's inventions), Todd effects a getaway and crosses half the globe to return to London and plan his revenge. He is already somewhat deranged, and, when the judge breaks free just as Todd is about to slash his throat open, the protagonist crashes into outright madness. Henceforth, Todd will slit any throat offered up to him, and Mrs. Lovett will cook the remains as food.

Bizarre as this may sound, Todd's dispassionate slaughter of innocents—good men wronged, as he was—is reminiscent of the behavior of horses butchered in American meat-process "farms." The animals aren't simply killed. They are mistreated so horribly that they become desperate to hit back at their tormentors. But they can't. The men who make their last hours of life unbearable are out of reach, so they turn on each other, kicking their hind legs in helpless rage at other horses, though they are victims, too.

---

* To chase metal is to ornament it, with a design created by artful indentations or even the use of precious stones.

Good, I got your attention. *Sweeney Todd* is not only Sondheim's *Porgy and Bess*: it's his *Threepenny Opera*. The entire show views society as incurably wicked, tilted in favor of those with power against those without. *The Threepenny Opera* is a comedy (at least as intended; modern productions often make it grim and doctrinaire) and *Sweeney Todd* is a tragedy, but both works believe that social evils cannot be exorcised, because those in power will always be the worst people in the population. The playwright Maxwell Anderson (whom we may recall as the author of *High Tor*, one of the subjects of Sondheim's four student musicals) thought this the only thing worth knowing about the very idea of government. In *Gods of the Lightning*, a play based on the Sacco and Vanzetti case (co-written with Harold Hickerson), an Anderson mouthpiece-character named Suvorin sounds the libertarian note in the tones of Jeremiah:

> SUVORIN: I tell you there is no government—there are only brigands in power who fight for more power! Till you die! Till we all die! Till there is no earth!

Todd, less vehemently, says something comparable, not about the state but about mankind in general, when a young sailor, Anthony, mentions saving Todd, whom he spotted floating on a raft:

> ANTHONY: It would have been a poor Christian indeed who'd . . . not given the alarm.
> TODD: There's many a Christian would have done just that and not lost a wink's sleep for it, either.

This marks a difference between *Sweeney Todd* and more politically minded plays: their perspective is legalistic while *Sweeney Todd*'s is humanistic. That is, the political works see catastrophe in the very existence of power structures while Sondheim's opera sees it in the nature of man. True, the first bit of scenery one glimpsed in the original New York *Todd* was a drop bearing a Victorian etching of a sort of beehive view of the class system from top to bottom: a power structure, to be sure. Still, it is Todd who frames the show's observation of evil, and he sees it as inherent in humankind, stopping short of the religious concept of a species corrupted by sinful creation. The corruption lies not in a view of sex but in a view of ethics: man, the show believes, has none.

Yet there are decent folk among the show's principals—Anthony (who, as Christopher Bond's equivalent of Mark Ingestrie, is the musical's Boy who Gets Girl); Johanna, the Girl, now directly connected to

Todd as his daughter; Tobias; and, perhaps, the Beggar Woman, a harmless wreck who was, before the brutalization that drove her mad, Todd's wife, Lucy.

All the same, it is the malefactors who give the show its flavor; it oozes with evil. These are, first of all, Judge Turpin, who convicted the innocent Todd to get control of his wife and is now prepping Johanna to become Mrs. Turpin; Beadle Bamford, in league with the Judge; and Todd's rival barber, Pirelli, an Irishman posing as an Italian to make his pitch for hair tonic intriguingly exotic. Despite a smallish role, Pirelli kicks the plot into second gear when he tries to blackmail Todd on penalty of exposure as an escaped convict. So Pirelli is Todd's first murder victim. But what to do with the corpse?

And that brings us to *Sweeney Todd*'s only amusing character, Mrs. Lovett, vastly expanded from the personality-less shopkeeper of the novel. What to do with the corpse? Well, "You know me," she says. "Sometimes ideas just pop into my head..."

And thus is born a strange union. On one hand, they become lovers, which we know from her allusion, in "By the Sea," to her "rumpled bedding" (an image used also in "Quiet," in the original version of *Candide*). On the other hand, he kills, she cooks, and man eats man: "God, That's Good!" is the chorus that opens Act Two. Ever since the 1920s, it was all but de rigueur for musicals to launch their second act with a perky number, usually a chorus. The first act might start with a book scene and only then reach the First Number, but after the intermission the audience needed a bit of pepping up.

The practice gave us *Carousel*'s "This Was a Real Nice Clambake," *My Fair Lady*'s "You Did It," and *Rent*'s "Seasons of Love," their effect greatly varying. "Clambake" is an atmosphere number, also a time-stater, as its lyrics make it clear that only a few hours have passed since Act One ended. "You Did It" is a plot number, recounting offstage events but also firing up the Boy Loses Girl as Higgins takes all the credit for the transformation of Eliza, who stands fuming and ignored and ready to rebel. "Seasons of Love" is an out-of-story carol in which the cast addresses the audience with a précis of *Rent*'s gospel of Love Thy Neighbor. Still, all three numbers reinvoke the spirit of musical comedy after the intermission's fifteen minutes of banter, texting, smoking, and drinking.

Sweeney Todd's "God, That's Good!," however, pursues the "musical thriller" aura by doubling down on the work's horror. This is an Eat Thy Neighbor number—and a plot number as well, for threaded into the soprano-alto-tenor-bass chorus are separate lines for Mrs. Lovett and Tobias, conducting their business, and a scene apart for Todd and Mrs. Lovett concerning the arrival of a special chair to send his victims down a chute leading to the basement. (This derives directly from a less advanced set-up in the 1847 novel.)

Todd worries and Mrs. Lovett soothes him till the chair arrives and is tested—all while the pie-shop customers continue to rave over the heavenly taste of Mrs. Lovett's meat pastries. Compared with *Carousel*'s clambake, *My Fair Lady*'s Embassy Ball recap, and *Rent*'s humanist anthem, this is one unique second-act opening, as Mrs. Lovett, her inventory exhausted, relaxes with a spot of ale, Todd gets ready to—oh look, here's his first customer—and the chorus tops off the number in their four-part harmony, the sopranos hitting seven high B flats in a row.

That scene provides a kind of blueprint for the music given to Todd and Mrs. Lovett, in a classic driver-and-facilitator scenario. Todd is the driver, for this is a Revenger's Tragedy: his story from top to toe. Mrs. Lovett is the facilitator, because she provides his infrastructure—the venue, the front for his murder spree, the elimination of the evidence, and moral support. So his music is that of an embittered victim-aggressor: couched in a low growl, intense, enraged. He philosophizes, he threatens, he gloats, a singular personage for the male lead in a musical, though not out of place in the opera world. By contrast, Mrs. Lovett's music is that of a cutup, promoted from the chorus of merry villagers because she shows some theatrical spark. She jests, she arranges, she passes pungent remarks. And she loves. She probably fell for Todd the first moment she saw him, husband and father though he was.

So they both have implausible dreams: he, the escaped convict, wants revenge on powerful enemies, and she wants to be a part of his crimes and commit her own. His dream is grandiose, hers domestic, no more—in a certain way of looking at it—than sensible housekeeping.

Thus, he is opera and she is musical comedy, a helter-skelter match. However, his music contains some comedy (especially in the duet that closes Act One, "A Little Priest") and hers contains some serious moments (as in her account of what happened to his family, "Poor Thing"). So the two may be said to blend at the edges. Still, the entire show really is a compound of discrepancies, a reflection of the lack of harmony in an industrialized society run by monsters. The sometimes screechy high notes we hear (from the Beadle in particular, but from others as well), or the jagged irruptions into the action by the narrating ensemble, or even the use of the Dies Irae* (first heard on "Swing your razor wide, Sweeney," then subtly varied

---

* A thirteenth-century plainsong melody set to words meaning "Day of Wrath" and used in the Catholic requiem mass.

throughout the score, for instance in Todd's salute to his long-lost razor, "You there, my friend," with the note relationships inverted). *Sweeney Todd* is a work unified by the extraordinary power of its driver, the man himself, and by the bond that Mrs. Lovett builds with him, despite his barely acknowledging her existence except when she is actively participating in his revenge plot. Everyone else in the piece offers forms of interference in his agenda, even the Beggar Woman, who is of course the real Mrs. Todd—or, rather, Mrs. Benjamin Barker, the name under which Todd was Judge Turpin's prey.

When *Sweeney Todd* opened, on March 1, 1979, at the vast Uris Theatre (today the Gershwin), the show revealed a shift in Sondheim-Prince practice, with a wholly new production staff. First, Boris Aronson had retired after *Pacific Overtures* and a *Nutcracker* for the American Ballet Theatre, both in 1976. (Aronson died in 1980.) Eugene Lee designed the set, essentially a backdrop of a London wharf behind what looked like the interior of a factory (and was: Lee constructed it from parts of a Rhode Island iron foundry). There was a walkway above the stage and a revolving module representing Mrs. Lovett's shop and flat and, on top, Todd's barber shop. Lee's wife, Franne, designed the costumes, Larry Fuller handled "dance and movement," and Ken Billington lit the action. All had worked for Prince before, but never on a show with a new score by Sondheim. Orchestrator Jonathan Tunick was a holdover from all the Sondheims from *Company* on, but this was a musical consideration, Sondheim's call rather than Prince's. And *Sweeney Todd* really did feel "different" from Sondheim-Prince thus far—much roomier, obviously (because of the Uris' gaping stage) but also somewhat in the grand manner, as befits a nineteenth-century melodrama. Even *Pacific Overtures*, on a bigger theme, was not physically as big as *Sweeney Todd*.

At 558 performances, the expensive production didn't pay off in its first New York run, though it has long since become profitable, in a "same old story" paradigm. Noël Coward had one, after his huge successes in the 1920s and 1930s. By 1950, it was: four months of good houses, then a mad sag at the box office as his lock audience was exhausted and, soon after, the closing notice. Sondheim's same old story, as I've said, runs thus: the original staging lasts somewhat over a year and loses money, but the show keeps getting done more or less everywhere and eventually becomes a classic. *Sweeney Todd* is even more than that: an initiation piece. When I was a tad, kids getting into the musical played the cast albums (or even the soundtracks) of, say, *Oklahoma!* and *The Pajama Game*. A generation later, they played *Mame* and *Cabaret*. Today, they play *Sweeney Todd*. It's the Little Golden Record of the millennium.

Merrily We Roll Along

Supremely ironic musical comedy on the bitch goddess Success, 1981.

Based on the play by George S. Kaufman and Moss Hart.

Music and Lyrics: Stephen Sondheim. Book: George Furth.

Original Leads: Jim Walton, Ann Morrison, Lonny Price, Jason Alexander, Terry Finn. Director: Hal Prince.

T his is the plot of Kaufman and Hart's comedy-drama *Merrily We Roll Along* (1934), in three acts with three scenes in each act. The action covers eighteen years, from 1916 to 1934:

ACT ONE

1916: Delivering his college valedictorian address, Richard Niles extols his "great friendship" with classmate Jonny Crale.

1918: Richard courts Helen, a simple soul unsuited to his intelligence and culture.

1922: Jonny, now an artist, introduces Richard to a new best friend, Julia Glenn, a writer. She tells him, "You're going to do great things in the theater." Richard's experimental off-Broadway piece got him nowhere, but now he's writing a Society comedy for Althea Royce, a trendy star. He has to live with his loathsome in-laws to do it, which harms his marriage, as Helen sides with their endless assaults on him.

ACT TWO

1923: At the opening-night party for the Royce vehicle, her earthy mother, a vaudeville veteran, mocks the tony airs of Richard's characters with her own loud antics. (Raising a glass, she shouts, "Up the chimney, boys!") Sensing that Richard and his star are involved, Helen walks out of the party and her marriage.

1924: Lurid headlines about lovemaking with Althea on a leopard skin rug bedevil Richard at his divorce hearing. Julia (who secretly loves him) urges Richard to get away for a vacation. Paparazzi scam a photo of Richard, holding up a leopard skin behind him, and he breaks down sobbing.

1925: Richard's bond with Jonny and Julia weakens because they aggressively deplore his writing contentless hits. What about that socially progressive "coal-mine" piece? Richard says it's not what people want. As he leaves, Julia sadly tells Jonny, "He's met The Crowd, and there he goes!"

ACT THREE

1926: Living on Park Avenue in bespoke tailoring with a Japanese manservant, Richard is the very glass of style. He neglects his pals—Jonny accuses him of "posing for those lousy pictures in *Vanity Fair* all day." And Richard has done harm: abandoned by Althea, her husband kills himself.

1927: Jonny has painted a portrait of Richard clutching Althea and a cash register. At a bon ton restaurant, he tries to make up with Richard, who socks him, starting a brawl.

1934: Like The Great Gatsby, Richard has a home on Sands Point ("West Egg" in the Fitzgerald novel). Now it is Althea's turn to sense that Richard is involved with another woman. At the height of a party, Althea attacks his talent. Fashionable playwright? No: "Fashionable prostitute!" In a fury, she hurls iodine into her replacement's face, blinding her.

These are the play's events in chronological order—but not in playing order, because *Merrily We Roll Along*'s narrative ran backward. As the program noted, "Each scene takes place at an earlier time than the scene preceding." Thus, the play's first act starts with the Sands Point party and the iodine incident, and the third act ends with Richard's graduation speech.

The authors' design was to show the audience, first, how their protagonist ended up and then, step by step, to isolate the mishaps that led a gifted but sensitive and even mousy artist to forfeit all rights to self-fulfillment. As the years recede, we see him fall out with his two best friends because they demand he live up to not his own expectations but theirs. They scorn the elite—The Crowd, as we saw Julia call it—but Richard enjoys being a part of it. "I like meeting Noël Coward," he tells Jonny, "and I like being successful."

More important, he adds, "I'm enjoying myself for the first time": because he was failing at serious work, taking menial jobs and sponging off his gruesome parents-in-law in an atmosphere of non-stop pushing and nagging. Then, at last, the authors pictured Richard finishing college in the certainty that ideals and friendship were all he needed. Because the young believe they are invincible.

It was perfect source material for Sondheim, with the "knowing what you want" problem, the "past creating the present" meme, and the chance to write a kind of newfangled version of good old musical comedy, substantial yet at times lighthearted, and very touching at the close. Comedy tonight, with a kick. Or: it was *Allegro* with a hero who never escaped from The Crowd, as *Allegro*'s hero finally does. Or: it was *Follies* in which Ben marries Sally and leaves her for Phyllis, who in this version is vicious—throwing iodine in someone's face in 1934 could actually cause blindness. It was a challenge, as all Sondheim's shows now were, and the first of the challenges was the updating. When the play *Merrily* opened, it was smack in the middle of the sophisticated 1930s, and a smart and ambitious fellow could make a name and fortune as a playwright. Moss Hart was a kid from nowhere; by 1940, he was a national treasure. However, in Sondheim's day the culture looked to not Broadway but Hollywood, so Sondheim and his librettist, George Furth (returning after *Company*, five shows ago), made their hero a songwriter who becomes a movie producer.

But is a movie producer in the 1980s at all equivalent to a playwright in the 1930s? The author of successful drama back then was a man of renown. "Eugene O'Neill" became a household term, the American for "major playwright" as "Caruso" meant "top opera singer" and "Lindbergh" meant "daring aviator."

However, in the musical *Merrily*'s 1980s, few knew or cared who produced movies. It mattered in Hollywood—that is, in the industry itself—but not in the cinemas. The rock stars of film were actors and directors, even certain soundtrack composers. What does a movie producer do, anyway, besides make deals? Producers can be extremely powerful, but they're not *famous*. And the play *Merrily* emphasizes that it is Richard's fame that grants him entrée into the cultural ruling class. The musical *Merrily* substitutes power for fame, making it a somewhat different story. Richard Niles gets to meet Noël Coward. His counterpart in the musical, Franklin Shepard, meets...who? Laverne and Shirley?

Before we go on, let's set forth the name changes the three leads underwent from play to musical:

PLAY	MUSICAL
Richard Niles, playwright.	Franklin Shepard, composer.
Jonathan (always called "Jonny") Crale, painter.	Charley Kringas, lyricist.
Julia Glenn, a sort of Dorothy Parker.	Mary Flynn, journalist.

Some of the changes from play to musical made the material more effective, especially in the shift from then to now. Instead of Jonny's picturing Richard as a Dorian Gray, Charley defames Frank during an interview on national television, a much more dramatic event. And Julia's phrase "The Crowd" gave rise to a number called "The Blob," on the hows and whys of the opinion-makers who run New York's arts scene.

In the play, The Crowd is simply the elite, of which George S. Kaufman was a willing member and Moss Hart an enthusiast. Indeed, Hart's favorite stunt was to set onstage replicas of the Names that his audience read about in Walter Winchell's column—Gertrude Lawrence; Harpo Marx; Johnny Weissmuller; Elsa Maxwell; Katharine Cornell's gay husband, Guthrie McClintic; and even Hart's mother-in-law, Kitty Carlisle's mom. In the musical, The Blob is a richer concept than The Crowd—not just the famous and talented but their vast coterie of friends and near-friends, who at times unleash destructive forces as they Make Their Opinions. This aspect, one of the musical *Merrily*'s most intriguing aperçus, got a bit lost; the "Blob" number itself was even cut during previews (though it was reinstated in a later revision).

One very important element of the play completely vanished in the musical—the lengthy scene in which we see Richard's peace of mind under siege while he boards with his grotesque in-laws. They do appear in the musical, briefly, characterized as intolerant and boring. But the play reveals them as instruments of Richard's destiny, for their cruelty drives him to seek financial independence, to be free of obligations to anyone who assaults his self-esteem. It explains why he becomes uncomfortable with Jonny and Julia, why he "sells out," and why his first marriage dissolves.

Worse yet, the musical altered the play's charming madcap Jonny into the hectoring, self-righteous Charley Kringas. The original Jonny, Walter Abel, became famous in his maturity as an authority figure, but in his twenties and thirties Abel was a romantic lead. When O'Neill's reboot of Aeschylus' *Oresteia*, *Mourning Becomes Electra*, became the talk of the town, in 1931, the Theatre Guild sent a second company out on the road, headed by heavyweights Judith Anderson and Florence Reed. And Walter Abel played Orin, O'Neill's equivalent of Orestes and one of the classic jeune premier parts. He is haunted, yes—it wouldn't be O'Neill if he weren't. But he is as well attractive and (sort of) powerful.

It would seem that Kaufman and Hart planned Jonathan Crale as a counterweight to Richard Niles: something solid and alluring to contrast with Niles' hesitant style. Act Two opens with Jonny in pajamas after a night with his current girl friend. After she leaves, Julia comes in, and while talking with her Jonny starts to change. A shot of the two of them, with

Abel looking toothsome in his pajama pants, was used prominently in the show's PR, a bold address of the public for 1934.

In fact, the simple act of showing male skin on stage, so common today, was a contextual signifier in the 1930s: something was up. Later, it was because director Joshua Logan was so closeted that his gay ID resided in the casting and unshirting of gleaming hunks; in *Merrily*'s 1930s, it was called "suggestive": advising the worldly that something beyond "normal" sex was in play. In other words, the play *Merrily* at least considers a homoerotic subtext in the relationship of Richard and Jonny. The musical's Charleys might be more effective if they did less kringasing and put some effort into charming us.

The only successful part of the musical in its original form was Sondheim's score, a combination of easy-listen melody and intricate classical construction. Using a number of melodic cells throughout the evening—as in *Sweeney Todd* but much more overtly—Sondheim combined and adjusted them, so that an improvised piano riff turns into a school song, "The Hills of Tomorrow" (heard in the original production but no longer in the revised show), then into Frank and Charley's carefree audition piece, "Who Wants To Live in New York?," and *then* into their soulful ballad, "Good Thing Going."

Yet the score came off as ingenuous musical-comedy music, appealing and impulsive. Unstudied. The old snark that Sondheim doesn't write "hummable" tunes never seemed as lame as it did here, and the plan to strip away the compositional devices as the show proceeded exactly matched the "youthening" of the characters. At length, we reached the happy, crazy juveniles who loved each other because they were going to conquer the world together, in "Opening Doors" and the finale, "Our Time." A Sondheim show can end in mixed feelings; this Sondheim show starts that way, but ends in love and optimism.

Unfortunately, when *Merrily* began previews, in October of 1981, at the Alvin Theatre, it played badly. George Furth's book, filled with glitches, would be vastly improved over the coming weeks. For instance, the musical's equivalent of the gigantic fistfight that broke out in the play's restaurant scene was, at first, simply a feeble snub: Frank haughtily turned away from Charley while seated at a banquette. By the time the show opened, on November 16, Frank, standing, ripped into Charley verbally and shoved him away, his rage at his old best friend at a shocking level of intensity. In fact, this was an improvement on what Kaufman and Hart had, as fistfights are almost never believable on stage. A shove can be incredibly effective, but a full-scale brawl has to be choreographed, and always looks it.

Anyway, *Merrily*'s book was not the problem: it was the production itself, because Hal Prince cast very young kids, apparently to suggest a high-school show, with these children enacting the follies of grown-ups. It was supposed to be endearing and touching, but most of the players came off as clumsy and unknowing. Not naive, as intended: incompetent. "They were amateurs," said the show's choreographer, Ron Field, in *Sondheim & Co.* "But that was the concept. And I went, 'Oh, well, if that's the concept let's pick the homeliest and awkwardest, and put them on this funny set. And then they're going to wear what? Wigs? Gray wigs? And...clothing, like from their mother's [*sic*] closets.... How come I don't get it?'"

Field had created the dances for *Cabaret* and *Zorbá* for Prince, and choreographed and directed *Applause* and an *On the Town* revival. He was used to working with Broadway dancers, who are, frankly, the best in the world at what they do. Never before did Field have to figure out how to move a cast of schmoos and kadiddlehoppers. There was a dance break in the first-act finale, "Now You Know," and, besides letting two chorus people try erotic this and that and hoping to keep the three leads looking professional, all Field could do with the corps was fold them into a conga line. And it still looked risible. But when Field approached Prince about this parlous state of affairs, Prince simply said, "Ron, we're not in trouble."

With all his experience, couldn't Prince tell from the audience reaction that they most certainly were in trouble? So many people walked out on *Merrily* that a joke ran around town that you couldn't get a cab at intermission. The public laughed at serious lines and ignored jokes, sure symptoms of a flop. Morale backstage was so bad that, at an early preview, James Weissenbach, who was playing Frank, couldn't hang a picture in his "new apartment" scene with Mary because the tech failed him; shooting a helpless look at Ann Morrison, he walked off the stage.*

Newspaper columns ran with tales of disaster, as they love to do, and there may well have been a pile-on by The Blob, which had endured five Sondheim-Prince masterpieces in a row in the 1970s and was fed up with genius. All the same, *Merrily*'s failure—very bad reviews and a two-week run—was largely *Merrily*'s fault. The sense of failure was so pervasive that RCA Victor, who had the recording rights, at first declined to go ahead, which would have made *Merrily* the only Sondheim musical not to get an original-cast album. Cooler heads, as they say, prevailed, and the recording was a hit.

Then, in 1985, Furth and Sondheim (with director James Lapine) created a revision in La Jolla, California, cast with grown-ups John Rubinstein, Chip Zien, and Heather MacRae (with Marin Mazzie as Beth). Now the high-school play atmosphere was dispelled, but so thoroughly that the frame of a graduation ceremony—a key link with the play *Merrily*—was dropped,

---

* He did come right back, but in the end he left the show, replaced by his understudy, Jim Walton.

losing "The Hills of Tomorrow." Furth tried to give the principals more profile, though Mary's writing career remained mysterious (exactly what does she publish?) and Charley was still a naggy twerp. In fact, both still see Frank as *her* husband and *his* songwriting partner for life, which makes them as selfish as they enjoy thinking he is. Frank wasn't put on earth to serve as a tool of their agendas; he needs to establish his own agenda and get into the dangerous Sondheimland of free will and its consequences. It's no doubt unhappy that his will includes taking on another man's wife—Gussie, married to the producer of Frank and Charley's Broadway show. But it's really Gussie who makes the moves, not Frank:

> FRANK: I could never live with you leaving Joe for me.
> GUSSIE: I'm leaving him for me.

In the 2012 Encores! concert staging, this scene was directed (by James Lapine again) very sensually, as Elizabeth Stanley's Gussie didn't just seduce Colin Donnell's Frank but took him apart piece by piece. Their transaction is built around a number newly written for the 1985 revision, "Growing Up," which begins as Frank's soliloquy—giving us a first chance to understand him—and then becomes Gussie's siren's song. The Encores! staging showed us, unmistakably, a being confronted by irresistible temptation. The musical's Frank is a strong man, but Gussie's wish to make him her alpha male was stronger, urged along in the music by a chromatic run (one of the score's melodic cells) that, when Frank sang it, was hesitant and thoughtful but, when Gussie sang it, became slithery and bewitching.

But then, all of the changes in the score made in 1985 clarified the action. A new opening, "That Frank," replaced the original's "Rich and Happy" with a different view of Frank, as sung by his Hollywood cohorts: he's *good* at producing movies, so no wonder he changed careers. "The Blob," cut on Broadway, as I've said, was reinstated, amplifying Gussie's character—a strategic improvement, as she is the musical's equivalent of the play's Althea Royce, not just a leading actress but the embodiment of the security and glamor that Frank wants to make his own. Royce is that famous excuse for artists who started off keen but failed in their second act, the bitch goddess Success. She lures you, corrupts you, destroys you—or so runs the myth. In truth, doesn't she give back to you what you give to her? Stay keen and don't die young. Be William Faulkner, not F. Scott Fitzgerald.

Or be Moss Hart. Frank is Moss Hart, or Oscar Hammerstein, or Stephen Sondheim: anyone with the intelligence and talent to make interesting things happen in the arts; and every single one of them has the right to define "interesting" on his terms. But Hart, Hammerstein, and Sondheim were adventurous in what they did, Hammerstein more than Hart and Sondheim more than Hammerstein. Richard/Frank is, in the long run, not adventurous.

He is successful. Again, it's *Allegro*'s Joseph Taylor Jr. as Dr. Feelgood, throwing away his skill—his soul—on la-di-da hypochondriacs. Joe Taylor is an everyman, a kid with growing pains and a yearbook page and anxieties. Franklin Shepard is special, which is why he attracts admirers who believe he will solve their problems. There's an excitement about him, and every time *Merrily* is produced with a charismatic actor as Frank, the show works. Otherwise, it strains for meaning, because the role is underwritten and only makes sense when we can *see* what Frank is: a savior.

Paradoxically, the musical *Merrily* is both very faithful yet rather untrue to its source. To repeat: in the musical, we lose a substantial piece of information about why the hero is so determined to achieve financial independence: to protect himself from the kind of beating he took during his first marriage. No one, we almost hear him cry, will ever own me again! But the musical also improved on that hero, trading the somewhat high-strung Richard Niles for the more fascinating Franklin Shepard, a wonder boy on whom everyone needs to project his or her fantasies. He's a savior, yes— but of no redemptive power whatsoever, because he's too self-absorbed to relate to others.

Is that why he gave up the very creative vocation of composer for the bureaucratic post of movie producer? Like so many Sondheim shows, *Merrily We Roll Along* raises more questions than it answers. But raising questions is the theatre's mandate. It may be that we're never going to know what drives Franklin Shepard, just as we never quite understand the Franklin Shepards we meet in life. The better we know them, the more they confuse us. One *Merrily* lyric runs, "It started out like a song." It always does, doesn't it?

Sunday in the Park with George

Possibly autobiographical study of the passion of the artist, 1984.

Music and Lyrics: Stephen Sondheim. Book: James Lapine.

Original Leads: Mandy Patinkin, Bernadette Peters. Director: James Lapine.

For many decades now, people in the lively arts have been decrying their seamy underside, the part the public is largely unaware of. "A grand profession but a dirty business" has been attributed to so many actors, opera singers, ballet dancers, and so on that, for all we know, it dates back to Aeschylus. The problematical "human" side of the arts industry takes in everything from lie-cheat-and-steal producers and two-faced playwrights to the "Darling, you were marvelous" first nighters in your New Haven dressing room who race back to Broadway to tell everyone you know, "My dear, his collapse is complete!"

The Blob is back. "We're in a business," James Lapine says, in *Sondheim & Co.*, "where they love nothing more than to build you up and tear you down," and it was The Blob that spread bad words about *Merrily We Roll Along*'s New York previews so relentlessly that, in effect, the critics reviewed the dish rather than the show itself. Sondheim told me that, at one preview, two men chased him up the aisle attacking the show virually into his ear, sheer venom, The Blob. And, of course, when Sondheim's next piece broke out of the Sondheim-Prince line to forge a new partnership with James Lapine, The Blob was quick to infer—and advertise—a rupture in Sondheim's relationship with Prince.

There wasn't one, and Prince would stage another Sondheim show some years later. Nevertheless, *Sunday in the Park With George* marks the start of Sondheim's third period, dominated by collaborations with Lapine. As both librettist and director, Lapine comes out of the off-Broadway experimental stage, as opposed to Sondheim's background in the Big Broadway of *West Side Story*, *Gypsy*, *Do I Hear a Waltz?*. His Prince shows of the 1970s form a quintet of unparalleled experimentation, true—but they were all the same carried out within a main-stage viewpoint, that belief that, historically, Broadway is where important American theatre happens.

Lapine's venue was offbeat—and he was unfamiliar with musicals in general. In *Look, I Made a Hat*, Sondheim mentions that Lapine didn't know Leonard Bernstein's *Candide* score, which is somewhat like a movie director not having seen *Bonnie and Clyde*. In fact, as Sondheim and Lapine discussed possibilities for a musical of their own, they finally arrived at a painting, Georges Seurat's *Sunday Afternoon on the Island of La Grande Jatte*,* in which various figures sit or stand on their day off: a company of strangers isolated in their thoughts on an in fact not vase-like but serpentine spot of land in the Seine. (The island is not in central Paris but to the northwest, after the river passes through the city's famous parts and curls back around toward St. Denis, about ten kilometers north of Notre-Dame.) Seurat's picture fascinates because it seems so full of something or other yet so still and unyielding, so...storyless. It's a mystery, Lapine and Sondheim thought. Something's missing. Then one or the other said, "It's the artist." He can't be seen, yet only he is aware of what he has left out: because he knows all the stories.

And that was the musical they wrote—or, at least, the first half of it, opening up the lives of the people in the picture from the viewpoint of the artist. In a bold move, the musical's second half jumps from the time of the painting, the mid-1880s, to a hundred years later. Again, the action revolves around an artist, apparently the great-grandson of Seurat, an American also named George. As Seurat was radical for his time, so is his counterpart, using electricity in his exhibitions as Seurat used pointillism, employing tiny dots of different colors instead of broad brush strokes of solid or slightly modified shades.

Sunday's first act, set, in effect, *inside* the *Grande Jatte* painting, has the advantage of Seurat's piquant imagination; he footnotes the painting for us even as he lives it along with his creations. The second act, set in a museum and then back on that island in the Seine, now crowded with high-rises, can seem antiseptic by comparison, but in fact the show's inner life is left hang-

---

* In my own translation of *jatte* from the 1988 *Le Robert* dictionary: "A rounded vase, very wide at the top, without edges or handles." Thus, the island was dubbed "The Big Vase."

ing at the intermission, and is resolved only at the evening's end. Here is the action in outline:

Act One: Distracted by his work, Georges neglects his mistress, Dot, and struggles for acceptance in the face of public scorn. Does no one understand how desperately he needs to substantiate his vision? His mother, his subjects, even Dot? Furious at Georges' refusal to give himself emotionally to any love but art, Dot—who is pregnant, presumably with Georges' child—leaves for America with another man.

Act Two: The politics and commercialism of the modern-art scene depress George. His predecessor died very young, unaware of how posterity would honor him; thus, George feels as lost as Georges felt unaccepted. Then, on La Grande Jatte itself, Dot appears to him just as she looks in the painting, heartening George with the same music with which she took her angry leave of Georges in Act One, the rejecting "We Do Not Belong Together." Only now it is "Move On," reassuring and forgiving. Better: understanding who he is. The familiar painting reforms itself as we watch, and, at the music's climax, in a gesture at once tender, epic, and shocking, Georges' subjects bow to George, in homage to the mission of the artist, redeemed and encouraged to continue his work.

This should explain why the show's halves, which seem to some onlookers to be two different musicals, in fact form a single continuity that isn't rounded off till the very end, when the trumpet sounds the two notes of the "Sunday" theme, terminally binding the old story with the new one. Further, a single cast plays the two sets of roles, though there is no relationship between the painting figures in Act One and the museum habitués in Act Two.* However, the same actor appears as Georges and then George, and one actress plays both Dot and George's grandmother, who takes part in his exhibit. The pairing is deliberately off-kilter, akin to that of Sweeney Todd and Mrs. Lovett, the man so obsessed and the woman so sportive: instead of Boy Meets Girl it's Musical Play Meets Musical Comedy. But then, *Sunday* is not a smooth work but a rough one, with odd parts, starting with those two "mismatched" acts. Most Sondheim shows are smooth—in

---

* For instance, Louis, the lovably boring baker of the painting, becomes Billy, a sarcastic art-world hanger-on; and Yvonne, an artist's lively wife in the 1880s, turns into Naomi, a scowling musician. There is one arresting parallel: the actress who plays Georges's mother in Act One reappears in Act Two as a writer on art—in fact, George's severest critic. Does this reference Sondheim's vexed relationship with his own mother? One of the mysteries of Sondheimland. Another mystery: for some reason, Lapine called both artists "George," though the first one is of course George*s* Seurat.

another word, consistent. In fact, most musical shows, period, are smooth, because rough confuses the public. It's so... surprising.

On the other hand, the music-theatre historian Scott McMillin, in *The Musical as Drama*, makes a powerful argument in favor of "disjunction" in the form. McMillin's thesis—which he acknowledges as a spin-off from Brechtian theatre—sees the rough musical, with its disconnects and unassimilated elements, as a reinvigoration of the Extremely Integrated Musical, with its homogenized art. Yes, integration creates persuasive storytelling—*Oklahoma!*, *Brigadoon*, *My Fair Lady*, *The Music Man*, *A Chorus Line*, with all their features in harmony. But the best shows combining dissonant features—*On the Town*, *Cabaret*, *Chicago*—are very much with us, ceaselessly revived. (*Chicago*, in its Encores!-to-Broadway staging, is now one of the longest-running shows of all time.) They seem fresh decades after their premieres because their McMillinesque disjunction makes them vital and exciting—unpredictable, like an unreliable friend of enormous charm. *On the Town*'s symphonic ballets dropped into a chase-me-quick farce, *Cabaret*'s intrusive (yet deviously relevant) nightclub numbers, and *Chicago*'s vaudeville-within-a-play move past Rodgers and Hammerstein's realism to revel in a vivacious surrealism, theatre piled upon theatre.

Thus, *Sunday in the Park With George* excites and touches us not through the *Oklahoma!* model (rocky romance + villain + community coalesces around hero = statehood) but through an innovative layout (Story 1 [art under siege] + Story 2 [art encouraged by love object from Story 1] = transfiguration) in which a narrative unfolds on two platforms, united at the very end.

So *Sunday*, the initiating work in Sondheim's third period, is in at least one way his most revolutionary show till that point—and, perhaps, of his entire career. It was also, when it opened, on May 2, 1984, his most puzzling. True, even some Sondheim devotées balked at *Pacific Overtures*, but that work is crowded with event and at times intricately detailed, a history in which the kings and battles are just out of sight, beyond the horizon. *Sunday*, on the other hand, is spare, very easy to follow. Those who found it perplexing were not prepared for its Story 1-Story 2-fusion-finale structure. But one could argue that the best theatre is the kind that one isn't prepared for. Sondheim's oeuvre as a whole recalls Denis Diderot's stated intention, in editing the *Encyclopédie*: "Changer la façon commune de penser" (To change the usual way of thinking). Sondheim has tried to change the usual way theatregoers think about musicals, to lead them into at times disjunctive art.

I say this even though the *Sunday* score is as character-driven as any in Sondheim—and expert character songs are what began to drive the musical when it entered its Golden Age, and what theatregoers are prepared for: "Bess, You Is My Woman Now," "Adelaide's Lament," "I Wonder What the King Is Doing Tonight." Georges's major solo, "Finishing the Hat," offers a massive credo for the artist who has, in effect, two souls: one for the physical specimen living in the world and another for the out-of-body creator living in the canvases where he re-fashions the world. And note that this song is composed partly of isolated nouns, images, sounds—"grass," "stick," "dog," "light"—in a reflection of Seurat's pointillism.

Then, in Act Two, (the other) George has "Putting It Together," in a completely different style, for George's art is different from Georges's. "Finishing the Hat" is a soliloquy, for the artist in his natural-born isolation. "Putting It Together" is a soliloquy set into an ensemble piece, for nowadays the artist must work the room, shake hands with the grants and commissions community, spark the PR circuits. This George would like to fly from it all, and, as he sings, he conjures up simulacra of himself (in black-and-white figurines that rise through the deck) to take his place in conversation with the crowd after his exhibition. Is it autobiographical? That is, is this Sondheim lamenting his position as the Broadway musical's maximum leader, taking a ritual pounding as his shows fail to top commercial charts? even as they (gradually, albeit) ascend to classic status? Must he debate with his detractors? Here, figurines, *you* talk to them.

Barbra Streisand was so struck by the reportorial accuracy of "Putting It Together" that she asked Sondheim to recast the lyrics for her to record as her own autobiographical lamentation. Powerful though Streisand is, even she must argue with executives, as Sondheim must with the Tired Businessman because Sondheim left out the cancan girls, or with The Blob, spiteful because his latest show tried to sneak by without Elaine Stritch's jazzamatazz one-liners.

And there is this odd event at the 1984 Tony Awards, when *Sunday* was up against Jerry Herman's *La Cage aux Folles* for not only Best Musical but Book, Actor, Score, Direction, Costumes, and Lighting. *Sunday* got two other nominations as well, but won only Sets and Lighting; *La Cage* took all the important laurels except Best Actress in a Musical simply because it had no leading-woman role. When Herman accepted his Tony for Best Original Score, he very defensively said, "There's been a rumor around...that the simple, hummable show tune was no longer welcome on Broadway. Well, it's alive and well at the Palace [Theatre, where *La Cage* was playing]!"

Everyone thought Herman was attacking *Sunday* and Sondheim, though Herman admired Sondheim scores and surely would not have been so uncollegial in so public an arena. More likely, he was venting because his last three shows—*Dear World*, *Mack & Mabel*, and *The Grand Tour*—had failed. In 1975, the Tonys had even gone so far as to nominate for Best Score

A Letter For Queen Victoria (which isn't a musical) and *The Lieutenant* (a rock opera on the My Lai incident that few if any Tony nominators would likely have seen in its 9 performances), just to avoid giving a nod to Herman's *Mack & Mabel* songs.

Yet folks believed that Herman's "simple, hummable show tune" was a slap in Sondheim's face, because, while his tunes are in fact hummable, they are not simple. Sondheim didn't merely intellectualize the musical: he intellectualized the music in the musical.

But let me return to that moment in *Sunday*'s second act, when the characters in the painting bow to their creator. As a director, James Lapine scorns the grand manner. It's another difference between his style and that of Hal Prince, who knows that great theatre has great moments, when the stage is electrified by a sudden shift in tone in the visual—a *coup de théâtre*, as the French put it. It could be the moment in *Company*'s "Side By Side" when, one by one, each of the men indicated his partner with a "take a bow" hand, leaving Robert to indicate . . . no one. Or the moment in *A Little Night Music* when the dinner party materialized in a table of guests facing upstage, in steely Madame Armfeldt facing down, and, behind them all, in a tapestry dropping into place from the flies: a suave assembly of the moving parts of baronial luxury.

No doubt Hal Prince would have made something sumptuous of the bowing in *Sunday*—it is, after all, the visual climax of an extremely visual piece. Lapine's crew, however, were directed to underplay their salute; there was no deep homage from the creations to their creator. Nonetheless, it remains a striking moment in the history of the musical, especially so in this possibly very personal work: when art thanks the artist. *Understands* him. "Art isn't easy" is a key lyric in the piece, sung by George; it could as well be sung by the audience: because art isn't supposed to be easy. It treats elements the mass public finds disturbing—irony, contradiction, malice, destruction. And notice that even Jerry Herman, whose shows are easy to enjoy, felt he had been isolated on Broadway. Well, life is short but art is long. You'll be happy later.

Into the Woods

Interlocked fairy tales, 1987.

Music and Lyrics: Stephen Sondheim. Book: James Lapine.

Original Leads: Bernadette Peters, Joanna Gleason, Chip Zien, Tom Aldredge, Robert Westenberg, Chuck Wagner. Director: James Lapine.

hree stories initiate the action. One is *Cinderella*. Another is *Jack and the Beanstalk*. The third is the authors' invention, *The Baker and His Wife*, into which *Little Red Ridinghood* was inserted.

A Narrator keeps the play moving along, providing explanations, backstories, and the like, and a very long First Number (beginning with "I wish") sets all three tales into play, with the principals separately *needing* something that will lead them into that unsettling bit of geography, the nearby forest.

That First Number is the title song, a rondo with an irresistible clip-clopping refrain that suggests the excitement (and anxiety) of taking off on an adventure. But what is the woods, exactly? It's a crucible, a learning or defining test. It's danger, temptation, treachery, sex: the unknown in all its forms. You daren't go, yet you must go. And it has its attractive or at least harmless side. "The woods are just trees," runs one of Sondheim's most amiably seductive lyrics, "the trees are just wood."

Nevertheless, there's nothing "just" about these characters. Jack is a little nuts. Cinderella has occult powers. The Baker and his Wife live next door to a Witch. And then the pair find themselves off on one of those scavenger hunts that Sondheim used to fashion in his youth. Only those hunters were scouring New York on a lark. In this show, the hunters are *in the woods*, where lives change or even end.

This second Sondheim-Lapine musical has, among other distinctions, the busiest plot in the history of the form. *A Funny Thing Happened On the Way To the Forum* runs a melee of a storyline, but it at least centers on a protagonist, Pseudolus, and his quest for manumission. *Into the Woods* has no clear-cut protagonist. Who is the essential figure? The Baker would appear to be the leading role, his quest (to sire children) the most far-ranging of the many in the show. But it is the Witch who drives the action, she who runs the scavenger hunt that occupies the Baker and his Wife for most of Act One. Further, the Witch is the star part: for Bernadette Peters in the original production, Julia McKenzie in London, Vanessa Williams in the 2002 Broadway revival, and Meryl Streep in the 2014 film version. True, the Baker's dramatic arc dominates the second act. But this really is an ensemble show with a few showy roles.

It is certainly a more unified work than the previous Sondheim-Lapine title, *Sunday in the Park With George*—though, oddly, it had a comparable "intermission problem." With *Sunday*, some felt that the second act lost the compelling fantasy of the first act. With *Into the Woods*, a few members of the audience thought the show had concluded at the end of Act One and had to be dissuaded from going home. True, the last thing one hears as the act ends is "Happy ever after!," while first acts are supposed to end suspensefully. Laurey spurns Curly to go off with Jed. Dolly vows to win her half-a-millionaire. *Chicago*'s Roxie fakes pregnancy—will she get off, after all?

Into the Woods' first act ends in a departure from the rules, something Oscar Hammerstein tried several times. Thus, *Show Boat*'s first-act finale offers the classic Boy Gets Girl, which more usually *closes* the evening. *Allegro*'s first act ends the same way, though in that case we have been warned that the Girl is not worthy of the Boy.

And *Into the Woods'* first-act curtain gives us a visual warning of sequelae to come: while the cast celebrates the "happy ending," a beanstalk suddenly shoots up to the sky. They don't see it—but we do, and while the first beanstalk led Jack to treasure and what appears to be his sexual awakening, a second beanstalk in a Sondheim musical is bound to prove problematic. In Sondheimland, few get even one beanstalk; two promises the surfeit of instability and disappointment, the growing old of *Follies*, the liquid nature of love in *A Little Night Music*.

As it happens, that second beanstalk allows the Giant's wife to descend to earth. She's a widow now, Jack is why, and she wants revenge. This sets off the tumult between appeasers and defiers that busies much of the show's second act. And of course fairy tales are rich in such hazards; they're like westerns with magic. There was much talk of the extent to which

Sondheim and Lapine were influenced by Bruno Bettelheim's study of children's wonder stories, *The Uses of Enchantment*, "simply because," Sondheim dryly observes, "it's the only book on the subject known to a wide public." And one needn't read Bettelheim to notice how fairy tales help children work out psychological anxieties of various kinds. One key passage of Bettelheim, right at the start of his book, does bring us closer to understanding how *Into the Woods* works, if only coincidentally: "Wisdom," he writes, "is built up, small step by small step, from most irrational beginnings. . . . The most difficult task in raising a child is helping him to find meaning in life. Many growth experiences are needed to achieve this."

Fairy tales specialize in those growth experiences; such voyages into the unknown are, for many children, their first taste of the world beyond the more or less intelligible one of home, family, and play dates with their coevals. The hazards of their lives entail day-to-day frustrations and penalties, little problems. No, you can't have candy for dinner. Don't ask Grandma why she has a mustache. Clean up your room or no *Legend of Zelda*.

Fairy tales, however, open up a cosmos in which the hazards are alien, the penalties conclusive . . . and there's always a wicked witch. *Big* problems. Fiction for grownups can be fraught with paradoxical or simply impenetrable characters—Dmitri Karamazov, say, flinging himself from mood to mood without transition, murderous yet technically innocent; or the nihilistic yet ultimately self-sacrificing Sydney Carton; and is Jay Gatsby truly wonderful or is he just attractive and Nick Carraway gay? But fairy tales present basic and consistent characters—the weak father and vicious stepmother, the gobbling goblin, the sweet little kids, the clueless king, the savior prince. And, yes, the wicked witch, whose address is invariably: *the woods*.

Thus, *Into the Woods* gives us a bunch of adults and adolescents who are like the children who appear in or listen to fairy tales. They behave oddly—Jack, when not climbing the beanstalk, thinks he's buddies with a cow. Cinderella is in league with birds who do her bidding. Little Red Ridinghood steals food. The Baker and his Wife seem normal, but they all have to undergo those growth experiences, directed by their "parent"—the Witch, who is, in the musical, not so much wicked as demanding.

Very demanding.

In fact, one of the show's charms is the way in which it humanizes fairy-tale icons. The storybookland that Bettelheim describes is a remote and dream-laden realm, but when the Baker's shop has a visitor, the Baker calmly tells his wife, "It's the Witch from next door," because, when you reside in a fairy tale, you have zesty neighbors. Further, we realize just how shadowy Jack, Red Ridinghood, and the other familiar figures always were before Sondheim and Lapine shed light on them—Jack is simple-minded yet, after his adventure in the sky, enlightened and poetic; Little Red is blunt and pushy; Rapunzel is an idiot; Prince Charming cheats on his wife. And it isn't even an irresistible romantic fling. It's sex, and then it's over. "How alive you've made me feel," the Prince says, leaving. And his momentary partner, the Baker's Wife, asks us, "What was that?"

And, to a hesitant vamp, she slithers into "Moments in the Woods," one of the score's many numbers that bubble up out of the action without warning. Musicals used to have song cues; here's one from Rodgers and Hammerstein's *Flower Drum Song* (1958), from the time when Sondheim was launching his career. The show is set in San Francisco, and, at a party, someone asks Pat Suzuki if she's going to move to Nob Hill. What? And give up Chinatown?:

SUZUKI: I've got to be where the action is.
GIRL: Where is that?

The brass unfurl in four snazzy chords, and Suzuki's off and running, in "Grant Avenue." Not only is the song embarrassingly supplementary: it hasn't even been nested properly.

They don't do that any more, and Sondheim's shows are one reason why. At that, *Into the Woods* might be his most integrated score, because the book runs through the numbers just as the numbers run through the book. Further, the show is emerging as one of Sondheim's most popular. It opened on November 5, 1987, at the Martin Beck Theatre, won enthusiastic reviews, ran 764 performances, and remains one of Sondheim's most performed titles. Above all, the show's endearing silliness mixed with calamity make it perhaps the richest work of Sondheim's third period, dark with death yet reaching a transcendently uplifting conclusion.

Assassins

Revue on the motivations of American president killers, 1990.

Music and Lyrics: Stephen Sondheim. Book: John Weidman.

Original Leads: Patrick Cassidy, Victor Garber, Terrence Mann, Eddie Korbich, Debra Monk, Annie Golden, Jonathan Hadary, Jace Alexander. Director: Jerry Zaks.

T his is a physically small-scaled show, assembling in songs and sketches the famous presidential assassins and would-be assassins of various eras, from John Wilkes Booth and Leon Czolgosz to John Hinckley and Sara Jane Moore, to have a look at who they were and what they wanted. The piece was first mounted at Playwrights Horizons on December 18, 1990 (with a critics' date of January 27, 1991), in a spare production using projections to create locale. Each of the characters appeared in the dress of his or her epoch, and the sheer unreality of this highest of crimes—the killing, in effect, of a country—was emphasized in the way they all had personal access to each other. Thus, in a scene in a saloon, Charles Guiteau (who killed James Garfield) ran into Samuel Byck (who hijacked a plane hoping to crash it into the White House to kill Richard Nixon), attired in the Santa Claus suit he affected. Unhinged as all of them are, Guiteau nevertheless has a sense of humor, and he sang a snippet of Christmas carol at Byck as they passed each other.

It's a simple show, but deceptively so, because the librettist, John Weidman, didn't simply assemble the killers: he analyzes them. This succession of seemingly unrelated scenes moving to and fro in time and space and veering in attitude from the comic to the shocking delves into what drives these people toward their evilly ultimate act. John Wilkes Booth avenges the humbling of the South, Czolgosz (who killed William McKinley) wants retribution for the oppression of the working class, Sara Jane Moore (who tried to kill Gerald Ford) thinks it's a joyride, and so on.

Then, too, juxtaposing figures from different ages gives the show a flavorsome theatricality in large and small ways. Small: in the bar scene mentioned above, Booth the actor is sitting at a table reading *Variety* (which wasn't founded till several generations after Booth died). Large: the last scene, the only one played (in the original staging) on a fully three-dimensional set, presented a room filled with shelves and boxes of books and one young man in a very sixties outfit of jeans and white T-shirt. After a few moments, the audience realized that this was the Texas School Book Depository in Dallas and the young man was Lee Harvey Oswald. As Playwrights Horizons' artistic director, André Bishop, wrote in *Assassins'* published text, "This moment inevitably evoked gasps of surprise and occasionally horror."

Even so, much of Weidman's script hews to the zany side of things, as in Guiteau's relentlessly glad-handing personal style—he's everybody's best friend, until he isn't—or the fantasy universe in which Byck resides. To return to that scene in the bar—a dump of a place—Byck asks the bartender if Nixon has been around:

BARTENDER: Who?
BYCK: President Richard Nixon.
BARTENDER: We don't get many presidents in here, pal.

And Guiteau, who bops in immediately after, calls out, "Barkeep, your wine list, please," as if sweeping into some fabled *boîte de nuit*.

All the mixing up of these enraged loons and their crimes is pure concept-show thinking, that unrealistic realism in which characters can commune though separated by space and time because it is their ideas that are communing. What brings together Byck and Guiteau—and Booth with his *Variety*, and Hinckley, Czolgosz, Giuseppe Zangara (who tried to kill FDR)—is not Weidman's playful side but their fury, mustered by Booth, the founder of their movement. In *Pacific Overtures*, Weidman's history is a development of transitions and revolutions. In *Assassins*, history stands still, as witness to something that never changes: the unfathomable malice of the born loser. The show counts a Balladeer among its cast, serving as a kind of narrator. But it is really Booth who gives these freaks their inane sense of mission. Back in that bar, Zangara furiously complains of his stomach pains, which nothing can soothe: "I give up smokes! . . . I move Miami! . . . I take appendix out! *Nothing! Nothing! Nothing!*" So of course:

BOOTH: Have you considered shooting Franklin Roosevelt?
ZANAGARA: You think that help?
BOOTH: It couldn't hurt.

Assassins' humor peaks in scenes between Sara Jane Moore and Squeaky Fromme, the one so scatterbrained and the other so calmly demented that they echo the antics of Lucy Ricardo and Ethel Mertz. Moore is so clumsy with a gun that she accidentally shoots her dog:

FROMME: You brought your *dog* to an assassination?
MOORE: What was I supposed to do with him, leave him in the car?

They're on their way to kill Gerald Ford, who happens along, stumbles in the clueless awkwardness he was famous for, and even pets Moore's dead animal:

FORD: Good doggie.

Unfortunately, audiences at *Assassins* seem at times to be uncomfortable about this aspect of the show. I've seen three productions, and even the funniest bits can elicit little reaction, as if no one wants to be the first to laugh out loud when the evening's topic is somber. Critics at the premiere appeared to dismiss the work's difficult subject matter and its intelligent treatment of that subject as if they were the same thing; mostly poor notices prohibited a transfer to Broadway. Ironically, the two-month run was not only sold out but the hottest ticket in town. *Assassins* immediately went on to other stages, and it finally got to Broadway, in 2004.

Perhaps this musical is enjoyable despite itself—a twist on the musical's time-honored mandate to be nothing *but* enjoyable. And, as most of the score is pastiche—country narrative, cakewalk, soft-rock ballad—it's one of Sondheim's most overtly tuneful scores, with none of the jagged, syncopated vamps that confuse the less venturesome listener (as in *Company's* "The Little Things You Do Together" and "Another Hundred People"). *Assassin's* songs hew closely to the dark side of Weidman's scenario even so, and they concentrate on the killers, though "How I Saved Roosevelt," a merry march episode using John Philip Sousa's "El Capitan," traces the actions of bystanders who foiled Zangara.

Then, in 1992, Sam Mendes directed *Assassins* at London's Donmar Warehouse in one of the first of the "smaller than the original" English Sondheim stagings that have become chic of late, both at the Donmar and the Menier Chocolate Factory and on off-Broadway as well. Mendes felt there was a hole in the latter part of the show that a song should fill, and Sondheim realized that nothing in what he had written expressed the popular reaction to news of each assassination in the days before social media made everything instantly viral. "The chain of grief" is how Sondheim puts it, and he wrote it into the show as "Something Just Broke," letting various unknowns tell us where they were and what they were doing when they heard the news.

Perhaps that's why the audience is so stunned when the lights come up on the Texas School Book Depository: Booth's murder of Lincoln is the first one, but Oswald's of Kennedy was the Big One, directly related to the personal feelings of at least some of the audience. From the very first notes of the opening, "Everybody's Got the Right [to be happy]," this is the scene that the show has been navigating toward, the act that outranks the others—the meanest one, the stupidest one, and of course the mysterious one, with an entire subculture of writing about just who (else) was involved. And once again, the concept-musical format allows the authors to set onstage two characters who could never have met, Booth and Oswald—who must be thinking, Who *is* this guy?

> BOOTH: I'm your friend, Lee.
> OSWALD: I don't have any friends.
> BOOTH: Yes, you do. You just haven't met them yet.

Not long after, all the other assassins came out from crevices in the set to add their pleas to Booth's. Oswald resists. "People will hate me," he says. Then Booth hits the shift key: "They'll hate you with a passion, Lee."

With a *passion*. Because, on one level, assassination on this grand a level is about becoming famous for more than fifteen minutes. Sondheim and Weidman show history's government killers longing for the headline of OSWALD KILLS KENNEDY as the *My Fair Lady* of murders, one destined to reaffirm them personally. *Assassins* uses a shooting gallery as its framing metaphor, but the show really sees—as many other works do—American culture conducing to show biz, as if fame were talent, individuality a production, notoriety a long run. Again, Sondheim likes to say, "Content dictates form," and, yes, violence guns the action. Still, doesn't everything in America revolve around one's billing and who gets the eleven o'clock song, in a Tocquevillian entertainment? So now we know who they were. What did they want? André Bishop tells us: "To reconcile intolerable feelings of impotence with an inflamed and malignant sense of entitlement."

Passion

Anxious, rhapsodic romance, 1994.

Based on Ettore Scola's film *Passione d'Amore*, itself drawn from Iginio Ugo Tarchetti's novella *Fosca*.

Music and Lyrics: Stephen Sondheim. Book: James Lapine.

Original Leads: Donna Murphy, Jere Shea, Marin Mazzie. Director: James Lapine.

Toward the end of the nineteenth century, as Romanticism was giving way to Modernism, there arose in Italy, around Milan and Turin, a movement known as the Scapigliatura. The term doesn't translate easily. *Una capigliatura* (without the *S*) denotes a head of hair with the implication that it's a fine one—a hairdo, say, fresh from the shop. *Una scapigliatura* is the opposite—a messy head of hair. The movement that wore that name denoted writers, artists, and musicians who were thus "disorderly" or "sloppy": because they rejected the conventional in all things. Their attitude, one might say, anticipated Groucho Marx's refrain in a song in the college film *Horse Feathers*: "Whatever it is, I'm against it."

Indeed, there was a lot of humor in the worldview of the Scapigliatura—or, at least, a lot of sarcasm. The scapigliati loved juxtaposing extremes, and their characters tended to nurture feelings of ambivalence, regret, and anger—an anticipation of many of Sondheim's people. Above all, the scapigliati abhorred Alessandro Manzoni's *I Promessi Sposi* (The Fiancés), the celebrated early nineteenth-century novel that put its two sweethearts through state and religious persecution, war, and plague yet never lost its oh, so measured narrative voice. No more *measured*, the scapigliati cried. Instead: anarchy!

And yet, as with so many artistic movements, the scapigliati included many exceptions and unaligned offshoots. Arrigo Boito, the most prominent of the scapigliati, collaborated with Giuseppe Verdi, himself a firebrand but conservatively so, nonconformist and old-fashioned at the same time. Boito even dug into the dictionary for his libretto for Verdi's *Falstaff*, giving it the most elaborate and fastidious vocabulary of the age, an act that could be seen as the very opposite of anarchy: literature.

However, the scapigliati were known not for making art with national treasures like Verdi but for edgy behavior and dying young. One such was Iginio Ugo Tarchetti, an ex-soldier who tried journalism and fiction. Under the spell of Edgar Allan Poe, Tarchetti favored Gothic tales, and his short novel *Fosca* (1869), though not fantastical, is somewhat macabre. Let there be a garden and it must be overgrown, filled with decaying trees and mutilated statuary, dead yet pulsing with some unnamed, insidious energy. Comparably, love is a force eager to consume the innocent, and Tarchetti built his tale around a soldier not unlike himself, caught between a beauty and a sickly horror of a semi-invalid who is forever letting off terrifying screams and going into convulsions.

Caught? Surely the soldier will choose the beauty. But, in Tarchetti's view, love does the choosing, and his soldier hero is drawn to the horror despite himself. "You shall learn about me," she tells him (in Lawrence Venuti's translation). "I need to be known, understood.... I am sick, on top of being ugly, very ugly.... Do not deny me your pity—show it, do not deny me!"

Fosca, named for the sickly woman, was unknown (and even untranslated) here when Ettore Scola's Italian film adaptation, *Passione d'Amore*, was released, in 1981. The movie became the source of Sondheim's third collaboration with James Lapine, the title shortened to *Passion*, and the word alone, basic yet rich in meanings, has so overshadowed the novel that the Venuti translation has been republished under Sondheim's title rather than Tarchetti's. Interestingly, the film virtually uses the novel as its script, so close is the adaptation, and the musical closely follows the film. It is a single idea in three formats.

The construction is tight, in a virtual three-person scenario, all but strangling in its own feelings. It's a vast change after the panoply of eccentrics that peopled *Sunday In the Park With George* and the activity-filled plot lines of *Into the Woods*. Opening with the soldier, Captain Giorgio Bachetti, and his beauty, the married Clara, in bed together, the musical wastes not a moment in getting to its topics. These are: the nature of love, how looks and charm introduce it into our lives, and how a shared sensibility urges it on. Giorgio and Clara are drawn together out of sheer physical symmetry, though they think of themselves as sharing a very finesse of affection. In novel and film alike, they make love in an abandoned cottage overrun with lizards and rodents, so crazed for each other they might as well be in a silken bower in Loveland. Or they become so entranced in a meadow that they ignore mischievous children who remove a plank from a watering outlet and (the movie omits this) soak them in the ensuing flood.

Fosca's bond with Giorgio is just the opposite, not physical but poetic, a mating of sensitivities. The other soldiers are coarse, especially in the musical. "They hear drums," she sings, "you hear music." And Sondheim carefully, subtly, distinguishes that music from the melody gushing from Giorgio's union with Clara. The two "musics" can't be too different, for passion is passion. Nevertheless, the show runs on the comparison between a love of two enchanting physical equals and a love unbalanced and crazy, a beseeching obsession.

As if in retreat from this difficult subject, the songs scarcely bear titles. After the resonance of "Being Alive," "I'm Still Here," and "God, That's Good!," it is bemusing to read *Passion*'s song list on the CD, devoted to "First Letter," "Second Letter," "Third Letter," to "Garden Sequence," "Trio," "Soldiers' Gossip," to "Flashback" and "Farewell Letter." Such modest nomenclature suggests a Neo-classical approach, but in fact the score is Romantic and lyrical in the extreme. Again, it soars for Giorgio and Clara in their solipsistic love feasts, then yields to Fosca's self-denying plaints, love bingeing on a fast. Still, this is a very singing score, almost an unbroken flow, the spoken dialogue tipped into the music like mezzotints into an ancient collection of sonnets.

And here's something odd: the plot of *Passion* is very reminiscent of Bellini's opera *Norma*. The titular heroine, a Druid priestess in Gaul, is the Fosca figure—difficult and vindictive, though of course Bellini's bel canto poeticizes her. Then, too, unlike Sondheim's musical, which tells Giorgio's story, the opera sees the difficult woman as the protagonist, and tells the tale from her viewpoint.

Norma's Giorgio is Pollione, like Tarchetti's hero an officer, of the occupying Romans, involved with Norma (and the father of her children). But Giorgio is cultured and sensitive, whereas Bellini characterizes Pollione as brutish, a conqueror like Rome itself. The Clara figure is Adalgisa, a Druid temple virgin, and, just as in *Fosca-Passion*, the soldier is drawn to the pretty one, not to the intense one.* In the end, though, Pollione, like Giorgio, is overwhelmed by something extraordinary in the character of Norma-Fosca, and he dies at the stake rather than be separated from her.

---

* There's a taste of *Follies* in this, too: Ben loves Sally but needs Phyllis.

Of course, in 1831, the year of *Norma*'s premiere, Italian tenor heroes were not made of Giorgio material. His type came along later, mainly in French opera, in the heroes of Massenet's *Manon* and *Werther*, for example: sweet and docile lovers, not fighters. As Sondheim sees him, Giorgio is above all a naïf, someone upon whom a character-changing experience can easily be imprinted. In *Look, I Made a Hat*, Sondheim greatly praised another of those trendy "little" London productions, a *Passion* at the Donmar Warehouse, calling David Thaxton the very embodiment of Giorgio: "He conveyed an innocent vulnerability not just through acting but by virtue of who he was .... He didn't seem to be a fully grown man; he was clearly someone on the brink of change."

This brings us to a major topic in the influence of the Sondheim shows—their need for performers who are more than the acting singers or singing actors of old, thespians nimble enough to slide into the niches of ambivalence and anxiety that hide in the psychology of the Sondheim lead. When the musical's Golden Age began, at about 1920, the stars weren't actors. They were personalities—Al Jolson, Fanny Brice, Fred and Adele Astaire, Marilyn Miller. They had talent, to be sure, as singers, dancers, comics. They were unique and irreplaceable. But they weren't actors in the sense of the people who appear in Shakespeare, Ibsen, O'Neill.

Came the revolution, in the 1940s—Rodgers and Hammerstein and their meaningful narratives with genuine character conflict. Not tiffs or contrived misunderstandings, but the war between incongruent worldviews, as with the two leads in *Oklahoma!*, *South Pacific*, and especially *The King and I*. Suddenly, those who played such roles had to justify characterologically nuanced texts. Why is *Oklahoma!*'s Laurey so uncommitted—but intensely so—to Curly? Is she a flirt? A feminist? Is it because she's a landowner and he herds cows? Does *The King and I*'s Mrs. Anna want to coach the King in democratic humanism or simply control him? Or consider shows written by others in the Rodgers and Hammerstein style—*Brigadoon*, for instance. Why does a hip New Yorker like Tommy want to live in an isolated Scots village made of fantasy and folklore? Is he what people seem like just before they join a cult?

So far, so good. But there was a second revolution, in the 1950s and after, with the habilitation of the Novelty Star—Rosalind Russell, Rex Harrison, Robert Preston, Richard Burton, Anthony Perkins: infusions of acting talent from outside the world of the musical. A live audiotape of the original *Camelot* reveals the secret of why this misconceived show, with its glorious score and dodgy libretto, played so well. Burton's Shakespearean grandeur mated with Julie Andrews' Noël Cowardesque light comedy offers another example of Scott McMillin's aforementioned theory of "disjunction," in which apparently inimical styles mesh through a kind of bonded disunion, a vitality of opposition.

Clearly, the musical was becoming enriched by a various expertise in its acting pool—and Sondheim's provocative characters created the third revolution. *Follies'* four leads function far more expansively than the traditional First and Second Couples whose heyday not only runs back to the so-called "first" musical, *The Black Crook* (1866), but continues well past the Rodgers and Hammerstein era. The First Couple has the romance, while the Second Couple gets to dance and wax sarcastic: *Kiss Me, Kate*'s Fred and Lilli, then Bill and Lois, from "So in Love" on one hand to "Always True To You In My Fashion" on the other. And, yes, there are variations, as with *The King and I*'s Mrs. Anna and the King, then Tuptim and Lun Tha: all four are serious, and an air of tragedy hangs heavy over them.

Nevertheless, Sondheim's approach provisions more meticulous character interaction, fluid and elusive. James Goldman's surrealistic *Follies* script gives its two couples choices to make on an almost line-by-line basis. Sondheim's *Follies* songs pin them down like butterflies on velvet...and yet. *Does* Ben love Sally? It's the very center of the show, the revisiting of the past, the reviewing of the choices, the life you should have led. Sally's so shallow that her choice comes down to the color of her dress. "I should have worn green," she tells us. Yes, that's why you're unhappy. You forgot to wear green.

Then, too, Sondheim's interests draw him to gifted, intense, or damaged figures. No performer from the era of *Good News!* (1927) or *Anything Goes* (1934) could have justified, for example, the two leads of *Sunday in the Park With George*, especially that art-absorbed painter who *does not share*. That's what makes him marvelous: he is almost literally made of art, art that Dot, his lover, admires. But it makes him impenetrable. Women look for a man who recalls to them their view of their father when they were very young, as a source of love and power. A supportive father creates the need for a supportive partner; a neglectful father leads to an unhappy relationship: the one Dot has with George. But a substitute relationship with a "good father" won't work for her. When Dot takes up with Louis, a genial baker, she notes, in the restless "Everybody Loves Louis," that the entire world appreciates the baker and *his* art, making cakes. He's so agreeable, so pleasant and available. Then comes the Sondheim zinger: "That's the trouble, nothing's wrong with him." Because interesting people are screwed up, and Sondheim writes about interesting people. Only interesting actors can play them.

Passion's three leads offer challenges, each in a different way, because— in true scapigliato style—they belong together while not belonging together.

That is, Giorgio and Clara are beauties. They deserve each other. But their passion doesn't last. That of Fosca and Giorgio does, eternally, as we learn in the musical's last seconds. Yet Fosca, anguished and the cause of anguish, does not, by the rules of love, deserve Giorgio.

Scola's film emphasizes these anomalies, casting the all but implausibly handsome Bernard Giraudeau as Giorgio and the steamy Laura Antonelli as Clara. Fosca was Valeria D'Obici. "A monster," Giorgio calls her, and Scola films her as one, with her hair pulled back and her teeth thrust forward like a vampire's.* One shot, devoted to another of Fosca's screaming faints, is immediately followed by a view of two skulls. Or: she literally kisses the hem of his uniform tailcoat, whereupon Scola shows us Giorgio and Clara in bed, cutting thence to Fosca banging on piano keys in rage.

The Scapigliatura wrote the preface to Modernism, and Sondheim is the musical's Neo-modernist, so no wonder he was attracted to the subject. Interestingly, the musical *Passion* is subtly diverted from the scapigliato atmosphere of the novella and film, losing some of their—here's that word again—disjunctive aspects. For example, the novella is narrated by Giorgio himself, and, in Scola's version, when the narrative is done, a dwarf, to whom he turns out to have been telling the tale in a tavern, gets up to leave, roaring with laughter as he goes. Why a dwarf? And why laughing? On one level, the scapigliato aesthetic needed to unnerve its audience with the bizarre. After all, the story is already unthinkable—Giorgio and Fosca sitting in a tree, *kay eye ess ess eye enn gee*. So why stack your bombshells? Why not, instead, try to naturalize the tale, leaving out the baroque vexations, smooth it down to its genuine feelings?

This is what the musical *Passion* does, in every respect. It subdues the grotesqueries of novel and film, and the original Broadway production underlines this in its casting. As Giorgio, Jere Shea was an impressive leading man, young but mature, not the novel's boy-in-uniform. Fosca was not a "monster" but Donna Murphy in dowdy makeup. Then, too, Tarchetti's Clara, a ravished nymph hoping for more, always more, was, like Giorgio, bumped up in age and experience. But then, it is difficult to find actors who suit character while commanding their share in a Sondheim score. Casting an Italian film is a cinch, because actors are chosen for their looks; movies are shot silent and dubbed later to create multi-lingual release prints. But one can't cast the musical *Passion* on looks alone, not least because the espressivo inherent in the vocal lines demands seasoned performers. To

---

* The actress was actually a looker, and Scola's casting her against type may have contributed to her Fosca's winning the David di Donatello Best Actress, Italy's equivalent of an Oscar.

repeat, Sondheim doesn't think of his shows as operas. Still, a narrative as intensely musicalized as *Passion* demands intensely musical performers. It's a truism, of course, but it reminds us to wonder where exactly Broadway ends and opera begins, especially after *Porgy and Bess*, *The Most Happy Fella*, and *Candide*.

Intensely musical performers, yes: who can also build character like a Method ace. That is the third revolution in who gets to be in musicals. It's worth remarking that the academic world first took interest in the musical after the Sondheim-Prince era, for those titles offered dense psychological and thematic content for critics and historians to explore at length. But more: the training, so to say, of a generation of actor-singers took off in these very shows, making them an academy in themselves. Sondheim thought that Donna Murphy gave one of the most persuasive auditions (for *Passion*) that he's ever seen. It was like Rodgers whispering to Hammerstein, when Yul Brynner came on stage, seated himself cross-legged, and broke into a Mongolian folk song to his own guitar accompaniment, "There's our King."

Indeed, there were great performances in musicals before Sondheim-Prince. But, from *Company* on, shows began to require unique performers as a rule, because the roles became unique—Robert, Ben, Désirée, Sweeney Todd and Mrs. Lovett. Perhaps an authentically scapigliato *Passion* musical would have ground up the gears of art, overloaded Broadway with information derived from twentieth-century Italian firebrands stuck in the nineteenth century. That's too much source material to juggle at once. Sondheim's *Passion* is startling, but not aggressive: it steals into the ear by degrees, just as Giorgio begins as a pleasantly ordinary youth and only gradually becomes haunted and focused. He moves from Clara, who is easy and acceptable. And he moves toward Fosca, who is utterly deranged.

Ettore Scola's *Passion* is startling and aggressive. He filmed Fosca's main entrance into the action gliding nimbly down the stairs to the officers' mess as if propelling herself forward. Destiny and death await; yes, she comes! But in the musical, she descended stealthily, as if wary of her own tragedy. Yet she cannot resist, for everyone needs a Giorgio (or a Robert, Ben, Franklin Shepard). Still, we already knew that *Passion*'s surprise is that Giorgio needs a Fosca.

It's a small piece, *Passion*. Tightly controlled yet all but gushing with music. Paradoxical, then. Of course there would be a ruined castle in the work—in book, film, and musical alike—because the scapigliati loved articulating their futuristic worldview by using Romantic memes (chivalry, ghosts, the fear of engulfment) in contemporary settings. And that is Sondheim's *Passion*, an old tale revitalized by the new style of Broadway actor-singers. What would the piece have been like with the most vivid opera people—Maria Callas as Fosca, say, with Franco Corelli as Giorgio and Anna Moffo as Clara? It's not an outrageous hypothetical, for Sondheim breaks boundaries. Though it won the Best Musical Tony award, *Passion* was not appreciated at first. *Norma* wasn't, either. Its premiere, at La Scala, was a disaster. Now it is regarded as a *summum bonum* of Italian opera. Or, to restate the thought by bringing it back to Broadway, Barbara Cook thinks *Passion* is, with *Sweeney Todd*, Sondheim's best music.

The Frogs

Ancient Greek humoresque performed in Yale University's swimming pool, 1974.

Based on the play by Aristophanes.

Music and Lyrics: Stephen Sondheim. Book: Burt Shevelove. Original Leads: Larry Blyden, Michael Vale, Anthony Holland, Jerome Geidt. Director: Burt Shevelove.

Expanded into a dry musical comedy, 2004. Book adapted by Nathan Lane. Original Leads: Nathan Lane, Roger Bart, Daniel Davis, Michael Siberry. Director: Susan Stroman.

First performed during one of the Athenian drama festivals in 405 B.C., Aristophanes' *The Frogs* follows the voyage of Dionysos—the god of drama and drink—into hell to bring back a great playwright to restore the vanished glory of the stage. I have laced the following synopsis with anachronisms, to suggest Aristophanes' many contemporary references and general zaniness:

PROLOGOS: Dionysos and his servant, Xanthias, visit Herakles, who gives directions to Hades. First, there's Charon's ferry:

> DIONYSOS: Is it expensive?
> HERAKLES: He takes Visa. You'll hear sweet music and meet enlightened theatre-goers. Before that, though, there's a vast bog filled with evildoers. Liars, cheats, patricides...
> DIONYSOS: And fans of *Glee* and Frank Wildhorn?

SCENE: The voyage across the River Styx.
KOMMOS: (usually a lament or disturbing passage): An offstage chorus of frogs.

SCENE: Dionysos and Xanthias gain hell's frontier.

PARODOS (traditionally the chorus' first entrance into the playing area, danced as well as sung): Spirits direct the pair to Pluto's palace.

SCENE: Pluto's doorkeeper, Aeakos, threatens Dionysos:

AEAKOS: Terrors await! Cyclops! Medusa! Jimmy Carter's man-eating bunny rabbit!

SCENE: A banquet. Aeakos whips Dionysos:

DIONYSOS: Augh! Oof! Misery!

AEAKOS: Bet you felt *that* one.

DIONYSOS: (sarcastically) No, I was quoting from Newt Gingrich's secret garden of love poetry.

PARABASIS (a choral hymn, detached from the play's action, on political events of the day)

SCENE: Pluto decrees that Euripides and Aeschylus vie for the chair of First Playwright.

AGON (a contest between opposing forces) Euripides begins; Aeschylus says nothing:

EURIPIDES: Another of his famous Profound Silences! He went completely Actors Studio after Tony Franciosa got here!

Aeschylus inspires with nobility, Euripides educates with realism, and, at length, Dionysos chooses to brings Aeschylus back with him to Athens.

EXODOS: Pluto wishes Dionysos godspeed, and a chorus concludes the work.

So. Burt Shevelove wanted to stage his own version of *The Frogs* in the swimming pool of Yale's Payne Whitney Gymnasium, and he asked Sondheim to supply the needed incidental score. There were only two songs as such, the opening "Invocation and Instructions To the Audience" and, near the end, "Fear No More," the words taken from *Cymbeline*—for, in Shevelove's version of Aristophanes, the two playwrights in the underworld were Shakespeare and Shaw, and their respective virtues lay in poetry as opposed to sociopolitics. (Shakespeare wins the Agon.) All the rest of the score was choruses—the kommos, parodos, parabasis (which did have some solo lines), exodos—plus an opening fanfare.

Thus, at Yale in 1974, *The Frogs* was a play with music. A show that doesn't let its characters vocalize isn't a musical, and that is a waste of Sondheim. Worse, the 1974 score wasn't recorded in full till much later, so few could assess it. Worst of all, *The Frogs* (Sondheim tells us in *Finishing the Hat*) was "one of the few deeply unpleasant professional experiences I've had." The dean of the Yale School of Drama, Robert Brustein, was one of the most disliked people in the theatre community; Sondheim insisted that he take no meetings with Brustein during production. But Brustein found another way to interfere. Though *The Frogs* was essentially a school play—the ensemble included students Meryl Streep, Christopher Durang, Sigourney Weaver, and Alma Cuervo—Brustein invited the New York critics to the premiere, which, because of incompetent set building, was in effect the only dress rehearsal.

So, in all, *The Frogs* did not go over and was seldom seen for a while. But Nathan Lane, Dionysos in a piano-accompanied concert version at the Library of Congress in 2000, thought the show would work as a full-scale musical if Sondheim was willing to expand the score with character and plot numbers. The result was "less an expansion," wrote Jesse Green in the *New York Times*, "than an explosion": for the piece was wholly reinvented, the music taking on the comic attitudes that had previously been confined to the script. Much else was repurposed. In 405 B.C., the frogs themselves provide a choral interlude and are not heard from again. In 1974, at Yale, they actively impeded Dionysos' mission by trying to swamp his boat. In 2004, at Lincoln Center in Nathan Lane's new version of the script, the frogs (who seek to lure Dionysos into becoming one of them) represent apolitical complacency, and the evening ended with Dionysos exhorting the audience members to keep an eye on their government. Thus, Aristophanes' consideration of what kind of theatre enlightens its public turned into an example of that kind: it was not realistic (like Euripides), but noble (like Aeschylus).

Here—again, in brief—is what Sondheim added to the largely choral *Frogs* music from thirty years before:

"I Love To Travel"—Dionysos, Xanthias, chorus. A plot number, as the two leads set off to find Herakles. The choral bits were from 1974, but Dionysos and Xanthias' duet was all new.

"Dress Big"—Bossy Herakles' character number, with Dionysos' interjections.

"All Aboard!"—Charon's solo, evoking the clammy darkness of the underworld.

"Ariadne"—a ballad, Dionysos' recollection of his late wife.

"Hades"—Pluto's character number, in an ancient musical-comedy trope: the comic whooping it up with the chorus girls.

"Shaw"—a plot number, as Dionysos introduces the prickly playwright, who arrives complete with entourage. Emphasizing Shaw's dry wit, the music stops every time he utters one of his patented quips, then starts up again right after. The song also provides a link with Aristophanes' play, as his Dionysos goes to Hades specifically to bring back Euripides, just as the musical's Dionysos intends to bring back Shaw. The agon between the writers comes as an unexpected development.

Except for "Ariadne," these are all comic numbers, even the glowering "All Aboard!." They go nicely with the choruses left over from Yale, yielding a score that is half-ceremonial and half-character-specific, a sensibly odd blend for a musical based on a play 2,500 years old.

Nathan Lane was obviously going to play Dionysos in his own adaptation of Shevelove's adaptation, and Xanthias was to have been Chris Kattan. Celebrated for his seven years on *Saturday Night Live*, Kattan maintained a lively trade in craziness, from his characters Gay Hitler to the deranged simian Mr. Peepers. This should have created an inspired moose-and-squirrel teaming with Lane: the one's traditional top-banana timing and intonation with Kattan's comedy-club improv style. After a few previews, however, Kattan was replaced by Roger Bart. In an interview with Geraldine Brown for the *Los Angeles Times*, Kattan—who was new to the stage—revealed that he had been told that he "didn't speak the language of the theater." But, says Kattan, "There was never a sit-down, let's-talk-about-it session. It was just over." Perhaps Kattan was too used to *Saturday Night Live*'s seat-of-the-pants extemporized format to key himself into the lock of Broadway rehearsal etiquette. Still, in the impetuous style of the old comedy musical of the 1920s, Kattan would have been right at home.

The Frogs, whose revision opened at Lincoln Center on July 22, 2004, is one of the few Sondheim shows to lack a cult. At the same time, it lacks a Sondheim anxiety figure, forced to make life-central decisions or, yes, later regret them. In this show, everybody's happy, even dour Charon. It's a light piece in all. It may be that the production number of the frog attacks and the Shaw-Shakespeare contest go on for too long. Nevertheless, it's an ingratiating score by—for once in his post-sixties shows—a merry Sondheim, carefree and accommodating.

Road Show

Parable on two American personalities, the builder and the destroyer.

Suggested by Alva Johnston's *The Legendary Mizners*.

Music and Lyrics: Stephen Sondheim. Book: John Weidman.

Seen in three versions. First as *Wise Guys*, 1999.

Original Leads: Nathan Lane, Victor Garber, Michael C. Hall. Director: Sam Mendes.

Second as *Bounce*, 2003.

Original Leads: Richard Kind, Howard McGillin, Gavin Creel. Director: Hal Prince.

Third as *Road Show*, 2008.

Original Leads: Alexander Gemignani, Michael Cerveris, Claybourne Elder. Director: John Doyle.

The journalist Alva Johnston was noted above all for his *New Yorker* profiles, in a series the magazine was famous for under its founding editor, Harold Ross (from 1925 to 1952). At first just a short essay but later expanding to multi-part studies running in consecutive issues, the *New Yorker* profile came in two kinds, one a look at prominent Names of the day, the other less well-known and even occult figures. Like the popular fiction series—Clarence Day's reminiscences of his youth that became the play *Life With Father*, or John O'Hara's *Pal Joey* letters—the *New Yorker* profiles were thought a main reason that people subscribed to the magazine, because they were entertaining and, at times, shocking. They were playful as well. Ethel Merman's profile was called "Little Sure Shot" (after the sobriquet bestowed upon her by Sitting Bull in *Annie Get Your*

Gun), Alexander Woollcott's "Big Nemo" (after Winsor McCay's comic-strip hero, a young boy haunted by fantastical dreams, known as Little Nemo).

Alva Johnston's profiles give an idea of the series' range, from Hollywoodites Darryl Zanuck, Wallace Beery, and the Warner Brothers to Albert Einstein, a fake Russian prince, and the secretary of the New York Society For the Suppression of Vice. Johnston profiled also Wilson Mizner, as "Legend of a Sport," in 1950, and Mizner's brother Addison, in "The Palm Beach Architect," in 1952. The two pieces were then combined into a book, *The Legendary Mizners* (the adjective became *Fabulous* in the English edition, as the Mizners were a strictly American legend), and Sondheim, then twenty-three, saw a musical in this odd pairing of con man (Wilson) and artist (Addison). In Sondheim's understanding, the pair had a "can't live with him, can't live without him but I'd rather" relationship, Wilson a man of great charm who never fails to let you down and Addison a tortured soul who somehow turns into Society's choice in the styling of mansions in Palm Beach. It's a foretaste, perhaps, of *Merrily We Roll Along*, if Franklin Shepard were a crook and Charlie his regretfully adoring brother.

The Legendary Mizners would thus have been Sondheim's first Broadway musical. But David Merrick had optioned the material: Irving Berlin was writing the songs, to a book by S. N. Behrman, known for social comedy and also Merrick's book writer on his first Broadway hit, Harold Rome's musical *Fanny*. However, Merrick's show never materialized, and Sondheim finally began work on his own Mizner musical in 1994, with John Weidman writing the book. As with Weidman's *Pacific Overtures* and *Assassins* librettos, the show would turn pages of history; the plan was to create a fun-filled musical comedy with a serious subtext on the nature of American capitalism in the years between the post–Civil War robber barons and the Great Depression: when capitalism worked (for some) and when it failed (for everyone).

Yet the focus was personal, not political. Wilson uses and cheats while Addison creates. Wilson leaps recklessly from the sports world to writing for Broadway and Hollywood; Addison finds something he's good at—design—and sticks with it. They love each other, they hate each other, they need each other. They feel complete only when together—as if American business only works with a combination of the unscrupulous promoter and the dedicated artist. The movies. Popular music. Fashion.

Let's get literary about it and quote Goethe's *Faust*:

> Two souls dwell, alas!, in my breast,
> And each would break from the other;

One is worldly, snatching at joys of love,
While the other soars, from dust of earth
To thoughts on high.

Or we can consult the popular side and note the parallel—one Sondheim relished—with the comical Bing Crosby-Bob Hope *Road* series in which two frenemies get into mischief in Singapore, Zanzibar, Morocco, and so on. There was always a girl—the same one, Dorothy Lamour—and a host of cutthroats and hostile officials, but the films were comic above all, and Sondheim's Mizners were presumably going to take their own road in a similar tone. Yet under the fluff there would be subtextual enlightenment: a show about America.

Somehow, Sondheim and Weidman had trouble getting the elements properly blended, and the show appeared in multiple forms on its way to being finalized. After a few readings, it was first given by the New York Theatre Workshop as *Wise Guys*. Then it went to Chicago's Goodman Theatre as *Bounce*, thence to New York's Public Theater, on November 18, 2008, as *Road Show*.

Let us summarize the differences among the three versions:

WISE GUYS: a vaudeville frame gives the two brothers direct access to the audience in the convivial Crosby-Hope manner. Third lead: Paris Singer (a real-life figure, heir to the Singer Sewing Machine fortune) for the Palm Beach sequence, when the brothers symbolize American entrepreneurism in a mating of gambler and technician.

BOUNCE: a black comedy. Vaudeville frame gone. Third lead: Hollis Bessemer, apparently Addison's lover, taking over Paris Singer's role. A leading woman is added, Nellie, played by Michele Pawk—the Dorothy Lamour gig, so to say. Former MGM star Jane Powell appears as Mama Mizner.

ROAD SHOW: similar to *Bounce*, but very compressed, centering on the brothers' relationship rather than on their symbolic place in American capitalism. Dorothy Lamour dropped. Addison's romance with Hollis more overt. Played in a single set with the ensemble watching and taking part as needed.

In all, *Road Show* took fourteen years of gestation, including nine years from the first performance to the premiere of the finished work, and the rewriting spun off many new songs that were then replaced by newer ones. The so very public revisions recall *Merrily We Roll Along*'s previews, inadvertently giving the public a message of desperation. In fact, *Wise Guys* through *Bounce* to *Road Show* comprised cutting away the amusing details of American history, from gold rush to Florida land boom (and bust) to reach the show's core: a bad marriage of two men who would rather die than divorce. Starting as an ironic musical comedy, the material finally asserted itself as a kind of sassy musical play, dour and depressed yet joking around all the same. *Bounce*'s irresistibly catchy title song turned, in *Road Show*, into "Waste" (the same melody, with new lyrics), now a sarcastic requiem for the brothers. Sondheim says that not till "Waste" did the show open with a number that clarifies its view of its two leads: Wilson may be charming but Addison is the good guy. Wilson is the rogue, the user, the creep. That's how the audience always saw it—and now the show saw it that way, too.

As I've said before, Sondheim's theatre concentrates on the mechanics of making choices, and the emotional physics of repenting those choices. To put it another way: If free will, then *Follies*. Some wrong choices wreck your life; others daunt you for a time. *Road Show* offers a classic case of the latter in a moment we've seen in plenty of movies, when the audience knows more than the characters do and sees them as catastrophically self-destructive. It's meant to be comic, at least in the Crosby-Hope films. In a Sondheim show, it isn't really comic. It has weight, because this isn't a silly movie. It's life.

This scene occurs during the brothers' sojourn in Alaska, digging for gold. After an assayer prices their strike at $24,300, they start for home. But the next boat doesn't leave till tomorrow morning, and, as the pair consider their options:

CARD SHARP (at the table of chance with fellow gamblers): I don't suppose you boys'd care to play a little poker?

We in the audience are thinking, Are they that stupid? Don't they know a setup when they see one? But no one listens to us:

ADDISON: Poker? Gee, I don't know...(He looks at Wilson)
BOTH MIZNERS (merrily): Why not?
CARD SHARP (to his fellows): All righty, move over, boys. We got some new blood in town!*

Disaster. Yet, to the extent that it is comic at all, it is sitcom humor, not character humor—that is, the fun is applied externally to a situation rather

---

* This is the scene as it was played in *Wise Guys*. The poker game occurs in *Bounce* and *Road Show* as well; it works out differently each time, always ending up with Wilson blowing their fortune away.

than allowed to arise on its own. Sitcom humor was prevalent in the fifties musical, Sondheim's launching pad—but his shows ran on character humor. Here's a sample, from *Gypsy*'s second act, when Rose, daughter Louise, and their troupe wind up in a burlesque house. As one of the strippers admires Louise's needlework on a costume, librettist Arthur Laurents sets up a terrific laugh, and note how the scenelet builds in not only power but character logic—you can't fight a mother—to reach the punchline. (My stage directions, not in the published script, derive from the audiotape of Ethel Merman's last night of *Gypsy*'s New York run):

TESSIE: My! Look at them ladylike little stitches! That miserable broad who makes my gowns must be usin' a fish hook!

LOUISE: What do you pay her?

TESSIE (Fast, businesslike, offering a deal):   Twenty-five bucks a gown and I provide the material.

ROSE (Quiet but strong):   Thirty.

TESSIE (Trying to bargain):   She's new in the business!

ROSE (Louder now):   Thirty!

TESSIE: Who're you? Her mother?

ROSE (Titanic):   *Yes!!!*

TESSIE (Immediately, total surrender):   Thirty. (Which gets a huge laugh, then applause, and briefly stops the show.)

Sondheim's musicals—whether he was composer-lyricist or just lyricist—almost never resort to sitcom humor because he worked with imaginative and resourceful book writers. I quoted the sitcom moment in *Wise Guys* to example a very rare moment when a Sondheim show behaves like standard fare. It's the exception that tests the rule, which, broadly stated, holds that Sondheim has reinvented the musical by opening it up psychologically and thematically while elevating its musical component. Many writers have called the musical "America's opera," meaning (roughly) that smart and gifted people tilted "musical comedy" into "music theatre": analytic, expressive, even overwhelming. Popular art is supposed to be disposable. But the great musicals keep coming back, too rich to collect at first hearing, second, third.

And that's altogether true of Sondheim's musicals. The main reason is probably the sheer abundance of first-rate music, just as with *Show Boat*, *Oklahoma!*, *Cabaret*. A classic show has a classic score. But there is as well the playability of the Sondheim people—the character depth that gives actors so much to develop. We never fully absorb these shows because there's so much *there* in them, which is not the case with many older classics—*Annie Get Your Gun* or *Kiss Me, Kate*, for example. They're wonderful entertainment, but they don't offer actors vast playing room. There's no ambiguity, no mystery. Take *Company*'s Robert: he was based more or less on Anthony Perkins, a longtime bachelor who did in fact eventually marry and start a family. Yet Perkins was gay; "longtime bachelor" used to be one of the many available euphemisms. Robert isn't gay, because gay men don't take an overnight with a stewardess—another euphemism, the equivalent of what "actress" meant a hundred years earlier: a sleeparound. Perkins' boy friend also married a woman after the two men broke up. Don't all these Complications in the Plot reflect our continual bewilderment about the curious niches of human sexuality, and doesn't that make *Company* eternally trendy?

Or simply consider the Beggar Woman in *Sweeney Todd*, a kind of nemesis figure, Mrs. Lovett's personal fury. The Beggar Woman is tied into the plot as such only near the show's end, but the first scene in fact establishes her as Todd's "lost" wife—at that in a chance line that we are meant to miss. It adds to her presence as a figure almost of another world—and doesn't she stalk Mrs. Lovett and her cuisine of horror out of a dim recollection of how envious the latter was of the Todd family? There are two drivelines in *Sweeney Todd*. One is Todd's revenge plot. But the other is Mrs. Lovett's passionate love of Todd, alluded to here and there but largely veiled—except to the Beggar Woman, who, when she was the happy young Mrs. Benjamin Barker, must have been aware of Mrs. Lovett's attentions to her husband.

Few of the famous musicals carry so much "intelligent design" (to borrow a phrase from the enemy) within their scenarios, so much inner life. For the first fifty years of its history—from, say, *Evangeline* (1874), the first famous integrated American musical, to *No, No, Nanette* (1925) and the like, the musical was simply not a subtle form.

Well, it is now. Sondheim elaborated the musical just as Beethoven elaborated symphony and Wagner elaborated opera. And, as I've said, the intellectual and academic worlds paid little heed to the musical till Sondheim took hold of it; now the intelligentsia has raised the form into a discipline all its own. It is often said that Sondheim is *the* author of present-day musicals, but, in truth, he is *the* author of musicals, period. There were prominent, influential, and just plain marvelous composers and lyricists before him—and there was Oscar Hammerstein, who reformatted the libretto as a platform of narrative power. But no one on the musical end recreated the musical as thoroughly as Sondheim.

Or we could put it more simply and say that Steve finally fixed the second act of *Allegro*.

Sondheim on Film

As if emphasizing a break between Sondheim's First and Second Periods, he offered no new shows between *Do I Hear a Waltz?* (1965) and *Company* (1970), five years that began with his last lyrics-only job on a new work and ended with the first of the Sondheim-Prince titles that introduced his mature composing style. However, Sondheim did take part in the cycle of original television musicals at this time, inaugurated on the grand scale by Rodgers and Hammerstein's *Cinderella* (1957) and Cole Porter's *Aladdin* (1958).* There were as well more modest efforts by less established names working in "smaller" music—fewer numbers and no commemorative LP.

Sondheim's contribution was *Evening Primrose* (1966), to James Goldman's script, from John Collier's story. It's a macabre piece in which two young people find love while hiding out from the world in Stern's department store (a real location, by the way). It turns out that an entire sub-population resides there, whiling time away in offtrack niches and pretending to be mannequins when a night watchman passes. Anthony Perkins played the Boy, an unsuccessful poet who hates life. He's a dropout, in sixties parlance, yet his establishing song, "If You Can Find Me, I'm Here," is somewhat jubilant. The Girl, played by Charmian Carr, is used as a maid by a Mrs. Monday (Dorothy Stickney), the stern leader of this bizarre tribe; worse, Carr never wanted the hermit's life: as a tot, "I just fell asleep in Women's Hats."

Perkins' hard sophistication and Carr's soft innocence create a bond of opposites, and the pair wants to depart and face life together. But Stern's is

---

* The cycle really took off with the Mary Martin *Peter Pan* (1955), though that production came from Broadway—and, in 1956, CBS presented *High Tor* with Bing Crosby and Julie Andrews, from the Maxwell Anderson play that Sondheim wanted to musicalize in college. Arthur Schwartz and Anderson wrote the score.

like Brigadoon. You *can't* depart. Their impassioned love duet, "Take Me To the World," offers a great example of Sondheim's "playwrighting" music, because it isn't just a romantic moment: the store's sound system picks it up, and we see the others (even the night watchmen) listening in alarm. When the citizens of Stern's personal Oz defy the Rules, the Dark Men are called, and, though Perkins and Carr make a run for it, *Evening Primrose's* last shot gives us the pair in a show window, transformed into genuine mannequins. Welcome to the Twilight Zone.

Good old Sondheim: offbeat even on television. It may seem odd that, for all his love of the narrative Hollywood soundtrack pioneered by Erich Wolfgang Korngold, Max Steiner, and Bernard Herrmann, Sondheim never composed one himself in that style. But then, he has no interest in creating "functional" music—to accompany, for example, battles, ships sailing the Spanish Main, or the New York skyline. Sondheim's music is social; he doesn't write about "things."

But he must have been flattered when Alain Resnais wanted Sondheim to "soundtrack" his 1974 film *Stavisky*, on the adventures of the Russian bond swindler who scandalized France in the 1930s, ever evading justice because of his links to the Third Republic's one per cent. Resnais had seen and loved *Follies*, especially the moment when John McMartin went up on his lines in the top-hat-and-cane number. Resnais saw Stavisky (played by Jean-Paul Belmondo) as comparable, hiding his fears behind a bon vivant's façade. The period setting gave Sondheim a chance to play in the world of pastiche that he loves, but there was some "suspense" music as well, as when a sedan prowls a roadway to anxious woodwinds over a busy bassoon line. (Jonathan Tunick handled the orchestrations.) Mainly, however, Sondheim covered the film's dressier aspect, as when Stavisky's wife, Arlette (Anny Duperey), pulls up at a fashionable resort in a Hispano-Suiza and gets out to pose like a model, all in white, from her floppy hat to the straps of her heels. So Sondheim wasn't writing about things: he was conjuring up the flamboyant chic of the age. The *Stavisky* music isn't narrative or functional. Rather, it's atmospheric, like a palm-court orchestra playing as you lunch. Further, Sondheim was able to give voice to three tunes dropped from *Follies*. (One of them, "The World's Full of Girls," has a tiny bit of vocal in the film, in French.)

Unfortunately, *Stavisky* is very dry in texture, deliberately made of short scenes without any sense of flow from one to the next. It's romance without sensuality, glamor without joy. Many of the characters narrate in voice-over, distancing us, and there is an odd subplot involving the legal status of Leon Trotsky, on the run from Stalin. Resnais intended *Stavisky* to explore the xenophobia rampant in France in the 1930s, which many historians see as having sabotaged the democratic processes of the Third Republic and all but invited Hitler to invade. Near the film's end, as Stavisky's little empire of fraud and grand larceny disintegrates, one of his business partners suddenly tells him, "You know what we will say? We will say that the French are right to mistrust *métèques* [a derogation for resident aliens], refugees, and Jews." Music would give too much flavor to a film that is less dramatic than polemical, so most of what Sondheim wrote, though recorded, was not included in the release print. But somebody was smart enough to issue everything on the soundtrack LP.

Sondheim wrote as well for Warren Beatty's *Reds* (1981), though Dave Grusin scored the battles and sailing ships, so to say. Sondheim's contribution was one of his most touching ballads, "Goodbye For Now." As this was to be the love theme for John Reed (Beatty) and Louise Bryant (Diane Keaton), who both end up in Russia near the start of the 1917 revolution, Sondheim used the first few notes of the "Internationale" to launch the melody. The *Reds* soundtrack LP included two different versions of the melody (without lyrics), but the film proper used a third reading, on piano alone, played by Sondheim himself. It occurs during the transition from New York to Provincetown, about forty minutes into the running time.

Sondheim would work with Beatty again, on *Dick Tracy* (1990), this time writing five songs. Amusingly, one of these was a piece for Madonna's character, Breathless Mahoney, playfully characterizing the Material Girl herself—"More," a catalogue number devoted to the theory that too much is never enough. *Dick Tracy* was further distinguished by its optics, faithful to the world of Chester Gould's comic strip yet utilizing the expansive artistry of the comic *book*, which, unlike the daily strip, takes in vistas when necessary. Gould's bizarre bad guys, named for how they look or act, were in place—Flattop, Mumbles, the pianist 88 Keyes (as Gould spelled it). But Breathless Mahoney, used in a storyline in 1945, was less a criminal than an unscrupulous opportunist who goes on the run with a fortune and ends up a killer. The film retained only Mahoney's name and blond coloring, reinventing her as a club singer big with gangland bosses. She, too, ends up heavily involved in crime.

Gould's strip was grim in tone, for all its boisterous grotesquerie, but the movie is a madcap, startled into delight by a comically over-the-top Al Pacino as mob boss Big Boy Caprice. Brutal yet elegant (albeit in strange, strange ways), Big Boy is Tracy's nemesis. Or is that Madonna's role? She does seem to want to steal Tracy from his eternal fiancée, Tess Trueheart. All this gives depth to a flat source, but even five Sondheim songs don't turn *Dick Tracy* into a musical, because of the way they are used.

The five are Sondheim at his best, and while they are all floor numbers or soundtrack voice-overs, he cleverly bends them toward character or plot commentary. For example, "Live Alone and Like It," heard almost in passing as a pop selection on a car radio, in fact questions why Tracy hasn't married Tess when they're so well matched. As we listen, we see a montage of Tracy and Tess caring for Kid, the waif they informally adopt.

So the song isn't quite heard. It's *seen*, not properly absorbed, and that's true throughout the continuity. The shootemup action never falters, often intruding on the singing or, in the effervescent "Back in Business," accompanying scenes of gangland mayhem that distract us from the music. Not till the closing credits is a number heard complete: Madonna finally gets through "More" from verse through chorus and "trio" (a middle section separate from the chorus) and back to a chorus. The songs are sewn into the screen like stitches on a dress suit, meant to disappear into the fabric. It creates a new kind of integration in which the numbers don't suit the story: they suit the editing.*

Leaving music and lyrics aside, Sondheim co-wrote a movie (with Anthony Perkins), *The Last of Sheila* (1973), a murder mystery with an extremely confusing plot. Sondheim also co-wrote (with George Furth) *Getting Away With Murder*, another murder mystery and a two-week failure on Broadway, in 1996. Recalling the many scripts Sondheim wrote for television's *Topper*, in the early 1950s, one wonders why he has never written his own librettos—though he does thrive on the alchemy of collaboration.

This is probably the right place to consider Sondheim's sole appearance as a professional actor, on television, in George S. Kaufman and Ring Lardner's spoof of the music-publishing business, *June Moon*, a hit on Broadway in 1929 and broadcast forty-five years later. Sondheim played Maxie, a song plugger cynical about the industry (Maxie on a fellow songwriter: "He's using his ideas up too fast. 'Montana Moon'—he uses a state and a moon in one song?"), but idealistic about love. In fact, Maxie is the deus ex machina who saves the show's romance from a scheming bitch (Susan Sarandon). Jack Cassidy, Estelle Parsons, and Kevin McCarthy are also on hand, indicating and overplaying like a community-theatre director's pets. Only Sondheim, albeit a bit stiffly, tries to keep the acting natural, underplaying his entire role. As he is often at the keyboard, both noodling and essaying some modfied "concerto style" (as they used to call it), the DVD (Kultur) offers a rare chance to see him as a pianist. He looks great, too, still

---

* Two very short scenes at the opera show us what looks like a Wagnerian mountain sequence. They would have given Sondheim a rare chance to pastiche nineteenth-century opera, but the bit was composed by Thomas Pasatieri.

in his earlier beardless period, though Maxie is the sort who never takes his derby off, even indoors.

The movie versions of Sondheim's shows are more or less faithful in their fashion, but the singing is scanted. On *West Side Story* (1961), they dubbed everybody but the ushers, though retaining the original choreography marked something of a breakaway at the time. There had been precedents—*Oklahoma!* and *The King and I*, for instance. However, *West Side*'s dancing hoodlums were a flighty theatrical conceit; Hollywood might easily have thought the whole thing too arty for real city streets on screen. The film also marked the first exposure of Sondheim lyrics to a mass audience.*

There was dubbing as well in *Gypsy* (1962), which gave an outstanding singing part to Rosalind Russell, a semi-vocalist who did in fact carry a stage musical, *Wonderful Town* (1953). However, that show's score was tailored (by Leonard Bernstein and Betty Comden and Adolph Green) to Russell's "Yes, I can't" singing voice: she knew how the music was supposed to sound, and somehow made it work. Apparently, she laid down *Gypsy*'s soundtrack vocals unaware that Lisa Kirk was going to be technologied in wherever more tone was needed. If you listen to Russell's "Rose's Turn," after the "Momma" hiccups, at "I had a dream," you will hear Kirk smoothly moving in on the track.

Disdained at first, the *Gypsy* movie has been gaining admirers. Certainly, no stage Rose has brought together her charm and command better than Russell, an extremely ingratiating performer who was uncompromising when playing difficult or even wholly unsympathetic figures (such as her Rosemary in *Picnic*). True, as far as Sondheim is concerned, this is more or less the Lisa Kirk *Gypsy*, which doesn't quite work. Kirk's style is dark velvet, while Rose is rough. Bette Midler, in the very, very faithful 1993 telecast (Lionsgate)—overture, dance music (by John Kander, by the way), Broadway orchestrations, and all—gives a cluttered performance overrun with gestures. It's *Charades Gypsy*. But she sounds great in the songs, biting into the words; the great Roses sing not just the Styne of the score but the Sondheim as well. Even Ethel Merman, no one's idea of a *diseuse*, nevertheless uses a word here or here to reach the character, letting all her rage loose on a single syllable—"rot"—in "Some People." Note, in Midler's *Gypsy*, a few star cameos—Andrea Martin as Mr. Grantziger's secretary, and Edward Asner to utter the immortal line "You ain't gettin' eighty-eight [*recte*: just "eight" in the published text] cents from me, Rose!" Sondheim himself delivered it on the original-cast disc, lovably accenting not *cents* but *me*, as if

* Fun Fact: In the opening sequence, as the Jets amble through a basketball court, one of them tosses a ball to one of the players. The latter later became Hollywood's least favorite stage father, Kit Culkin, sire of Macauley.

implying that she might get eighty-eight cents from someone else, perhaps Adele Dazeem.

A Funny Thing Happened On the Way To the Forum (1966, on MGM Video) was directed by Richard Lester, who was trending at the time for the zesty pacing and quasi-surrealistic atmosphere of the first two Beatles films, *A Hard Day's Night* and *Help!*. Lester must have seemed the ideal match for *Forum*'s avid bedlam, but he cut the action up in jumpy editing; the storyline is already jumpy enough. A forerunner of the rock video and the whirling-dervish camerawork of *Moulin Rouge* and *Chicago*, Lester's *Forum* has been excoriated as a movie about not a slave seeking manumission but a director showing off. Then, too, *Forum*'s original playing style was pure burlesque, an above all theatrical communication. Even while using stage veterans Zero Mostel, Jack Gilford, Phil Silvers, and Alfie Bass (the first replacement Tevye in London's *Fiddler on the Roof*), Lester made his *Forum* so *movie* that the comedy comes off as alien in its own neighborhood. And look how much Sondheim is missing: "Love, I Hear," "Free," "Pretty Little Picture," "I'm Calm," "Impossible," "That Dirty Old Man," and "That'll Show Him," all cut.

As for Tim Burton's *Sweeney Todd* (2007, on Warner Video), it does rather fail as a musical, though it's brilliant as sheer filmmaking. Extremely atmospheric, it boasts the very look of a dressy society—the men in waistcoats, scarf ties, and top hats—erected above throwaway unfortunates sinking into comatose despair in every alleyway or condemned to death for nothing at the age of ten. Yes, we actually see the latter happening. Interestingly, Mrs. Lovett's establishment, which we imagine as an unseemly hut, is a neat little corner house, nicely kept up with half-curtained windows, though the interior is squalid.

The score is mostly intact, though numbers are truncated. And there are deviations from the Broadway scenario, as when Judge Turpin (Alan Rickman) invites young Anthony (Jamie Campbell Bower) into his house only to terrorize him, or when the visit to Fogg's asylum ends up very differently than in the show. Further, Tobias (Edward Sanders) is not a short grown-up doing "young" but a little boy (as in the non-musical *Sweeney Todd* films, discussed in the discography). He can sing well enough, as can the Anthony and Johanna (Jayne Wisener), who even gets "Green Finch and Linnet Bird," the sort of number—a lesser character's "get to know me" solo—that movies always used to cut when adapting shows. But then, Burton uses it as a plot piece situating Johanna, Anthony, and Turpin in the action.

However, Burton wouldn't let his Mrs. Lovett (Helena Bonham Carter, Burton's partner) oppose the geeky gravity of Johnny Depp's Todd with her role's traditional music-hall jesting. This loses the McMillinesque disjunction of tragedian and goofaround that makes this material so vitally lopsided. Burton's film is too consistent for Sondheim's art, where irony and paradox reign, as in life. One built-in problem in the American musical generally is its adherence to the ideal of integration even as truly realistic musicals have pulled away from the Rodgers and Hammersteinian unities of Community, Soliloquy, and Dream Ballet. Life isn't integrated; why should art be different?

Then, too, most of Burton's principals are non-singers, and *Sweeney Todd* is not a score one can act one's way through. Depp in particular has no weight in his tone, though his role is the Madam Rose of leading men, the utmost divo role. Todd's salute to his razors and his mad scene after his unsuccessful first assault on the judge lack the character's Dostoyefskyan intensity just when it is most apropos, and while "A Little Priest" works better, Depp's higher lines are cut or spoken.

I for one thought surely Burton would use the camera's intimacy to isolate the moment when, in Todd's first scene with Lovett, she recognizes him. This is a story loaded with recognitions—Pirelli's of Todd leads to the first murder and seals the criminal pact of Lovett and Todd. Toby's spotting Pirelli's purse leads to the unraveling of the pact. Todd's realizing just who the Beggar Woman really is leads to his moment of the ancient Greek anagnorisis: when the protagonist knows all, inspiring the traditional pity and terror as his story ends. So the moment when Mrs. Lovett—who has been like Rapunzel, lo these fifteen years, waiting for Todd's return—realizes that he has just walked into her shop is epic, the narrative's launching pad. And Burton must be aware of all this, for by the time of "There Was a Barber and His Wife," she knows. You see it in her eyes.

Into the Woods (2014) is far more successful as both Sondheim and as a film, partly because cinema can show us all the magic that stage cannot. We see the castle, the beanstalk, the giantess—at least, we see just enough of her to know what she appears to be, a very Sondheim way of seeing. Think of Hapgood in *Anyone Can Whistle*, Robert in *Company*, Ben in *Follies*. We see them, yes—but how well? How well do we know any of the interesting people in our lives? It recalls Ibsen's scathing denunciation of his fellow Norwegians in *Peer Gynt*, when the Troll King observes that, among men, they say, "To thyself be true." But among trolls—meaning among the hypocrites Ibsen saw all about him in Norwegian society—they say, "To thyself be true...*enough*."

Into the Woods' magic centers on the Witch, and director Rob Marshall gives Meryl Streep the works. She doesn't enter a house: she blows the door in. She doesn't exit: she gazungles into a twirly mist and then evaporates.

Though not known as a singer, Streep throws out a tremendous reading of "The Last Midnight," so balefully glorious that we realize that you can't simply sing or simply act your way through a Sondheim part. These roles are dramatic *and* musical.

The casting is offbeat. Little Red is less argumentative than usual, rather prim and sensible. The original, Danielle Ferland, delivered "You can talk to birds?" with a mixture of suspicion and belligerence; Marshall's Little Red just asks for information. Jack isn't a musical-comedy guy but, like Tim Burton's Tobias, a real little kid. The two princes are absurdly handsome but very human—though, again, we see them but not *quite*. It's challenging, as Sondheim generally is, because, as this is a movie, everyone "is" his or her role. The original Broadway cast struck me as too theatrical even for theatre, in an "Upper West Side of Manhattan culturati" way. The whole show could have taken place in Zabar's.

But the movie gets real. For the first time, *Into the Woods* takes us *into the woods*, not into a set with a backstage and Pop at the door. A tangle of flora. Fog. Swamp. Most of it's dark even in daytime: the place of crucibles, of testing and mysteries. There's an almost spiritual feeling to the action now, reminiscent of Thornton Wilder's *The Bridge of San Luis Rey*. Wilder uses the novel to inquire, in overtly religious terms, why his handful of characters met death when, while traversing a gorge, their bridge collapsed. Wilder's conclusion, never directly stated, is that each had unknowingly finished his life's work: there was no reason for any of them to go on living.

Into the Woods is the opposite: everyone's starting out. The movie's physicalizing of the woods emphasizes this, as you see just how spooky and unexplored free will is. It's the Sondheim challenge: are you ready for the consequences of your life choices? And to be true to thyself? As Ben says, "It's knowing what you want, that's the secret."

A Selective Bibliography

First of all there are Sondheim's two lyric collections, published by Knopf, *Finishing the Hat* (2010) and *Look, I Made a Hat* (2011), and not just because of the lyrics. Here we have an artistic testament in the form of notes on the shows, on each song, on his predecessors, especially lyricists (e.g., "Lorenz Hart—Jaunty and Careless"), and on the writing and producing of shows generally. Cut songs and songs created for incomplete or unknown projects abound, as do tales of life among the savages backstage. Thus the books are half-and-half: one half the lyrics themselves and the other half Sondheim's (to quote one of the two subtitles) "Comments, Amplifications, Dogmas, Harangues, Digressions, Anecdotes and Miscellany."

Sondheim is the most eloquent of all songwriters at what the craft is made of. Some of them have little to say on the matter, instinctive rather than intentioned in their art. If you ask Sondheim why, in "Waiting For the Girls Upstairs," Ben and Buddy recall the stage doorman as Max while, in the past, their younger selves call him Harry, he'll tell you that it reveals the twisty enchantments of memory, and how hard it is to be certain about What Happened. But ask, say, Richard Rodgers why the unusual phrase starting on a major seventh in "This Was a Real Nice Clambake" (at "Galloped down our gullets") turns up again in "What's the Use of Wond'rin'," and Rodgers would have no answer.

Sondheim's mini-essays range widely, from "Critics and Their Uses" to "Awards and Their Uselessness," and the books are copiously illustrated, not least with stage shots of various productions. Two pages taken from the *Anyone Can Whistle* souvenir book, however, come from the pre-Broadway issue, and thus make do with rehearsal "candids." It's a piquant selection, with everyone in street clothes trying to look theatrical: Sondheim revving up Lee Remick while Arthur Laurents and Angela Lansbury seem miffed; Sondheim at the keyboard, Remick and Lansbury assuming "characteristic" poses. There's even a snap of Lansbury with Henry Lascoe, who kept undermining her confidence during the testy tryout and then died of a heart attack before the New York opening.

Also essential is Craig Zadan's *Sondheim & Co.* (Harper & Row, 1986), whose first edition dates back to 1974, relatively early in Sondheim's second period. The book's strength lies in its interviewees: Harold Prince, Arthur Laurents, James Lapine, Leonard Bernstein, Angela Lansbury, Bernadette Peters, Len Cariou, Hermione Gingold, Flora Roberts (Sondheim's longtime agent), Thomas Shepard (Sondheim's longtime cast-recording producer), and Sondheim himself. All speak quite freely about their experiences, and the latest edition runs through the San Diego tryout of *Into the Woods*. Zadan narrates skillfully, but it's the communicants recounting their adventures in Sondheimland that make the book basic to Sondheim study. We get Michael Bennett reflecting on the difference between the Roberts of Dean Jones and Larry Kert; then Anthony Perkins goes backstage on opening night to hear Jones say, "I tried to make that part mine but I couldn't." That's odd—has there ever been a better Robert than Dean Jones? Perkins—whom they more or less made the role on—remarks, as others do, that Roberts are "always unappreciated," and he was "happy I wasn't in it."

More: we learn that the concert called *Sondheim: A Musical Tribute* was originally to feature the "I'm Still Here" of Ethel Merman. No: it needs a second-rater, or a first-rater who never quite topped out. Merman held all Broadway in fee. It was Nancy Walker who got the spot, and that's perfect: a superb talent too often mired in swamp shows like *Copper and Brass* and *The Girls Against the Boys*, though she finally reached national celebrity as Mrs. Morgenstern, mother of Valerie Harper's Rhoda. Yet more: We get Ron Field flabbergasted that no one else on the *Merrily We Roll Along* production is worried about the amateurish cast. "I can't believe," he says, imaginarily speaking to the staff, "you don't know what I know." Finally Hal Prince fires him, and Field replies, "Thank you."

Last of the essential books is Ted Chapin's *Everything Was Possible: The Birth of the Musical* Follies (Knopf, 2003), based on notes Chapin took when, still in college, he served as a production assistant on the show, rather as Sondheim did on *Allegro*. There have been many books devoted to the making of a show, from *Show Boat* through *Fiddler on the Roof* to *The Producers*, but Chapin's stands out for its narrative vitality. He has a novelist's touch in characterization: Fifi D'Orsay is high-strung and given to muttering; Gene Nelson is game if overparted; Alexis Smith is pleasant, but don't push your luck. (One wonders if Phyllis' "I went my own damn way and don't make waves" was written after Smith was cast.) Chapin doesn't deal with the writing of *Follies*, but with its production, from the days leading up to the first rehearsal all the way to the recording session, with an account so experiential that, as the out-of-town premiere nears, we feel as keyed up as the cast.

The book's wealth of detail will fascinate *Follies* buffs. Jon Cypher, not John McMartin, was to have been Ben. The Loveland showgirls' pastoral dresses were so wide they had to be hung in the flies backstage and carefully lowered onto the performers. The Sally and Margie in "Buddy's Blues" were originally two men in drag (and a photo documents the casting). We hear about the famous and very prescient review in which Harvard undergraduate Frank Rich saw *Follies'* nostalgia in a crumbling theatre as the "funeral" of the American musical. We read an early version of the "Girls Upstairs" lyrics (at today's "Girls on the run ...") that isn't in *Finishing the Hat*. We see Sondheim coaching the performers, adept at addressing a glitch "with precision and without hesitation"—but then he tells the Sally and Margie that they both "*do* love Buddy." I thought Sally married Buddy dispassionately, on the rebound from Ben. And Chapin himself speaks to the "problem" with James Goldman's libretto with "Jim's brand of humor is very subtle and not joke-oriented at all," which does run against the musical's oldest tenet: whatever else you do, you have to be funny. Indeed, this is why, till relatively recently, the form was called "musical comedy."

Michael Bennett insisted (vainly) that Hal Prince call in Neil Simon for a fun-me-up of one-liners. So *Follies* isn't a laffs show in the end—but what other title provokes such loyalty, memories, wonder for its players as well as for the audience? Way at the end of Chapin's book, the original Young Buddy, Harvey Evans—who left high school to dance for Bob Fosse in *New Girl in Town*, where he was featured in a softshoe pas de trois with Gwen Verdon and Harvey Jung, and took on show after show, including *Anyone Can Whistle*, thereafter—announces how his gravestone will read: "Here lies Harvey Evans. He was in *Follies*."

Moving on: a very useful work is *Broadway Song & Story* (Dodd, Mead, 1985), transcribing Dramatists Guild panels and addresses. Sondheim's two biggest first-period titles, *West Side Story* and *Gypsy*, get the panel treatment, with all three authors and Jerome Robbins on the first and just the three authors on the second, as Robbins was unhappy with differing views on how *West Side Story* came about. There is also a panel on "The Anatomy of the Theater Song," with Sondheim, Jule Styne, Betty Comden, and Sheldon Harnick, and twenty-two pages of Sondheim alone on "The Musical Theater," in which he finds a very apt explanation for why his shows gain wide acceptance only eventually: they are "unexpected" art.

When folks anticipate one kind of entertainment and you give them another, they rebel reflexively, though they may come around after getting used to your style—even if one can never really "expect" what Sondheim will do next. Each of his shows is different not only from conventional musicals but also from each other.

Sweeney Todd has a "making of" book, too, on the legend and its adaptations: Robert L. Mack's *The Wonderful and Surprising History of Sweeney Todd* (Continuum, 2007). Like others, Mack adduces *Hangover Square* to an understanding of how Sondheim expanded his theatre into opera in his *Sweeney Todd*; considering it as a revenge tragedy, Mack says it has "far more in common with Aeschylus' *Orest[e]ia* and Shakespeare's *Hamlet* than . . . with [the stereotypical crime melodrama] *Maria Marten.*"

Years ago, if you asked someone if he had read *Treasure Island* or *Ivanhoe*, he'd say, "No, but I read the Classics Comic." We call them "graphic novels" now, and Thomas Peckett Prest's novel has made the journey (Classical Comics, 2012), available in both "original text" (that is, using the author's words) and "quick text" (simplified) versions. The comic, running to one hundred sixty pages of art, is stunningly brought off. Other titles in the series take in Shakespeare, the Brontës, and Bram Stoker's own *Sweeney Todd, Dracula.*

Now to biographies. Hugh Fordin offers *Getting To Know Him* (Random House, 1977), on Oscar Hammerstein. A number of the subject's confederates—including Agnes de Mille, Joshua Logan, and Mary Martin—spoke to Fordin, giving the book a flavorful Broadway atmosphere. Sondheim, too, shared recollections, and also wrote an introduction, which begins "I didn't know him well, but he saved my life." For Leonard Bernstein, a secondary mentor to young Steve, try Jonathan Cott's *Dinner With Lenny* (Oxford, 2013), twelve hours of conversation catching this ebullient polymath at his best. He leaps from topic to topic—Ella Fitzgerald's "Rock With Me," forgotten monologuist Ruth Draper, Sting's Mack the Knife, Herbert von Karajan on his deathbed, begging Bernstein to take over the Berlin Philharmonic. Hammerstein was known as "Ockie" and Bernstein as "Lenny," and there the apparent resemblance ends; one can imagine how different the two mentoring experiences were for Sondheim, Hammerstein so methodical, focused, heterosexual and Bernstein so mercurial in a gay stream-of-consciousness rap. Both men had a competitive side, yet both were generous. So there is resemblance after all.

For Jerome Robbins, Amanda Vail's *Somewhere* (Broadway Books, 2006) does the job nicely—and note that she chose a Sondheim lyric (or word, at any rate) for her title. Some critics want to pry loose from the Sondheim canon the works he did not compose, but this is to misunderstand how central the writing of lyrics is in the writing of musicals. It assumed that the music is the driver and the words no more than facilitate, but would another lyricist have substantiated as well as Sondheim did *West Side Story*'s potent blend of mean-streets grunge and fantasy romance—with "The Jets Song" on one hand and "One Hand, One Heart" on the other? *Somewhere*, in a place so grim and hopeless, is a magical image. And would another lyricist have given *Gypsy*'s Rose words that clarify, for our hearing, a personality that she herself doesn't understand?

Meanwhile, back at the ranch, Arthur Laurents discusses his innumerable sexual conquests, his delight in being nasty to friends and strangers alike, and other high jinks of the professional enraged queen in *Original Story By* (Applause, 2001). The author of three Sondheim librettos and a lifelong intimate, Laurents is very much a part of the Sondheim story, though we should note that Sondheim finally did get fed up with him and terminated the relationship.

Kurt Weill makes a valuable study in conjunction with Sondheim, because both men were classical composers who worked in the popular theatre. True, Weill did write symphonies, a concerto, string quartets, and such; Sondheim concentrates on narrative forms. But Weill did come to feel, as Sondheim does, that music theatre needs to be *theatre*, while the opera house of his day was too often about the music only.

There are other parallels. Weill's pacifist *Johnny Johnson* (1936) strikes me as not only daring but daring in the way Sondheim's *Assassins* is, dealing with a major national issue in a tone that toggles between serious and comic. Foster Hirsch's *Kurt Weill On Stage* (Knopf, 2002) is an invaluable guide through Weill's "musicals," from the opera ones to the operetta ones to the play ones to the snazzy jazzy ones. More parallels: Weill's *The Firebrand Of Florence* and Sondheim's *A Little Night Music*: the costume operettas. Weill's *Street Scene* and Sondheim's *Sweeney Todd*: the operas. In biography, I'll recommend my own *Love Song: The Lives of Kurt Weill and Lotte Lenya* (St. Martin's, 2012). Lenya was Weill's "voice"—at least, she became so after his death, leading the Weill Revival in recordings and stage appearances. But is there a Sondheim voice? Elaine Stritch in "The Ladies Who Lunch?" Len Cariou in Sweeney Todd's mad scene? Bernadette Peters? Some songwriters do have these authenticating deputies. Cole Porter has Ethel Merman and Bobby Short. Kander and Ebb have Liza Minnelli. Johnny Mercer has Johnny Mercer. But Sondheim?

Three books on Hal Prince take us through his career rather than his life. Carol Ilson's *Harold Prince* (Michigan, 1989) moves from *The Pajama Game* to *The Phantom Of the Opera*, quoting extensively from interviews, press reports, and the like. The book is big and thorough, and uncovers many interesting tidbits. Does anyone in the house remember that Prince was impersonated in a show many years ago, and was "furious" (his word) about it? Does anyone recall who impersonated him? It was Robert Morse, as one Ted Snow in *Say, Darling* (1958), the "not really a musical" with Styne-Comden-Green songs that came out of Richard Bissell's experience co-writing the *Pajama Game* book. One wonders if this is at all connected to Prince's firing Morse after the 2002 *Show Boat*'s Toronto tryout, in favor of a very miscast John McMartin.

Foster Hirsch again proves an intrepid guide, in *Harold Prince and the American Musical Theatre* (second edition, Applause, 2005), which goes up to the reunion of Sondheim and Prince on *Bounce*. As the subtitle suggests, Hirsch places Prince historically, analyzing his predecessors and colleagues with Hirsch's own insights. Ilson does not deal much with the notion of the concept musical, suggesting that *West Side Story* might be the first in the line. This would not be the *Allegro-Love Life-Cabaret-Company* concept musical, obviously, but rather a musical that develops out of an idea—*Romeo and Juliet* in a Manhattan slum—that bends all the musical's arts to its will. This reminds us how slippery the term "concept musical" really is. Hirsch's use of it tends more to the orthodox. He also brings in arcane little surprises, as when Dorothy Collins recalls that, one night, Yvonne De Carlo didn't want to take part in "Who's That Woman?" and "just sat on the edge of the stage"—which, Collins thought, was perfectly in keeping with her character.

Prince issued his own take in *Contradictions* (Dodd, Mead, 1974), too short a book for all that he should have had to say even partway through his career, just after *A Little Night Music*. He does share his backstage with us, noting that, in 1954, *The Pajama Game*—a full-sized show—cost only $169,000 and paid off in fourteen weeks. But Prince also tells us, "A play should be budgeted so that it can exist at sixty percent capacity," thus anticipating, again, what we might call Sondheim's Catch-22: his shows may not pay off in their first production but they will become classics, uniting him, albeit loosely, with such figures as Franz Schubert, Hector Berlioz, and Gustav Mahler.

It is as if Sondheim's works skip the hit-or-flop script and progress directly from their (so to say) entrance to the ovation at the curtain call. Back in the old days, musicals either banked or failed. There were no major "artistic" musicals—that is, as folks perceived them—till *Cabin in the Sky*, *Lady in the Dark*, and *Oklahoma!*, all in the early 1940s. Even then, they were only arguably art. It was *West Side Story*—that title alone—that imposed upon the form the belief that there were musicals and there were *musicals*, great ones, genius ones. Then came Sondheim-Prince and that dangerous term "concept show," and by 1975 or so everyone viewed the musical differently. Now it *was* art, no argument, and fit for critical study.

So we turn to academia. Mark Eden Horowitz, a librarian (of Congress) rather than a professor, gives us *Sondheim On Music* (revised edition, Scarecrow

Press, 2010), whose first half is an interview with the composer himself, helped along by musical examples. It's arresting to hear Sondheim speak about popular music with classical understanding, because my driveline, again, is that Sondheim wrote art for Broadway. This is not about the difference between opera and the musical. It's about the richness of meaning we find in the term "music theatre," because American culture has too much there in it to be limited by category. Weill discovered this, to his shock, when, fresh off the boat from Europe, he saw a dress rehearsal of *Porgy and Bess.* One doesn't have to write *either* an *Aida* or a *No, No, Nanette.*

We have then Joanne Gordon's *Art Isn't Easy* (Southern Illinois, 1990), Stephen Banfield's *Sondheim's Broadway Musicals* (Michigan, 1991), and Steve Swayne's *How Sondheim Found His Sound* (Michigan, 2005), each with a different approach and each, like Horowitz, enriched by input from Sondheim. Swayne explores influences on Sondheim. Banfield takes apart specific aspects of Sondheim's composed shows. Gordon, also concerned only with Sondheim the musician, provides a general walk-through of each title. Thus, Gordon pauses to note that all of those characters blundering in and out of the playing area of *Into the Woods* suggest not the Brothers Grimm but a Feydeau comedy, even Kaufman and Hart. "There are no revolving bedroom doors," Gordon notes, "but in its intricate design the plot more closely resembles French farce than the clear linear didacticism of the traditional fairy tale." Gordon also emphasizes Milton Babbitt's role in the formation of Sondheim's style, encouraging him to fashion large-scale works out of small musical cells. She quotes Sondheim: "If you look at a Bach fugue you see this gigantic cathedral built out of these tiny little motifs."

It's Composition 101: from Beethoven on, the endless development and transformation of key musical phrases became central to late-Romantic music—anti-Bach yet very aware of him—to the point that Wagner could erect the four operas of the *Ring* on virtually a single theme, the Rheinflow heard at the start of the sixteen-hour epic, to create new themes that are altered in turn. Some of the serious Sondheim scores adopt this practice to an extent, *Sweeney Todd* and *Passion* in particular. Leonard Bernstein used a comparable (but simpler) procedure on *Candide* and *West Side Story,* using, respectively, a single four-note and three-note theme to launch many of the numbers.*

---

* *Candide's* four notes are easily heard at the start of the "Paris Waltz" and the Act One finale in the 1956 score; a variant launches the overture. *West Side's* ur-theme, a tritone resolving a half-step up, gives the first notes of "Maria" and "Cool" but turns up in other places. While we're pausing, on *Pacific Overtures* Joanne Gordon quotes *Opera News'* critic, one Ned Brinker—your reporter himself, writing pseudonymously for reasons that now elude me.

Banfield's more detailed survey breaks everything down to niche consid-
erations. On *Pacific Overtures*, he offers mini-essays on "The Orientalist
Tradition," "The Phrygian Matrix and Stylistic Unity," "Ritual Form and the
Mimetic Interlude," and so on. Another definition of the concept musical:
"a show in which 'linear' plot is abandoned or downgraded in favor of vignettes." Swayne devotes three pages to the topic, quoting six different
sources of definition, none of which addresses its unique mashing of the
linear and the spatial to give all characters access to the playing area
whether or not they are "present" in the actual storyline. Banfield incorrectly traces the concept musical back to *Love Life*, which added the commentary vaudeville only after *Allegro* introduced the commentative chorus.
And the "vignettes" theory suits only certain concept musicals. Still, it is
refreshing to see critics attempting, like Aristotle, to describe what they
see in the development of an art rather than try to dictate to it—like the
"cool" movie-loving Broadway-musical haters of the late 1960s who demanded Broadway switch its sound to rock, trying to impose their will
upon it. Let the artists make the revolutions.

In 2014 there appeared *The Oxford Handbook of Sondheim Studies*, edited
by Robert Gordon. Twenty-eight writers, mostly academics, deconstruct
the subject on such matters as "Sondheim and Postmodernism," "The
Prince-Sondheim Legacy," "*A Little Night Music*: The Cynical Operetta," and
"Queer Sondheim" (on the gay content, obviously, from his interpolation
into an off-Broadway revue of 1964, *The Mad Show*, of "The Boy From ..."
through the added gay Robert-and-Peter exchange in *Company* and the
relationship of Frank and Charlie in *Merrily We Roll Along* to Addison and
Hollis' romance in *Road Show*). Tackling the "visual world" of Sondheim's
shows, Bud Coleman doesn't mention the concept musical, though striking
stage pictures have been embedded in the format from the start. Part of
what made *Allegro* unique was its design, allowing the action to "dissolve"
cinematically from scene to scene with no break in continuity. Set changes
in the 1940s were generally executed during blackouts while the orchestra
cranked out the last tune heard till the scenery had been changed and the
lights came up as the conductor signaled for a fadeout. *Allegro*'s black
curtains and furniture on an otherwise open stage without painted backdrops and side pieces, the next set of actors moving into view as the previous set departed, allowed the show to establish a tempo of playing energy
otherwise unknown to most musicals of the era.

Speaking of *Allegro*, Raymond Knapp's *Sondheim Studies* essay reassesses
the Hammerstein-Sondheim relationship. As Knapp sees it, Hammerstein
accepted a "compromise" between artistic completion and commercial success, while Sondheim rejects compromise. This leads to an intriguing

comparison of *The Music Man* and *Anyone Can Whistle*, as Knapp reveals how divergently the two treat common elements. Just for starters: in both, a stranger arrives in a small town, engages romantically with a local caretaker (librarian; nurse), and promotes a phony product (the band; conformism therapy). And of course *The Music Man* is in the Rodgers and Hammerstein style; *Whistle* is very much post-R & H in its edgy satire, a mode R & H adopted only once—in the second act of *Allegro*.

Elsewhere in the book, Matt Wolf tracks "Sondheim on the London Stage" (but watch out for captions accidentally switched on page 217). Like Sondheim himself, Wolf praises David Thaxton's "scalpel-sharp take" on *Passion*'s Giorgio. Wolf loves also Judi Dench's "aching, shimmering" Désirée at the National, along with Julia McKenzie's Sally at the Shaftesbury, trying to revive "a love affair that exists mostly in her mind." But there's a lot in that *mostly*, isn't there? Because *Follies* shows Ben now admitting his love for Sally and now denying that love. Which is it? Does Ben know? Did James Goldman? Even: are such things knowable? This is *post*-post-R & H.

Geoffrey Block's essay examines the differences between *Smiles of a Summer Night* and *A Little Night Music*, and also those between *Passione d'Amore* and *Passion*. Had the adaptation of *Night Music* been more faithful, the musical would have ended up earthier, darker, sexier, with an emphasis on the two servants, Frid and Petra. As I've said, Frid is a compelling presence in the film; he all but overwhelms it with a coarse ease of life utterly beyond the more socially evolved characters. Sondheim's decision to cut his solo, "Silly People," reduces him to little more than a walk-on and also deprives the public of the chance to review the show's metaphor of the night's three smiles. While noting the loss, Block very originally points out that further cutting "Two Fairy Tales" means Anne and Henrik never get a full-scale duet, a strangely innovative treatment of operetta lovers. Then, too, it keeps their romance shady till we learn of it unequivocally (in dialogue) in the second act.

True, *Night Music* already has a great deal of singing before the plot gets going (with the visit to the theatre), and the "Now/Later/Soon" trio takes up all the listening room the public can handle. "Silly People" could be reinserted in performance (and, rarely, has been), but "Two Fairy Tales" would elongate the exposition fatally. Then, too, it's a delicate piece—Block calls it "talky and somewhat impersonal" because Anne and Henrik sing constantly interlocked lines about imaginary figures to describe themselves. It's awfully oblique (though quite charming), and while "Indian Love Call" wouldn't work well in that spot, it's at least a direct statement of the kind audiences respond to. At any rate, "Two Fairy Tales" found a home in Craig Lucas' Sondheim pastiche *Marry Me a Little*.

I've always been struck by Georges's Mother in Act One of *Sunday in the Park With George*, because she reappears in Act Two as young George's critic—a touch motherly, but in the long run not helpful. I thought it odd at the time that there appeared to be no other such parallels in the show's double casting. But Olaf Jubin's contribution to *Sondheim Studies* finds subtle correspondences for just about every *Sunday* player. For instance, we tend to see Jules, Seurat's fellow artist in Act One, as Seurat's frenemy, narrow and ungiving. Yet, as Jubin reminds us, Seurat calls him "a fine painter," genuine praise from someone as explosively, fastidiously artistic as Seurat. So Jules must have something—and, in Act Two, that actor then turns into Bob Greenberg, head of the museum. He's professional rather than creative yet someone who must comprehend the art in order to curate it. But does he? Jubin feels that his announcement that the refreshments await the guests is his key line: "Jules, the minor artist, has been reduced to the role of a domestic," perhaps to tell us that Jules in fact isn't a fine anything after all.

As for biography, there is only Meryle Secrest's *Stephen Sondheim* (Knopf, 1998). Back in 1980 or so, I had a firm offer from Harper & Row for such a book, but only if Sondheim was willing to speak of his personal life. To change the wording, he would have to come out. He didn't want to then, but he changed his mind later, and Secrest quotes him in a deceptively simple line: "I was never easy with being a homosexual, which complicated things." It's simple because of the legal problems of those days, but a lot resides in that *complicated*. Being gay adds mysterious content to one's profile, because even tolerant straights don't understand anything about gay life. Wouldn't Gay Sondheim create a rival "text" overshadowing Sondheim the composer or Sondheim the arts revolutionary, or even just Sondheim the author of musicals with an interesting premise—shows that aren't intended to be revolutionary at all (but turn out to be, because that's what happens when you take Oscar Hammerstein's reforms to the next level)? Sondheim was forthcoming in talks with Secrest, allowing her to give a very readable and complete picture of the man. No doubt there has been no other Sondheim biography because there is no need for one.

A Selective Discography

With shows as rich as these, it may not be easy to isolate the most intensely haunted of *Follies* recordings or even place the Catalan *A Little Night Music* in the Sondheim canon. However, his first score, to **Saturday Night**, is a cinch. Preserving the 1997 world premiere, First Night's disc is historic but superseded in every respect by Nonesuch's taping of the 2000 New York staging. Nonesuch offers more music in a bigger orchestration (by Jonathan Tunick, souped up for the CD), taking in two numbers written for the Chicago production by the Pegasus Players, in 1999, "Montana Chem." (on stock prices, the show's maguffin: the characters care about it, but we don't), and "Delighted, I'm Sure," a throwaway bit that existed solely as a lyric when the show was written, in 1954. (Sondheim finally set it forty-five years later.) Then, too, Nonesuch offers a full set of notes and lyrics; First Night lacks even a synopsis. Its cast (all unknowns, even if Gavin Lee later punched out walking up, across, and down the proscenium in the stage *Mary Poppins* in London and New York) is respectable. Nonesuch's gang is rather better, though I miss the playful eccentricity we would have heard from the cast had the show gone to Broadway with—just for instance—Carol Haney, Grover Dale, Sheila Bond, Jimmy Sisco, and Sidney Armus. Even in "So Many People," a ballad that sounds very like the Sondheim of the Hal Prince era, David Campbell and Lauren Ward are affecting but never quite take over this romance of mingled yearning and contentment. Still, the show's tunefulness comes through quite nicely.

Many people relate to **West Side Story** through the 1961 film, but the original Broadway cast (Columbia) is unbeatable. Among Jerome Robbins' many infuriating qualities was indecisiveness, especially in casting, but when he chose his players at last they truly fulfilled a vision of who the characters were, and one hears it in every note. A letter from Sondheim to Bernstein in the latter's published correspondence (Yale) tells us that Columbia's Goddard Lieberson increased *West Side*'s pit for the disc to thirty-seven (from twenty-eight, according to Steven Suskin in *The Sound of Broadway Music*), and the conductor, Max Goberman, drafted from classical precincts, shapes the music as well as anyone, including Bernstein himself with a crossover cast (DG). The latter—José Carreras, Kiri Te Kanawa, Tatiana Troyanos, and Marilyn Horne (for "Somewhere")—do rather suffer from terminal opera kaboom, but, paradoxically, DG's *The Making of West Side Story*, the DVD on the sessions, is worth a detour. After "America," Bernstein says, "That may be my favorite song in the show," so now we know. Sondheim doesn't appear, but we do get Te Kanawa's "Somewhere," just for the fun of it, not included on the LPs or CD.

West Side's 1958 London cast is a curiosity, because it came out in segments. The sweethearts, Don McKay and Marlys Watters, got an EP (HMV) of four numbers conducted by Lawrence Leonard, who led the pit at Her Majesty's Theatre. You have to scramble to get the other leads. The Riff, George Chakiris, is on a *West Side* Society LP. David Holliday, who played Gladhand, then a Jet, then Tony, can be *seen* on the Society cover photo of the Prologue, but sneak over to two Music For Pleasure *West Side*s to hear his Tony, with Diane Todd and then Jill Martin. (The Todd disc features Tony Adams, a replacement Riff.) These London studio casts of Broadway and West End titles vary greatly in expertise, though such major names as June Bronhill, Shirley Bassey, Patricia Routledge, and Adam Faith took part. Buffs love them for their endearingly clueless habit of leaving out important numbers—one LP drops "America," another "Somewhere." The only complete *West Side* is on Jay's double-CD set, with the sole reading of the overture. And note that the movie's fiddling with the score—bringing the boys into "America"* or tacking a coda with a *piano* high G onto "Something's Coming"—has been creeping into revivals. In 2009 on Broadway (Sony), Matt Cavenaugh sang the coda with an extra phrase, then rose to a good strong high A.

Gypsy is unusual in claiming no fewer than five Broadway cast albums, from Ethel Merman (Columbia) through Angela Lansbury (Victor), Tyne Daly (Electra), and Bernadette Peters (Angel) to Patti LuPone (Time/Life). They're all good, and the later ones give the fuller readings. But Rose was made on Merman from top to toe, and, whether she knew it or not, she *was*

---

* "America" was written as a dispute between a pro–Puerto Rico Anita and an assimilating Bernardo, backed by the girls and boys, but Jerome Robbins wanted an all-girl number on Broadway. The original lyrics are in *Finishing the Hat*.

Rose, especially in the ruthless self-belief under the appealing façade. Lu-Pone's CD is noteworthy in including cut numbers made by the cast in Jonathan Tunick's orchestrations, so this is the fullest reading of all. One of these extras is "Smile, Girls," written because Merman didn't have enough to sing in Act Two— as I've already said, just her third of "Together Wherever We Go," a tiny reprise-bit of "Small World," and "Rose's Turn." "Smile, Girls" isn't a great number, but it's great *Gypsy*, showing us what Rose is like as a theatrical coach—remember, at the show's end, it's what Louise wants her to do with the rest of her life.

The above are the famous *Gypsys*. Let's pay a visit to secret *Gypsy*: the Kay Medford reading (Music for Pleasure). It's another of those English studio casts; Medford was then in London as Mrs. Brice in *Funny Girl*, and someone must have thought it equiponderant to record Medford as a second stage mother. But she was really a dramatic actress who took non-singing roles (as in *Paint Your Wagon*, a City Center *Carousel*, and *Bye Bye Birdie*) or finagled her way through vocals (as in replacing Pat Marshall in *Mr. Wonderful*). Medford wasn't a singer per se, and Rose is the musical's Brünnhilde.

Even so, this *Gypsy* is no fly-by-night affair. The smallish band plays an adaptation of the original orchestrations, and there is a valid supporting cast. There's even a Pop, for his one spoken line. But there's no Rose in any real sense, because Medford tries to act her way through the score, singing its Sondheim but not its Styne. She resorts to bizarre field expedients, such as lengthening the sound of the last syllable in a phrase (e.g., "I had a dreeeeeemmm-uh"), to suggest theatre excitement. It's not laughable or a disaster. It just isn't correct. Rose isn't one of those "mother" roles, like the one in *Funny Girl*, where personality rules. Rose is the greatest singing challenge in the classics sweepstakes, because there's so much Styne, so much Sondheim. Rose-Marie is just music. Roxie Hart is just lyrics. Rose is a chemistry of the two. As for the important number that, as British custom demands, the LP left out: it's "Little Lamb."

The most recent of the prominent Roses comes to us also on an English recording: Imelda Staunton, at Chichester in 2014 and then in the West End (First Night). Her portrayal was a sensation, and she produced a surprising amount of voice in the numbers, as she hadn't in such earlier Sondheim roles as the Baker's Wife and Mrs. Lovett. The disc is personable in general, the two girls joking around merrily in "If Momma Was Married." But something is missing: vocal tone. It is not enough to be able to sing this score with command, as Staunton does. Rose must produce an attractive sound, and Staunton's timbre lacks appeal. This is why one always returns to Merman-as-Rose. These songs were written specifically for that singer's incomparable instrument.

I want to speed through to Sondheim's second period, but let's dally with one of the outstanding Sondheim non-original-cast albums, that of the 2001 Pasadena Playhouse revival of **Do I Hear a Waltz?** (Fynsworth Alley), led by Alyson Reed and Anthony Crivello. *West Side's* Carol Lawrence plays the jaded pensione proprietor, and there is a splendid orchestra of twenty-one (cut down from the 1965 pit) under Steve Orich, who effects a wonderful rallentando in the overture at the first full-out statement of "Someone Like You." The Broadway troupe (Columbia) is very well sung, but this cast is more characterful. Crivello, without Sergio Franchi's exhibitionistic blitz, nevertheless makes "Take the Moment" seductive, then passionate, with a stunning climax rising to a high A flat, and, in the title number, Reed really sounds like a lifelong wallflower suddenly asked to lead the cotillion.

As I've said, that title song was originally staged with the ensemble, though only Leona sang. But it's a gateway number, leading to a "new, improved" Leona, and ancient rules of musical comedy demand that the chorus sing along, for a swelling of the show's emotional arc.* The Pasadena *Waltz* reset the action entirely at the pensione and, anyway, had no ensemble to join in on anything. Yet there were revisions. "Bargaining" was cut, and the now-famous cynical version of "We're Gonna Be All Right," dropped (as I've said) at the insistence of Richard Rodgers' wife, who felt she had been lyric-shamed, was reinstated along with song's verse, not heard on Broadway. Note that the Pasadena CD includes the 1965 overture (albeit shortened), which did not make it onto the original album.

Most important, Pasadena reprogrammed "Everybody Loves Leona," a sorrowful "coming to terms with myself" solo, dropped in 1965 because Sondheim felt it telegrammed character intel instead of dramatizing it. We know what Sondheim means. In *Brigadoon*, Tommy doesn't sing to us of how he misses that Scots village; instead, we see him haunted by it, in others' reprises of the first act's songs. Still, "Everybody Loves Leona" is an arresting way to connect us with the heroine's failure to hear more than a chorus or two of her waltz. It's also one of the best lyrics in the show. And before we leave the 1960s, let's note an amusing mishap on the original cast of *Anyone Can Whistle* (Columbia): at 1:39 of the CD cut of "I've Got You To Lean On," Angela Lansbury accidentally jumps in too soon. (Just by the way, there's great stereo separation on this particular cut, too.)

---

* A perfect example is *Show Boat's* "Why Do I Love You?," a duet turned into an ensemble when bystanders—visitors at the Chicago World's Fair, actually—simply join in. Rodgers and Hammerstein generally banned the practice as illogical, though *Allegro's* very busy chorus does take over "You Are Never Away" from the hero. One year before *Waltz, Hello, Dolly!* (1964) employed the usage throughout the evening.

Entering concept-musical territory, we should first consider **Allegro**, Rodgers and Hammerstein's third show and the pioneer of the movement. This is a difficult work to record excerpts from, as the original cast (Victor) demonstrates, for *Allegro* was designed to be, above all, a staging, not simply a composition. Lacking the show's open playing area filled with traffic as each scene "dissolved" into the next; and lacking the trade-off among the singing ensemble, the dancing ensemble, and the speaking roles, all working in a kind of chaotic unity; and lacking the character interaction that defied time and space, we have ten cuts of music theatre without the theatre. There are textual problems as well: Joe's parents distract us with "A Fellow Needs a Girl" just when we want to get to know Joe himself; or Joe's college date offers a sort of love ballad, "So Far," then vanishes forever.

Worse yet, Victor's *Allegro* did not sell well, a shocking comedown for R & H after Decca's *Oklahoma!* and *Carousel* helped acculturate the cast album in American life. True, *Allegro*'s music doesn't compare to theirs—but it also doesn't extract well. It's worth noting that, in 1948, a few months after Victor released its *Allegro*, the record industry was feverishly transferring its 78s onto the new LPs and 45s (all the more so because an orchestra strike prohibited new recording for almost all of 1948), yet Victor let *Allegro* languish on its instantly outdated shellac discs. The performance did not come out on LP till 1965; even now, on CD, it doesn't sound like the experiment that sparked two generations of nonconformist musicals, especially those by Sondheim. It apparently doesn't even use all of the thirty-player orchestra heard in the Majestic Theatre during *Allegro*'s run, because interesting contrapuntal effects are missing.

The recording's poor showing hurt *Allegro*'s reputation, for cast albums are more than souvenirs. They trace a show's profile as artwork. A show without a valid recording is a ghost—but finally, in 2009, Sony released a two-CD *Allegro* from overture to finale, with lots of spoken dialogue and all the musical bits, no matter how small, to vitalize the narrative. The cast is fancy—Patrick Wilson as Joe, Audra McDonald and Nathan Gunn as his parents, Judy Kuhn for "So Far," Laura Benanti as the unworthy wife, Norbert Leo Butz as Joe's sidekick, Liz Callaway as the sympathetic nurse, and even Oscar Hammerstein (on an old tape) as the Philosophy Professor in a college scene.

Larry Blank conducts a solid performance, with a disciplined group for the very tricky seven-part choral encore of "You Are Never Away" and an exhibition cut of "The Gentleman Is a Dope." The latter, the show's best-known number, gives us a Hammerstein thinking almost in Sondheim terms, ironic and discontented. Rodgers, too, sounds unlike himself, creating a verse entirely out of one measure of four descending notes repeated twenty-two times without variation and launching the refrain on a b flat minor ninth chord, a doozy of a start. The number made a star of Lisa Kirk, who sang it in a trenchcoat in front of one of the production's several black traveler curtains, a rare moment in this vivacious staging in which the Majestic's playing area was closed off for something intimate. Back on Victor, Kirk sounds fine in a stand-and-deliver way; Callaway and Blank have more content.

Sony does have a problem in a somewhat recessed orchestra; not every detail comes through. For example, there's a wonderfully strange episode in "One Foot, Other Foot," a remarkable depiction of the exultation of a little boy who has just learned to walk. He shouts, he marches around the yard looking for mischief to get into, he feels the stirrings of liberty and individualism for the first time. The number catches all of that in a gala chorale—and then, suddenly, the orchestra cuts out except for the tympani, muted yet pounding under a chant-like section (at "Especially made for you..."). When the song's main strain returns, the quixotic tympani rhythm is folded into the orchestral texture. Victor leaves this last bit out entirely, and while Blank's percussionist plays it, one has to strain to hear it.

Nevertheless, Sony has reinstated an all but lost title of great influence. Immodestly, I'd recommend inspecting the series of *Allegro* stage shots I put together for *Rodgers & Hammerstein* (Abrams, 1992), with access to all the Vandamm keysheets of the Broadway and touring production as well as amateur snapshots taken during the Boston tryout, to get an idea of how this extraordinarily visual show behaved. The pictures reveal how time and space were smudged to emphasize the parable-like story in a unique staging plan— another way of defining the concept musical, whose narratives often take on the iconic nature of the fable. Is *Company*'s Robert a person or a symbol?

Note that Sondheim himself took part in this *Allegro*, delivering its most important speech, in the finale, just as Joe is about to make the decision of his life—to leave material success behind for personal fulfillment. And of course this is a key Sondheim notion: that we create our lives with the application of free will. Yes I said yes I will yes. Ironically, *Allegro*'s characters are virtually nothing like Sondheim's. The hero is corny, his parents are lovely, and though his wife fails him, it's partly because she sees life differently than he does. In *Allegro*, everyone knows how he wants to live (though Joe is thirty-five when he finally attains that knowledge). In Sondheim, many are permanently confused. *Allegro*'s form inspired Sondheim, but his content is his own.

Though Sondheim was around for *Allegro*'s rehearsals, he told me that he doesn't recall the finished show all that well, as he had had to return to college early in its tryout. Still, there's a taste of *Allegro* in **Company**, if only in its use of an open stage populated by characters coming and going freely in one another's lives. And is Marta's "Another Hundred People" a complement to "So Far"—a look at dating etiquette from a love object with, paradoxically, no real vocation in the narrative? While admiring Dean Jones' fervent Robert in the original cast (Columbia), we should listen as well to Anthony Perkins, for he was after all the man the authors had in mind for Robert. The Jackpot label CD'ed two Perkins LPs from the late 1950s, *Tony Perkins* (Epic) and *On a Rainy Afternoon* (Victor) on a single disc. Is this the real Robert—sincere and pleasant but uninflected? The mysterious stranger as best friend, in old and new standards to a soft-jazz combo? "The World Is Your Balloon," from *Flahooley*, is typical, with a lively flute descant over the vocal and an improvisational piano break. Nice. But while the song is optimistic, Perkins is oddly noncommittal. On the *Flahooley* cast album (Capitol, Angel, DRG), Barbara Cook and Jerome Courtland thrill the same number with personal involvement.

Victor's cover art shows Perkins smiling as he strolls along the Central Park Mall, deserted in the rain: Robert alone, happy to be so. Yet we turn to Perkins' 1960 appearance in Frank Loesser's *Greenwillow* (Victor, Columbia, DRG) and hear him tear mightily into the surging "Summertime Love" and "Never Will I Marry." The latter is a kind of parergon to *Company*, Robert's credo till the scene with Elaine Stritch wrenches him toward the resolution of "Being Alive." Perkins was a puzzling character, moving from Quaker (in the film *Friendly Persuasion*) to *Psycho*, gay in life and then straight in marriage. Yes, the authors asked him to play Robert—but did they perhaps also make the role on Perkins in the first place, inadvertently using stray bits of Perkins' ambivalent sexuality? There is something uncanny about Robert, something "off" that never gets defined. Robert "doesn't have the good things and he doesn't have the bad things," says one of the other men. "But he doesn't have the good things." What exactly does that mean?

Two *Company* DVDs give us the show in full true, Image with pungent support (including Patti LuPone's Upper West Side Evita of a Joanne) for Neil Patrick Harris' straight-arrow Robert in a New York Philharmonic concert staging. Image gives us also the 2006 Broadway revival, with a less colorful group behind Raúl Esparza's nuanced Robert and director John Doyle's idiotic notion that actors in musicals should supply their own instrumental accompaniment.

Returning to the old idea that musicians play and actors act, *Company: Original Cast Album* (New Video Group) a look at the recording sessions, lets us study Sondheim at work. A perfectionist, he catches one of the "You Could Drive a Person Crazy" trio on a wrong note in a tricky scat pattern, and is as involved in coaching the drama as the music, an auteur of shows. Watching Dean Jones sing "Being Alive," his features so animated and in the moment, reminds us how intense he was in the role—and note Elaine Stritch's grin early on, delighting in this ultimate Stritch part (even if she has trouble satisfying the bigwigs in the "Ladies Who Lunch" takes). This documentary was to be the first in a series of reality tapes of Broadway recording sessions, but the producer suddenly left for work in Hollywood, and this was the project's only issue.

Capitol's Dick Jones wanted to record all of **Follies'** expansive score, but the label balked at a two-LP release, and numbers were abridged or missing.* Not till 1985, fourteen years later, did *Follies* get a full reading, when Victor took down a New York Philharmonic concert. This is the *Follies* that most effectively habilitated the all-star treatment, running to Betty Comden and Adolph Green for "Rain on the Roof," Elaine Stritch for "Broadway Baby," Phyllis Newman to lead "Who's That Woman?," Liliane Montevecchi for "Ah, Paris!," faded Metropolitan Opera diva Licia Albanese for "One More Kiss," and, lo, Carol Burnett for "I'm Still Here." Burnett gives it a grand slow build, with aplomb. Again, however, isn't this more properly the anthem of a third-rater?† Burnett is too big for the spot. It's about survival against odds, not deserved success.

The Philharmonic's four leads are George Hearn, Lee Remick, Mandy Patinkin, and Barbara Cook, and while it is an article of faith among *Follies* buffs that the original 1971 quartet is *hors concours*, this is very flavorful casting from top to bottom, and the audience reactions recall a very special night (actually two, September 6 and 7, with cuts drawn from each to perfect the release). Paul Gemignani conducts on the grand scale—hear him pull the Philharmonic back for a Big Statement of the main theme at the first forte in the Prologue, usual in *Follies* performances today but not heard in 1971 (led by Harold Hastings, Hal Prince's longtime house conductor).

This is not a note-complete *Follies*, however. The delightfully bizarre bundling of three numbers that caps "Broadway Baby" was omitted, along

---

* Jones produced wonderful cast albums, wedding the music to anchoring dialogue to "artifact" a show. His *Ben Franklin in Paris* (Capitol, DRG) is exemplary: the Mark Sandrich Jr.-Sidney Michaels score is not on the cult list, yet it jumps out of one's speakers so theatrically one can almost see Robert Preston going through another of his period impersonations in wholly contemporary style. Thomas Z. Shepard, also known for catching the spirit of a show on disc, handled most of Sondheim's Broadway cast recordings, from *Company* through *Sunday in the Park With George*, though the most recent titles were produced by Tommy Krasker.

† As I said earlier, Sondheim used Joan Crawford as his model. But the song ends up telling us of someone who never really made it, not someone who, like Crawford, was big enough to tie with Greta Garbo and Norma Shearer as Queen of the Lot at MGM and win a Best Actress Oscar (for *Mildred Pierce*).

with the "Bolero d'Amour," a lush ballroom piece composed by not Sondheim but the show's dance arranger, John Berkman. Yet the performance
resonates with the confidence of a work that, though disputed when new,
is now a classic and knows it. The 1971 recording is bound into *Follies'*
doleful story; this 1985 concert revels in its star turns, not least when Patinkin's high-energy Buddy himself provides the voices for the fake Margie
and Sally in his Follies turn and snaps like a firecracker. He even goes into a
show-stopping cakewalk tempo at the last strain, as if to take the entire
hall with him when he exits. With excellent stereo separation and the whole
Stavisky soundtrack LP transcribed as a bonus on the CDs, this *Follies* is all
but essential.

The DVD release of the concert (Image) cuts out much of the performance to include rehearsal footage, though we do get Sondheim, recalling
that "One More Kiss" was the first number written, as he wanted to explore
the pastiche platform and thus started out with the oldest model, the Rom-
berg-Friml love waltz (though the music more truly echoes late Franz
Lehár, at the time, say, of *Paganini* and *Der Zarewitsch*). The various performers' musings lack originality, though they present a valid Beginner's
Sondheim, and Elaine Stritch tells a funny divorce story and, indicating her
carryall, says, "I heard the cameraman say, 'Move the bag'—I thought he
was referring to me." Once the concert begins, though, the tape really takes
off, giving us a guide to staging this epic without sets or (mostly) choreography. The camera takes us backstage as the "Weismann Girls" await their
cue during "Beautiful Girls," and, as they appear, one by one, perfectly
timed, we feel the excitement of the event—Burnett, then Cook, Comden,
Montevecchi in fantastical black chic, Newman, Remick. *Follies* tends to
attract the big talents, but this has to be the most distinguished cast in the
show's lifetime.

However. The concert ultimately tries to cheer the show up—and the
Sally, all but comatose at the end in 1971, is now calmly ready to abandon
her dream of Loveland, while Phyllis tells Ben, "I'm glad we came." No, she
isn't. A reprise of "Waiting For the Girls Upstairs" followed, as if the four
leads were nostalgic rather than discontented, and Weismann delivered a
sermonette leading into a full-chorus "Beautiful Girls" finale.

Is *Follies* the *Show Boat* of the millennium, forever to be remodeled? The
1987 London *Follies* (First Night) offered a wholly rewritten book (by James
Goldman, frantically pepping up the tone), while Sondheim contributed
four new numbers and changed a few of the old songs' lyrics. It was musical-
comedy *Follies*, a Peter Pan *Follies* that won't grow up. Phyllis' confession
of adultery in "Could I Leave You?" was now a mere threat. Ben's Folly, the
new "Make the Most of Your Music," staged on a Ziegfeldian staircase as

the choristers leaped out of a vast piano, didn't implode climactically. So he isn't a fraud, after all? Even "Broadway Baby" was soft-grained, a croon. In 1971, Ethel Shutta was defiant, and in 1985 Elaine Stritch goofed and gloated. But Margaret Courtenay in London sounds tender; it's supposed to be an anthem, a De Sylva, Brown, and Henderson ode, like their "The Birth of the Blues" and "The Best Things in Life Are Free."

Oddest of all is the album's omission of the opening music, the most atmospheric in the history of the musical and a potent link between Sondheim and the classical world in its Erik Satie-esque evocations. To be fair, London's *Follies* played very well, with more attractive scenery (by Maria Björnson) than the original had, and the twenty-one-man pit was expanded for the recording to thirty-two, with two harps. But of the lead quartet— Diana Rigg, Daniel Massey, Julia McKenzie, and David Healy—only McKenzie leaves her mark, creating an unusually aggressive Sally. She also suggests what a crossover *Follies* might sound like, with her near-operatic instrument.

A two-disc set made on the 1998 *Follies* at New Jersey's Paper Mill Playhouse, now with Laurence Guittard, Dee Hoty, Donna McKechnie, and Tony Roberts (TVT), includes the "Broadway Baby" three-voice coda and the bolero. It also returns us to major star cameos, missing from the London cast. Phyllis Newman and Liliane Montevecchi are held over from the Philharmonic, Kaye Ballard sings "Broadway Baby," and, as originally staged, Ann Miller tackled "I'm Still Here" while moving from stage right to stage left and back as she gradually came forward in a kind of career-defining March to the Footlights. Once again, an expanded pit (of thirty-six players) lends a symphonic atmosphere to the grander pieces, and Jonathan Tunick himself conducts. The album's best feature is an appendix of eight numbers, six titles cut before the New York premiere and two alternates for Phyllis' Folly. True, these songs have been taken down elsewhere. But TVT presents them as cast recordings, using the Paper Mill people with the full orchestra. When Guittard and McKechnie work their way through the dropped "Pleasant Little Kingdom" to its revelation that Ben has been in love with the wrong woman all his adult life, we can virtually hear the music breaking into "Too Many Mornings" (as it originally did) and visualize the staging.

The 2011 revival (PS Classics), which originated in Washington, D.C., offers Bernadette Peters, Danny Burstein, Jan Maxwell, and Ron Raines in a roomy reading that programs a great deal of dialogue. Oddly, while the production itself used a repurposed book, the two discs use cut-down versions of the 1971 libretto. It makes one wonder if the pendulum will swing back to welcome more faithful *Follies* revivals. The performance is quite good, strengthened by James Moore's excellent conducting and superb sound engineering to capture boutique refinements in Tunick's orchestra-tions. One year after this release, the saga of the *Follies* discs was brought full circle when Bruce Kimmel's Kritzerland label reissued the original cast in a remastering designed to lift the haze that had hung over the tapes since 1971.

Considering **A Little Night Music**, one might start with Maurice Ravel, for his influence on Sondheim's style is most acute in this work. Pierre Boulez, usually dry and uncommitted in the Romantic composers like Wagner, is excellent in the French Impressionists, and Boulez's complete Ravel set (Sony) with the New York Philharmonic and Cleveland Orches-tras is ideal, especially for the *Night Music*-like *Valses Nobles et Sentimen-tales* and *La Valse* (which finds echo also in the more sweeping climaxes in *Follies*). The more one hears Ravel, the more Sondheim sounds like a French Impressionist himself. The *Night Music* film (Henstooth Video) has a rotten reputation, but its opening and closing sequences preserve the original staging (in a replica production at Vienna's Theater an der Wien). Further, it's interesting that the project attracted one of the era's most prominent movie stars, Elizabeth Taylor, to play Désirée. It was perhaps another sign that Sondheim was becoming a cultural icon, someone whose proximity lent one prestige. It's a little like knowing Beethoven.

I spent some time with *Night Music* recordings in *Anything Goes*, my his-tory of the American musical, so let us explore only the Barcelona cast album, as it sheds light on the nature of Sondheim's genre. Spanish zar-zuela, very little known here, is a unique form, too rich to match up to a simple definition. Where to start? Think of *No, No, Nanette* performed by opera singers. There are very serious zarzuelas as well, but the point is that zarzuela is a form of musical with a highly elevated vocal complement. So we expect *Musica Per a una Nit d'Estiu*, sung in Catalan (on the K label), to be a sort of operatized Broadway. Then, too, the many stage shots in the CD booklet give us a cast that looks "opera": less pretty than able. And, right at the start, as the Liebeslieder Singers assemble in cadenza, we hear even more swank vocalizing than the score calls for.

As the zesty performance progresses, however, we realize that this is no operatic Sondheim, no zarzuela-izing of a musical. The orchestra is cut down a bit from the Broadway pit, without a harp—so important in this music—and the cast is drawn from not zarzuela initiates but actors who either sing just well enough or less well than that. Désirée, indeed, is a di-seuse. So this isn't zarzuela style at all, but an attempt to catch Sondheim in his own sphere, that of "music theatre," that elusive form pitched somewhere between musical comedy and operetta wherein the music matters but the drama matters, too. But the music matters. This is what Sondheim brought to Broadway from *Company* on: a genre that scarcely existed before him. There are a few instances: *The Threepenny Opera*, or Ravel's short opera *L'Heure Espagnole*—yes, Ravel again, the ghost looking down on Sondheim's shows and wondering why he never uses the jazz that Ravel so loved about American music.

No *Night Music* cast album includes "Silly People," but George Lee Andrews gives us an original-cast performance on *Sondheim: A Musical Tribute* (Warner), a benefit evening held at the Shubert Theatre on the "Weekend in the Country" *Night Music* set in 1973. Andrews' cut was left off the LP, but it's on the CD (Victor), along with Nancy Walker's slow-build-from-resigned-to-titanic "I'm Still Here" and an "aww" cut of Sondheim himself playing and singing "Anyone Can Whistle." The audience thinks it's his confession, but Sondheim doesn't care whether he can whistle or not. As I've already said, it's not his song; it's a song for a character in a show.

Pacific Overtures (Victor) is never mentioned among the great cast albums—*Gypsy*, say, or a house favorite, *Jamaica*, which zooms right out of your speakers with Caribbean magic. (And *Jamaica*'s composer and lyricist, Harold Arlen and E. Y. Harburg, are Sondheim favorites.) No doubt folks fail to register *Pacific Overtures'* disc because it lacks an Ethel Merman or Lena Horne to anchor it in the memory; on one level, show biz is about fame. Even so, the original *Pacific Overtures* is a tremendous performance, far outclassing the British opera cast (Victor), indifferently sung and undramatic, and the 2004 revival (PS), with an underpowered Reciter from B. D. Wong and a tiny pit (rescored by Tunick, and very adroitly; but still). Note that "Welcome To Kanagawa" has added words, for Sondheim felt that some of the jokes didn't land. "We're always open," the madam cries, as she and her cohort glide away; that's a new line. The original Broadway production was taped for viewing in Japan; the intrepid may find it online.

Sweeney Todd's original cast (Victor) preserves Len Cariou's ravening gargoyle; the DVD (Warner), caught on tour with some replacement casting, offers George Hearn's barber, opposite the irreplaceable Lansbury. *Sweeney* buffs should sample the 1936 English film—primitive, but of a rough vigor—with the symmetrically named Tod Slaughter as Todd. From a distance, he looks, most asymmetrically, like Cyril Ritchard.

BBC television revisited the legend in 2006. Like Christopher Bond, scenarist Joshua St. Johnston gave Todd an explanatory backstory: he suffered as a child in Newgate debtors' prison, so his first victim is an evil jailer. Ray Winstone plays Todd as oddly impassive, though his motivation for serializing his bloodlust is jealousy of the young boy friends of appetitive Mrs. Lovett (Essie Davis). It's an arresting production in all, but without

Sondheim's score the story feels shrimped down; the opera is social, political, epic. By its end, with the stage all but soaked in death, we're exhausted. But when the BBC version ends, we're simply puzzled. "Why did you do it?" the chief investigator asks Todd: "I must know." But all Todd says is "Because I could...and then...I couldn't not." So he doesn't know any more than we do.

Sondheim buffs treasure the first **Merrily We Roll Along** album (Victor), but the two-disc sets representing the expanded score of the revision(s) tell us more about Frank, who is, after all, the protagonist. Comparable to *Company*'s Robert in the emphasis on his friendships and a certain air of mystery, Frank has not emerged as a great actor's challenge, as Robert has. But then he lacks a "Being Alive," a finish, because *Merrily*'s reverse chronology makes a climactic number impossible; the show climaxes at eight o'clock, not ten-thirty. On Jay, Maria Friedman's intensity makes Mary almost the lead with a very dramatic cast from a staging in Leicester, while Colin Donnell, an excellent Frank for Encores! (PS), is let down by a mostly soggy group. Maybe it's time to stop casting Charlie as a nebbish and let a Pippin play him. Kyle Dean Massey or Bobby Steggart in horn rims is what Kaufman and Hart had in mind for that character in the first place. As with *Pacific Overtures*, the original *Merrily* can be found online if you know where to look.

Sunday in the Park With George's two recordings mislead us because of their scoring. The original cast (Victor) was beefed up with a large string section, and the 2005 London staging (PS), another of those chic chicklet mountings, went with a tiny chamber pit. Even with two instruments added for the recording, the sound is feeble. But the DVD (Image) took the show down exactly as it was originally performed and is thus the only record of how the music sounded. Of course, this very visual piece must be seen to be savored, and, further, the pairing of Mandy Patinkin and Bernadette Peters gives us a typical Sondheim couple: the guy is crazy and the girl is dependently independent. It's Hapgood and the Nurse of *Anyone Can Whistle*, *Follies*' Ben and Phyllis, a crimeless Todd and Mrs. Lovett. *Passion* switches the genders.

Into the Woods. Here, once again, we have a DVD of the original staging (Image), though the London production, directed by Richard Jones in designer Richard Hudson's wall of doorways that suggested the inside of a cuckoo clock, made much more of the blithely dire atmosphere of the traditional fairy tale. In New York, the characters looked like New Yorkers in costumes; in London, they looked like illustrations from an antique volume of Grimm. The London production was also funnier than New York. At one point, Julia McKenzie's Witch came up through the floor to her waist, in a little outfit that made her legs about two inches long, to prolonged laughter in the house. The London cast album (Victor) is also a humdinger in sheer sound, as Jonathan Tunick's scoring comes through with all Sondheim's niche underthemes intact. Note, too, the interpolation of a new song, "Our Little World," for the Witch and Rapunzel, to explore the show's central motif of the rapport between parents and children. Unlike some other Sondheim additions for London (such as *Follies*' "Country House" and *Assassins*' "Something Just Broke"), it sits comfortably in the compositional style of the rest of the score.

Into the Woods' 2002 Broadway revival (Nonesuch), led by Vanessa Williams, makes small changes here and there and allows both Princes to double as wolves (the new Wolf plays opposite the Three Little Pigs). But why doesn't Williams put on a "wicked" voice as the Witch, before her transformation? This show is partly about the lack of security in human relationships. In Rodgers and Hammerstein, stability is threatened, then reclaimed. In Sondheim, there is no stability. It seems only logical that the driver of *Into the Woods*' plot start as one thing (the evil Witch—and she should sound like one) then turn into something completely different (a glamor goddess). Anything can happen in the woods: that's the problem.

Assassins is a rare later Sondheim show *not* orchestrated by Jonathan Tunick. The original, off-Broadway cast sang to a mere three-person band but recorded (Victor) to Michael Starobin's very sizable scoring, later used in the first Broadway airing (PS), in 2004. How to choose? The later disc offers interstitial music and dialogue, creating real theatre atmosphere (and includes the added "Something Just Broke"). **Passion** is somewhat comparable, though it starts on Broadway (Angel), then moves to the smaller venue (PS), with Rebecca Luker in for an ailing Melissa Errico. Most impressively, Angel added twenty-six extra strings to the Broadway pit, a possibly unprecedented expansion in the history of cast albums. Still, I think the 1996 London cast (First Night) is the best *Passion* of the three, very intensely portrayed by Michael Ball and Maria Friedman. A DVD (Image) preserves the Broadway premiere, and the commentary track gives us Sondheim, Lapine, and the three leads. That sounds historical, though in the event they don't have all that much to say.

There's a studio reading of **The Frogs** in its first, short version (Nonesuch), paired with the four **Evening Primrose** songs, but the 2004 Lincoln Center *Frogs* (PS) wipes it away. More than an extension of the original, the revision turns a play with incidental music into a full-fledged musical, and Aristophanes' characters burst into life—the aggressively ebullient Herakles (Burke Moses); the saturnine Charon (John Byner), with all the charm of a Triffid; party boy Pluto (Peter Bartlett); and of course Dionysos (Nathan Lane) and Xanthias (Roger Bart), ham-and-egging their way through the underworld. Note, too, that the typical PS production's notes, lyrics, and stage shots create virtual theatregoing, far beyond Nonesuch's bare-bones display.

Wise Guys was not recorded, but **Bounce** (Nonesuch) and **Road Show** (PS) give us a chance to watch Sondheim and John Weidman readjust the work's values as they tighten it. *Bounce* is flouncier, starting with an old-fashioned overture—hurry music, then a bright up-tune ("The Game"), then a ballad ("The Best Thing That Ever Has Happened"), almost as if it were the 1950s and *Bounce*, not *Saturday Night*, were Sondheim's first-to-be-written title. Interestingly, the overture concludes with a playoff between "Gold!" and "Boca Raton"—meme-ing on the only two enterprises that the two Mizners work on together. As the story unfolds, we hear great character resonance in the leads' voices, Howard McGillin eagerly charming, destructive not because he wants to be but because it's just something that's in him, and Richard Kind soft as flannel: a matinée idol and a teddy bear. Michele Pawk, the Girl of all epochs, comes and goes almost like the characters in *Candide*, turning up wherever she needs to, and Gavin Creel, as Kind's boy friend, offers a sweet sound to contrast with everyone else (except in a sudden twisty outburst at the end of "Talent," too tasty to spoil here). Conductor David Caddick leads a big orchestra, though *Bounce* itself seems small in scale till the gradual buildup of a huge ensemble on "You."

In Wagner's *Ring*, which opposes two lords of the world in Wotan (king of the gods) and Alberich (king of the nihilistic Nibelungs), Wotan is spoken of as "light-Alberich." So Alberich is "dark-Wotan"—and *Road Show* is "dark-*Bounce*." There is no overture this time. The show just starts, the gleeful "Bounce" now deflatingly re-lyriced as "Waste." Alexander Gemignani's Addison is as gentle as Richard Kind's, but Michael Cerveris proves a colder Wilson than Howard McGillin—and note that, in "Addison's Trip," the doom-laden messages that sabotage Addison's projects are delivered by Cerveris, in sepulchral tones. But we do hear more from the Mizner family, and "That Was a Year" ("I Love This Town" in *Bounce*), setting forth just how destructive Wilson can be, gives more narrative specifics now. At the same time, the brothers seem almost symbolic figures in *Road Show*. *Bounce* uses them as foils in a comedy; *Road Show* places them in a semi-comic drama of archetypes—the gay man whose inventiveness enriches the culture and the straight who takes advantage of what's already there.

Sondheim's acting gig in **June Moon** is available on Kultur, and his one full-length soundtrack score, for **Stavisky**, is, as I've said, paired with *Follies in Concert*. *Stavisky* the film is available only in Europe, though Region 1

DVDs used to be on sale in Canada (Maple), without English subtitles. Completists will want to view it, possibly following along with the screenplay in English translation (Ungar), but Resnais left out too much of Sondheim's tracks. This is fine music all the way though, and the main-title theme, urged along by a haunting rhythmic pulse, is a wonder, so intense yet so oddly noncommital: romantic and biting, playful yet criminal, an enigmatic smile and a hands-in-the-pockets posture. It was destiny: Sondheim's life-long love of film noir led him to this moment, when he could in effect compose the theme song for an entire genre.

Ever since **Side By Side By Sondheim** (Victor), revues of his songs have proliferated, partly to explore his extensive trunk material. Some of these have storylines, for instance the two-character **Marry Me a Little**—the title a dropped *Company* number, of course—folding unused songs into a Boy Never Actually Meets Girl, though, in concept-show style, they move around in the same "space." We have original (Victor) and revival (Ghost-light) casts, with a slightly different rotation of numbers, both with piano only. One of the revues, **Sondheim On Sondheim** (PS), features commentary by the composer himself, explaining how his art works. In anthology discs, Varèse Sarabande has the two best collections, both of arcane material. *Sondheim at the Movies* gives us the alternate version of "The Glamorous Life" written for the *Night Music* film (because the Liebeslieder Singers had been dropped and Elizabeth Taylor couldn't manage the number alone). The sequence became a montage of Désirée's adventures while Fredrica sang in voice-over. An arresting change: the "glamor" was finally substantiated, as the lyrics abandoned Désirée's sarcasm in favor of her daughter's idolatry, dreamy and lilting over an accompaniment of rushing triplets, the sound of delighted anticipation. Even as the screen revealed the dreary offstage of a life on the margin of the arts, the song told us of beauty and truth, captured in terms perfect for the girl's age and the era in question. Note, for example, her use of "recite," meaning "speak dialogue" and, more broadly, "act," a usage that bears an outdated and European flavor.* This new "Glamorous Life," too lovely to lose, found its way to the stage. The 1995 National Theatre *Night Music* (Tring), built around Judi Dench, troubled to unite it with the old one, ingeniously intermingling sections of the two. They strengthen Désirée as not only actress and lover but mother, a wonderful one. The first thing she tells Fredrica on seeing her again is "Darling...you're much prettier, you're irresistible." That's a mother to remember.

---

* Opera buffs will recognize it as the first word of the introduction to the famous "Laugh, clown, laugh!" aria "Vesti la Giubba" in Leoncavallo's *Pagliacci*. "Recitar!," it begins, with savage irony: "Play your part!"

Further auditioning *Sondheim at the Movies*: Gary Beach and Liz Calla-way give us the *Evening Primrose* songs with more voice than we hear on the Nonesuch reading with *The Frogs*—and this is important music in that it gave us a first taste of the "tricky" Sondheim, anticipating *Company* and his second period. Varèse includes also four of the five *Dick Tracy* numbers, with Randy Skinner tapping his way across the screen through stereo-speaker bas-relief in a very rousing rendition of "Back in Business," led by Alet Oury. Most interesting is "(Love is just) Sand," an insinuatingly sexy piece from **Singing Out Loud,** a movie musical that was never made, done to a T by Christiane Noll. You'd never guess her day job is singing operetta till she glides into a high-soprano descant on the second chorus.

The other Varese CD is *Unsung Sondheim*, which gave us our first experi-ence of *Saturday Night*, five years before the first staging. As well, there are dropped numbers from shows we know. Michael Rupert joins the ranks of Roberts lending their very timbre of voice to our attempt to catch up with this most elusive of characters; if *Company* were an opera by Richard Strauss, Robert might as well be Keikobad.* Rupert's solo is "Multitudes of Amys," a precursor of "Being Alive," fascinatingly outgoing for so re-pressed a figure.

The cut *Follies* number is "That Old Piano Roll," in which Buddy tries to "restart" with Sally—and she seems to respond. That's odd; hasn't she felt "wrong" with him from the beginning? Perhaps the staging was supposed to show us how alienated she is from this loser. It's Ben who has the daddy power. Or does Sally love Ben not because he has winner control but be-cause she simply loves him? Harry Groener and Lynette Perry make the most of the number; *Follies* buffs will recognize the melody from the show's overture (which is in fact the second number, played to mimed action after the curtain is up, though it is a medley of the type usually employed to start the evening).

From *Anyone Can Whistle* we get Kaye Ballard and Sally Mayes in for Angela Lansbury and Lee Remick in "There's Always a Woman," a challenge number in driving 3/4. The disc contains also a number Sondheim wrote for a proposed adaptation of Jules Feiffer's *Passionella*, which of course was finally realized by Bock and Harnick as the last act of *The Apple Tree*. Judy Kaye amusingly shades her normally gleaming tone for a woebegone feeling (albeit with a gala climax) in "Truly Content," an exact counterpart to *The Apple Tree*'s "Oh, To Be a Movie Star." Sondheim sees the scene as a lilting

---

* The ruler of the spirit world in *Die Frau Ohne Schatten*. Keikobad's influence per-vades the action, but, now commanding, now leading from behind, he never actually appears. One might say that, as with Robert, we know him except when we don't.

waltz; Bock and Harnick make it a jaunty fox trot. Yet both Kaye and *The Apple Tree*'s Barbara Harris are playing the exact same character in almost exactly the same way. Another excerpt from the aforementioned *Singing Out Loud* is "Water Under the Bridge," in which Debbie Shapiro Gravitte suggests Eydie Gormé singing Burt Bacharach in a Joni Mitchell mood. But the disc's sweetest morsel is the final cut, "Goodbye For Now," from *Reds*, which the other Varèse CD gives us in an instrumental. However, it's one of Sondheim's tenderest ballads, hungry for its vocal, sung here by Liz Callaway. Note the flute theme that punctuates the number; it's a cool understatement of the turmoil hidden in this fragile music, on the love of John Reed and Louise Bryant, separated by history and, at length, his early death. Though Sondheim doesn't orchestrate his music, he does write out all the arrangements himself, and "Goodbye For Now" would be incomplete without this quaintly regretful little descant.

Last of all the discs is Sondheim the performer, on private acetates and demos. PS Classics collected two separate units entitled *Sondheim Sings*. Volume One draws largely on *Forum*, *Whistle*, *Follies*, and *A Little Night Music*, but Volume Two backs up to catch young Steve's earliest compositions. As a vocalist, he's rough, especially at the top and bottom of his range. But he knows how the various types of songs are supposed to sound, whether sentimental or stentorian, and he gives each one all it needs. He is as well a much better pianist than many composers. Cole Porter—who made a few commercial cuts as well as demos, always accompanying himself—was a terrible pianist, with a hunt-and-peck right hand and a secret-message left one.

Of course, what interests us primarily is the material itself, almost entirely unavailable elsewhere—a birthday song for a friend, numbers from school shows, Steve's own "Do I Hear a Waltz?," three numbers for *The Last Resorts*. The songs created for story-and-character projects are more absorbing than the others, reminding us that Steve is less a songwriter than a playwright. They are also more tuneful. In a helping of *Saturday Night*, "In No Time At All" paired with "A Moment With You," we hear A strains suggesting the syncopated vocal line and colloquial poetry of Irving Berlin, though the release recalls the Rodgers of the Hart years. It's an archival cut, too, as "In No Time At All," musically a near-twin of "A Moment With You," bears different lyrics that seem to have vanished from *Saturday Night* as currently performed (and the words do not appear in *Finishing the Hat* with the rest of the show's verses).

After the sophistication of the mature shows—*Company*'s ambiguities, *Sweeney Todd*'s ur-themes in restless development, *Passion*'s profane confessions—it makes for offbeat listening to encounter Steve at his start. As we listen, he slips back into his twenties, auditioning his *Last Resorts* songs for Jean Kerr and her homophobic-shithead critic of a husband, Walter. They didn't like his work, and there would be others such. Did Steve know how tough it would be, at first, to find his way in the theatre? "Wish I knew my place" is a line from one of the apprentice shows he wrote for Oscar Hammerstein; surely he did know. "When a true genius appears in the world," says Jonathan Swift, "you may know him by this sign, that the dunces are all in confederacy against him."

INDEX

Note: Page numbers in **bold** indicate the primary reference to a title.